Spy War in South Asia

Spy War in South Asia

Intelligence Failure, Reforms and the
Fight against Cross Border Terrorism
in Pakistan, Bangladesh, India and
Afghanistan

Musa Khan Jalalzai

Y

Vij Books India Pvt Ltd
New Delhi (India)

Published by

Vij Books India Pvt Ltd
(Publishers, Distributors & Importers)
2/19, Ansari Road
Delhi – 110 002
Phones: 91-11-43596460, 91-11-47340674
Fax: 91-11-47340674
e-mail: vijbooks@rediffmail.com
www.vijbooks.com

Contents

Introduction

Pakistani intelligence agencies are dancing to different political and regional tangos within the rim of controversial counterterrorism and national security approach, which evinced the country in the eyes of international community as an irresponsible state-supporting terrorist groups and financing proxy war in neighboring states. This illegal business of jihadism destroyed economic, political and social infrastructure, and caused loss of face and self-abasement. From Nepal to India and Bangladesh, all regional players raised their voices against Pakistan's double political and diplomatic role in dealing with Kashmir and Afghanistan. After 9/11, Pakistani agencies vacillated between continued sponsorship of extremist groups and cracking down on radical anti-state groups. Pakistan never strived to destroy terrorist infrastructure instead hoping to nurture them and use them in the future against its neighboring countries.

In Afghanistan, Pakistan's primary goal is to prevent India from gaining ground and obtaining too much influence. Terrorist incidents in Pathankot, Uri and Pulwama exacerbated the level of tension between the two states. Indian Interior Minister immediately issued a statement in which he termed Pakistan as a terrorist state, while Indian Defence Minister Manohar Parrikar and other Hindu leaders demanded the change of no first use policy of nuclear weapons against Pakistan. The case is not so different in India. Manoj Joshi and Pushan Das have further illustrated some aspects of Indian intelligence operational mechanism:

> "The Indian intelligence system emerged as an extension of the police system to track and counter the Indian national movement during British rule. This is a legacy and structure that it has not quite broken out of to meet the challenges

of modern intelligence-gathering. It carries the burden of an intellectual infrastructure that has failed to build competencies essential to intelligence operations in a vastly different environment than the pre-Independence era. The lack of a dedicated intelligence cadre and the continuing practice of staffing intelligence agencies with police officers have resulted in agencies playing down the importance of language specialists, social scientists, technical specialists and cyber analysts".

With the Afghan war came to an end in 1990s, jihadists returned to Pakistan with a new ideology of extremism and militancy, which later on challenged authority of the state and law enforcement agencies. The Inter-Services Intelligence (ISI) never tried to intercept their violent actions against civilian and military installations. The ISI's intransigence and remorselessness to cooperate with civilian intelligence agencies on national security issues often prompted internal tug-of-war. This unending tug-of-war forced former Prime Minister Nawaz Sharif to restructure the IB and make it more effective to counter ISI's influence in democratic institutions. The greatest challenge Prime Minister Nawaz Sharif faced was on national security front where miltablishment was not happy with his national security approach and his silence over the arrest of Indian spy Kulbhushan Jadhav.

Reports from Netherlands confirmed spy war between India and Pakistan when Judges started investigating the espionage case of Mr. Kulbhushan Jadhav. On 18 February 2019, Reuter reported hearing of Jadhav case at the International Court of Justice amid a sharp spike in tensions between the two nuclear-armed neighbours, after a suicide attack on an Indian military convoy and renewed fighting in Kashmir. Mr. Jadhav was arrested in Baluchistan in March 2016 on charges of espionage and sentenced to death by the country military court in 2017. War in Kargil also exposed weak operational mechanism of the intelligence agencies of India and Pakistan. To investigate the Kargil war, several investigative committees were formed to spotlight weaknesses and incompetency of ISI and RAW.

In India, the Kargil Review Committee found that human

intelligence aspect of Indian intelligence agencies was weak. On one point the committee pinpointed a major success of RAW-intercepting the telephone conversation between General Musharraf and his then Chief of General Staff Lt. Gen Aziz, which provided crucial evidence to international media that the operation was being controlled from military headquarters in Rawalpindi. Experts perceived it as a major intelligence success. The Kargil Review Committee made the assumption that the critical failure in intelligence was related to the absence of information on the induction and de-induction of battalions and the lack of accurate data on the identity of battalions in Kargil during 1998. It indicated that the intelligence structure and the state of intelligence gathering were inadequate to assess available intelligence, manage the overload of unconfirmed background information or gather sufficient tactical intelligence to suitably warn the system.

The Mumbai attacks (2008) unveiled a number of terrorist tactics that prevailed in the country. Those tactics and the way terrorists targeted civilians and the police were new to RAW and the IB. Once again, in Delhi, intellectual circles and policy makers started debates with the assumption that counterterrorism operations had been influenced by weak intelligence analyses in the country. They also raised the question of check and balance, while the bureaucratic and political involvement further added to their pain. The exponentially growing politicization, divides within ranks of all intelligence agencies including RAW and the IB and violence across the country painted a negative picture of the unprofessional intelligence approach to the national security of India.

Intelligence expert and analyst Janani Krishnaswamy in her research paper noted some aspects of India's intelligence failures: "The central intelligence agencies have earned the wrath of the government for failing to sufficiently warn local agencies. Why do our secret intelligence agencies fail repeatedly? Is it because of (a) lack of adequate intelligence, (b) dearth of trained manpower in the intelligence sector, (c) failure to apply latest sophisticated technology in surveillance, (d) lack of proper intelligence sharing between the Centre and the states, (e) lack of action on available intelligence, (f) the current state of political instability or (g) the lack of sensible intelligence reforms? In the aftermath of the terrorist attack at Dilsukhnagar in Hyderabad, India's secret intelligence agencies were subject to an intense inspection. Heated political debates over the construction of the National Counter Terrorism Centre (NCTC), a controversial anti-terror hub that was proposed in the aftermath of 26/11 attacks, was stirred up after five years".

There were reports in yesteryears that Pakistani intelligence had established spy networks in some states of South Asia to closely monitor India's intelligence, political and military activities. On 10 October 2014, Analyst and expert Animesh Roul in his paper (Terrorism Monitor Volume: 12, Issue: 19) noted: "India's intelligence agencies have been investigating an espionage network reportedly run by Pakistan's external intelligence agency, the Inter-Services Intelligence (ISI), from Sri Lankan soil. The ISI uses legitimate government structures like the Pakistani High Commission and Consulate located in Colombo and Kandy, respectively, as staging grounds for anti-India activity. Pakistan has long used neighbouring South Asian countries like Nepal, Bangladesh and the Maldives as bases from which to attack India".

On 18 March 2018, Dawn reported Major General Asif Ghafoor, the Director General of the Inter-Services Public Relations (ISPR) interview with Gulf News. In his interview, General Ghafoor warned: "India is busy in fomenting unrest through terrorism using Afghan soil," he told Gulf News, mentioning Kulbhushan Jadhav—an Indian spy in Pakistan's custody—as an example. "So we are not having any let-up in safeguarding against Indian threat. While threat remains from India, both in conventional and sub-conventional domain, our biggest challenge is to maintain this stability with the threat still residing inside Afghanistan coupled with economic difficulties."

In-times-gone-by, Indian journalist Vinnet Malhotra asked former RAW Chief and former Adviser to Prime Minister's Office, Mr. Amarjit Singh Dulat about the Pulwama attack and India-Pakistan military clashes, he said: "This was a horrendous attack, terrible tragedy but something like this was waiting to happen." He castigated the killing of people in Pulwama. Mr. Dulat also disclosed about the conversation between him and General Dependra Singh

Hooda saying "When villagers come out in support of militants, there's very little the army can do". When asked about Pakistan's link with the Taliban, he said "It is natural for Pakistan to support Taliban; I don't know why we don't do business with Taliban".

On 28 February 2019, journalist and expert Vijaita Singh reported a dossier handed over to Pakistani authorities by Indian government on Jaish-e-Muhammad activities, a terrorist group based in Bahawalpur: "A dossier handed over by India to Pakistan mentions nine specific instances, in the past two years, when Jaish-e-Muhammad (JeM) was conducting rallies and religious congregations to recruit men to the terror outfit. India said these activities were conducted "right under the nose of the Pakistani establishment," even though it was banned by the Pakistani authorities in 2002. The outfit still features at serial number 3 in the list of 67 terror organizations proscribed by Pakistan's Ministry of Interior published on the website of National Counter Terrorism Authority. The Ministry of External Affairs said that a dossier was handed over to Pakistan with "specific details of JeM complicity in Pulwama terror attack and the presence of JeM terror camps and its leadership in Pakistan."

Indian intelligence failed to identify the right place where Jaish-e-Muhammad's fighters were deployed inside Pakistan. The fact is, the camp bombed by Indian Air Force was closed in 2005, and there were no casualties. Intelligence experts pointed at lack of professional approach to intelligence information collection in India. Pakistani expert and journalist Najam Sethi in his editorial piece of Friday Times (01 March 2019) argued:

> "Pakistan and India are, legally speaking, at war. This war broke out when Indian airplanes crossed the international border into Pakistan and dropped some bombs deep into Pakistani territory on an alleged "terrorist" camp. Strangely enough, this camp stopped existing after 2005, so the bombs didn't kill anyone in 2019. In response, Pakistani jets dropped some bombs across the Line of Control (LoC) in Occupied Kashmir, which is legally disputed territory. But Pakistan isn't saying who or what was targeted. So, naturally, the bombs didn't kill anyone. Indeed, in the one week that

India and Pakistan have been at war, no one has been killed. But nationalist passions are running high on both sides. Curiously enough, though, these are largely being expressed in newsrooms and social media platforms while both "warring" governments are conspicuous by their relative restraint. What a war! Is this a war"?

In Bangladesh, intelligence infrastructure also faces numerous challenges of operational mechanism, countering foreign espionage and domestic extremism. Directorate General of Forces Intelligence (DGFI), National Security Intelligence (NSI), Special Security Force (SSF), and the Border Security Bureau (BSB) are operating in a reluctant mood. Collectively, they are responsible for safeguarding vital national interests, physical protection of very important persons (VIPs), and territorial integrity of the country. The DGFI, NSI, and SSF report to the Prime Ministers, while the BSB reports to the reconstituted BGB, an entity under the Ministry of Home Affairs. To bring intelligence under democratic control in Bangladesh, several investigative committees and forums were established in yesteryears to reform the fractured intelligence system of the country, and introduce reforms to make it professionalize.

The Failure of Afghan intelligence agencies to defeat the Taliban deeply gloomed international community that consequences of wrongly designed counterinsurgency and counterterrorism strategies were consistently substandard. Disorder and complications the United States and its allies created in Afghanistan were more evident than ever before. Criminal negligence of CIA, Pentagon and NATO allies on making Afghan intelligence professional helped Taliban and the ISIS terrorist groups to exploit weaknesses and incompetency of the National Directorate of Security (NDS) across the country. Through their appalling and unsuccessfully engineered strategies and military adventures, the CIA, MI6, the NATO spy agencies facilitated the rise of a new terrorist group (ISIS) that never existed prior to the war on terrorism in Afghanistan. The US civilian and military intelligence fashioned a strategic mistake-reasoning that military action can put the state back in order, but unfortunately failed. However,

Islamic State (ISIS) and the Taliban also perceive a need to collect and process advance information to protect their networks against the theft of their strategic, defence and political secrets. This book highlights operational mechanism, reform packages, and failures of intelligence agencies in India, Bangladesh, Pakistan, and Afghanistan. I am highly indebted of my friend Rohan Vij who considered my book for publication.

Musa Khan Jalalzai

March 2019, London

Chapter 1

The Changing Fight of Indian Intelligence Agencies:
Jihadism in Kashmir, Reforms, and Bureaucratic Stakeholdrism

Intelligence organizations of the twenty first century make outstretched distinction between operations, analysis, and functions. Field officers collect intelligence information, analysts analyze information, and processors categorize it to help policy makers in designing military strategies. Any civilian or military government that wants to professionalize its intelligence infrastructure, and prevent it from decaying needs statecraft, which is comprised of economic power, and a strong military force and mature diplomacy. The case is quite different in India and Pakistan, where emerging contradictions in the state system, ethnic and sectarian divide, and failure of intelligence and internal security strategies generated a countrywide debate, in which experts deeply criticized the waste of financial resources by their intelligence agencies in an unnecessary proxy war in South Asia. Intelligence reform in India has been the most controversial issue as reform committees have been hijacked by political and bureaucratic stakeholders.[1]

In fact, the challenges India faces are to bring its intelligence agencies under democratic control and introduce security sector reforms have become more complicated when stakeholders adamantly refuse to change the culture of unnecessary spying on neighbouring states. The principal debate among these stakeholders also starts with the assumption that counterterrorism, and counterinsurgency decision making has influenced by intelligence analysis. When we read books and journals on Indian intelligence studies, we come across several counterinsurgency controversies of the state-the way it fights insurgents in Kashmir and Punjab provinces.[2] Indian analyst Srinath Raghavan exposed the failure of Indian intelligence to report the infiltration of Chinese PLA commandos into the Indian Territory in May 1962:

"On 06 May 1962, about 100 Chinese troops, in assault formation, advanced towards an Indian post in the Chip Chap valley in the Ladakh sector. In the event, the Chinese backed off without attacking. The next flashpoint was the Galwan valley in Ladakh where Indian forces established a picket on 4 July. The Chinese responded swiftly. By 10 July the PLA had surrounded the post, sealed all possible withdrawal routes, and advanced within 100 yards of the post......Meantime, the eastern sector of the frontier (now Arunachal Pradesh) was getting active too. In response to an Indian attempt to establish a post near the Namka Chu River, the Chinese occupies the bridge dominating the river".[3]

The nucleus of Mr. Srinath Raghavan argument inculcates us about the Chinese army attempts to crossed the Indian Territory when Indian intelligence failed to report to the centre on time. However, in his Indian Express analysis (2016), Mr. Pradip Sagar notes some aspects of intelligence failure during the Kargil war and the Uri terrorist attacks: "Many former Indian army Chiefs of Staff and Directors Generals of Military Operations had unanimously felt any large-scale Pakistani military intrusion in Kargil because it lacked infrastructure and logistical support. This perception was formed after analyzing confrontation in 1948, 1965 and 1971, when the Indian army dominated Pakistani forces in the area. There was also minimal cross-LOC military activity. Additionally, considering the challenging terrain and weather conditions, the Indian military mindset underestimated the Pakistani threat in Kargil. After Uri, a look at why intelligence failures happen: Eighteen soldiers died at Uri, marking one of the worse Indian intelligence failures of recent times".[4]

The biggest Indian intelligence failure occurred in 1999 in the Kargil war between India and Pakistan, in which RAW failed to report infiltration of Pakistan army units into the region. Military, civilian, domestic and foreign intelligence agencies failed to spotlight Pakistan's military unit's movement in the region. Indian analyst Prem Mahadevan in his research paper (2011) spotlighted important aspects of intelligence failures in Kargil war. Pakistani forces crossed Indian border while Indian intelligence was unable to spotlight their locations: "During the summer of 1999, India and Pakistan fought a 10-week limited war in Kargil, a remote area of Kashmir. Fighting broke out in May, when Indian troops discovered that a number of armed men had crossed the Line of Control (LOC) and entrenched themselves on the Indian side. Over the following weeks, the Indian army learned that these gunmen were not Islamist guerrillas, as it had first assumed, but Pakistani soldiers in Mufti. A security crisis erupted, with allegation of 'failure' being thrown at the Indian intelligence agencies".[5]

During the last three decades, there have been tenacious efforts in India to introduce security sector reforms in order to bring intelligence agencies under democratic control, but notwithstanding the last reform proposals of the Naresh Chandra Committee (2012), democratic governments in the country could not succeed to bell the cat. Since the end of the Cold War and the disintegration of the Soviet Union in 1990s, internal conflicts in India deeply impacted the performance of its intelligence mechanism. The emergence of sectarian mafia groups, and new terrorist organizations like the Daesh and Taliban further embroiled Indian intelligence agencies in an unending domestic violence.[6]

The long and interminable fight of the Research and Analysis Wing (RAW) and the Intelligence Bureau (IB) with domestic separatism and international terrorism brought about many changes in the attitude of its stakeholders and policy makers to control their self-designed operational strategies that caused misunderstandings between India and its neighbours. In states like Kashmir, Orissa, Chhattisgarh, Jharkhand, and Assam, several separatist and terrorist groups emerged with new tactics, while the recent Pathankot and Pulwama terrorist attacks generated a new debate about the failed strategies, weak security approach, and power politics within the intelligence infrastructure. These and other incidents showed that intelligence review committees, reports and political parties were right in their criticism of the operational flaws of the agencies.[7]

The Mumbai attacks (2008) unveiled a number of terrorist tactics that prevailed in the country. Those tactics and the way terrorists targeted civilians and the police were new to RAW and the IB. Once again, in Delhi, intellectual circles and policy makers started debates with the assumption that counterterrorism operations had been influenced by weak intelligence analyses in the country. They also raised the question of check and balance, while the bureaucratic and political involvement further added to their pain. The exponentially growing politicization, divides within ranks of all intelligence agencies including RAW and the IB and violence across the country, painted a negative picture of the unprofessional intelligence approach to the national security of India.[8]

The perception that the agencies decide whatever they want without restricting themselves to the advisory role causes misunderstanding between the citizens and the state. Moreover, numerous intelligence committees like the Henderson-Brook Committee on the Indo-China war and India's defeat in 1962; B S Raghavan IAS Committee on the failure of intelligence during the 1965 Indo-Pak war; L P Singh Committee; K.S Nair Committee; and the 1999 Kargil Review Committee and, the Ram Pradham Committee on the intelligence failure during the 2008 terrorist attacks in Mumbai have taken place after every big perceived intelligence failure.[9]

In spite the establishment of several investigation committees into the failure of Indian intelligence in yesteryears, and the reform packages passed by parliament, the RAW, IB and military intelligence are still dancing to different tangos, and never been able to respond to a series of terrorist attacks (14 February 2019) of Pakistan based extremist and terrorist groups in Kashmir. Janani Krishnaswamy (2013) in her research paper on the causes of Indian intelligence failure diverted public attention to the causes of failures:

"Why do our secret intelligence agencies fail repeatedly? It is because of (a) lack of adequate intelligence, (b) dearth of trained manpower in the intelligence sector, (d) lack of proper intelligence sharing between the centre and the state, (e) lack of action on available intelligence, (f) the current state of political instability or (g) the lack of sensible intelligence reforms? In the aftermath of the terrorist attack at Dilsukhnagar in Hyderabad, India's secret intelligence agencies were subjected to an intense inspection. Heated political debates over the construction of the National Counterterrorism Centre (NCTC), a controversial anti-terror hub that was proposed in the aftermath of 26/11 attacks, was stirred up after five years. Are such organization reforms sufficient to fix the problems of the intelligence community? Intelligence reviews committees and politicians constantly assess the performance of intelligence agencies and underline numerous failures within the intelligence system".[10]

In addition to these committees, several investigative reports were prepared to spotlight the failure of RAW, MI, IB and other civilian and military agencies in response to major terrorist attacks against India. Lack of legal and parliamentary oversight has been a very complicated issue since the Kargil war as several stakeholders refused to allow the judiciary and parliamentary committees to investigate the ooze. More than 70 percent of Indians do not know about the basic functions of their country's secret agencies, because the cover of secrecy often serves as a blanket of immunity from legal action, accountability and misuse of taxpayers' money.[11]

The operational incompetence of the Indian intelligence has now become legendary as it failed to defend the country during the Kargil, (1999) Mumbai (2008) Pathankot (2016, and Pulwama (2019) attacks. They even get away with failures in violence-infected regions such as Kashmir and Assam. This way of intelligence mechanism has raised many questions including waste of money and resources.[12] The alleged involvement of Indian intelligence agencies in Bangladesh and Nepal generated controversial stories in print and electronic media. In Afghanistan, Pakistan says that Indian intelligence agencies use the country against Pakistan, and recruit Afghans and Pakistanis to carry out terrorist attacks in Baluchistan. Afghan military and political leadership rejected the argument, and said India is the best friend of Afghanistan.

Terror attacks, whether in Assam or Kashmir, have exacerbated by the day, which lead policy makers to the conclusion that the involvement of intelligence agencies in proxy wars across borders causes major terror incidents in the country. Amidst all these failures and incomplete intelligence stories, Prime Minister Narendra Modi decided to bring his own team of experts in order to introduce reforms of security sector and bring intelligence under democratic control, but he also needed to understand the difficulties faced by his predecessors. He also needed to find out why RAW and the IB lack cryptanalysts who break enemy codes and ciphers despite India's aggrandizement in the field of computer technologies.[13] This deficit is in a stark contrast to regional trends where state agencies have been hiring an ever-greater number of experts. In an Indian Express article in 2014, journalist Praveen Swami noted: "India's over five-year efforts to monitor encrypted traffic-run by mainly military-staffed National Technical Research Organization-has failed to make progress in decrypting even chat programmes used by terrorists, like Viber and Skype."[14]

The Kargil Review Committee found that human intelligence aspect of Indian intelligence agencies was weak. During the Kargil war, RAW succeeded in intercepting the telephone conversation between General Musharraf and his then Chief of General Staff Lt Gen Aziz, which provided crucial evidence to international media that the operation was being controlled from military headquarters in Rawalpindi.[15] Experts perceived it as a major intelligence success. Moreover, the Kargil Review Committee also criticized military intelligence for its failure related to the absence of updated and accurate intelligence information on the induction and de-induction of military battalions, and the lack of expertise to spotlight military battalions in the Kargil area in 1998.[16]

The committee further criticized lack of fresh information, which makes it impossible for an intelligence agency to make an accurate judgement of the looming threat.[17] According to Indian intellectual circles, rivalry among the intelligence agencies and the issue of appointment in war zones or violence-infected areas has badly affected counterterrorism efforts across the country. In a country like India where credit-snatching influences intelligence analyses, there is no way to judge the accuracy of collected intelligence information.[18]

Pakistan's intelligence targeted security forces of India and Iran in February 2019, and killed 50 Indian and 30 Iranian soldiers. Irani General Yahya Safavi blamed Pakistan's Inter-Services Intelligence (ISI) for supporting terrorist groups in Iran. Terrorists carried out attack on a bus carrying security personnel of the elite Islamic Revolutionary Guard between Zahedan and Khash. The Jaish ul-Adl terrorist group, which is linked to al-Qaeda and based in Pakistan claimed responsibility. Gen. Safavi told newspapers: "These criminal outlaws were from one of the tribes of Baluchistan who had been trained on suicide operations in the neighbouring country, and the neighbouring country and the ISI should account to the Iranian government and nation and the IRGC how they have crossed the borders of that country and why this neighbouring country has turned into a safe haven and a place for the training and dispatch of these infidel terrorist groups (to Iran)."

Analyst Mr. Saikat Datta also believes that Pakistan-based terror group, Jaish-e-Mohammed (JeM), was involved in the killing of Indian security forces in Kashmir. However, India withdrawn the 'Most Favored Nation' status from Pakistan. "I want to tell the terrorist groups and their masters that they have committed a big mistake. They have to pay a heavy price," Indian Prime Minister Narendra Modi said after an emergency cabinet meeting. "If our neighbouring country thinks that it will succeed in creating instability through such acts and conspiracies in our country, they should stop dreaming." Finance Minister Arun Jaitley said: "The Most Favoured Nation status stands withdrawn and the Ministry of Commerce will issue the formal notification. India will make all available efforts to ensure Pakistan is isolated."

The deadly ambush by a Jaish-e-Mohammed suicide bomber on a CRPF convoy travelling along the Jammu-Srinagar highway near Latoomode, Avantipura, marked a disconcerting escalation in the insurgency in Jammu and Kashmir. Car borne suicide attacks were briefly seen in the valley last in the 01 October 2001 attack on the J&K assembly, but thereafter nipped in the bud through a series of concerted and successful counter measures. Mr. Saikat understands that due to the lack of security sector reforms, Indian law enforcement agencies are dancing to different tangos:

"The absence of security reforms over the last five years has been given as a key cause for the latest security lapse. Experts say the last time India undertook major reforms was after the Kargil war with Pakistan in 1999. Since then, incremental changes were made after the Mumbai terror attacks in late 2008. However, India's key intelligence agencies, the Intelligence Bureau (IB) and the Research and Analysis Wing (RAW) have been mired in controversies. Last year, a fracas in the Central Bureau of Investigation saw a key senior intelligence official dealing with Pakistan named in a corruption complaint. However, no effort was taken by the government to either remove him or set up an inquiry. The lack of credible Special Forces and special operations capabilities has also haunted the government for years. While there were reports of setting up a Special Operations Division along the lines of the US Special Operations Command, nothing substantial came of this idea."[19].

In 2008, more than 10 Pakistani terrorists attacked Mumbai and killed over 160 people. After every attack, the government of India made lukewarm attempts to introduce reforms in security sectors, but due to the influence of internal stakeholders all dreams vanished. Pakistan needs to tackle extremism and deal with any groups engaged in militant action not only because other nations demand it but for its own welfare. As Prime Minister Imran Khan stated that Pakistan lost tens of thousands of people to militancy, paying a price higher than that of any other country, therefore imperative is that the country tackles the problem. We must however also look at the past and learn from it. Having highlighted these and other intelligence failures, analyst Anurag Paul argued:

"The attack on a 78-vehicle military fleet killing 40 Central Reserve Police Force (CRPF) in Pulwama district of Jammu & Kashmir on February 14, 2019 seems to be an indication of failure of inputs from Indian Intelligence agencies. In today's ever-changing world order and geo-political dynamics, there is need of information sharing and multi-agency co-operation. There are many intelligence agencies in India of which the best known are the Research and Analysis Wing (RAW), India's external intelligence agency and the Intelligence Bureau (IB), the domestic intelligence agency. The Intelligence Bureau, the oldest intelligence agency in the country responsible for India's internal intelligence also handled external intelligence until 1968. The intelligence failure of Sino-Indian war and Indo-Pak war paved the way to establishment of RAW. RAW predominantly formed to counter China's influence; over time it has moved its focus to India's other traditional opponent, Pakistan. After the Pakistan-backed Mumbai terror attacks in 2008, the security and intelligence architecture was overhauled in the country. The National Investigation Agency (NIA) was created to probe terror cases and the National Security Guard established regional commando hubs. Coastal security was strengthened and the Multi Agency Centre (MAC) of IB started working to improve coordination among various Central and state security agencies".[20]

During the last 15 years of war against terrorism in Afghanistan, Pakistan and India have been engaged in an intense intelligence war-targeting their diplomatic missions in Kabul and blaming each other of sponsoring terrorist groups in Baluchistan and Kashmir. India believes that Pakistan supports Kashmiri groups including Lashkar-e-Taiba and Hezbul Mujahedeen to carry out attacks against its armed forces, while Pakistan understands that India supports TTP, Daesh and Baloch nationalist to disrupt its peace efforts in Baluchistan province. The two states are also involved in an unending proxy war in Afghanistan, where they have turned Afghan society into two rival camps.

Terrorist incidents in Pathankot, Uri and Baluchistan exacerbated the level of tension between the two states. Indian Interior Minister immediately issued a statement in which he termed Pakistan as terrorist state, while Indian Defence Minister Manohar Parrikar and other Hindu leaders demanded the change of no first use policy of nuclear weapons against Pakistan. Those statements set forth a hot debate among nuclear experts. In their Observer Foundation research paper, Mr. Manoj Joshi and Mr. Pushan Das highlight some important misgivings of the Indian intelligence in combating terrorism and militancy:

"There are currently 14 intelligence agencies operating in India with different and sometimes overlapping mandates. Most of these 14 intelligence agencies have come into being as a response to changing strategic environment and shortcomings in the intelligence framework on several occasions. Following the debacle of the 1962 war with China, the Directorate General of Security (DGS) was set up within the Intelligence Bureau (IB), with its operational unit, the Aviation Research Centre (ARC), tasked with obtaining intelligence on China. Following the failure of IB in the 1965 war against Pakistan, the government decided to hive off external intelligence under a new agency, the Research & Analysis Wing (R&AW) and linked the DGS with it. The biggest problem has been the lack of co-ordination amongst the intelligence community in India. Each agency looks out for itself and guards its turf zealously. There is need for strict guidance and supervision to ensure that there is cooperation and coordination. Former Union Home Minister P. Chidambaram enforced co-ordination at the apex level after the Mumbai attacks of 2008, but after his departure, the new Home Minister has not kept up the process. Since the Home Minister has a vast repertoire of responsibilities, there is need for a Director National Intelligence, or a Minister, to arbitrate between agencies and promote greater collaboration between them".[21]

Indian experts warned that the Pulwama attack caused consternation due to intelligence failure. As we have already stressed the need of reforms in Indian intelligence infrastructure, the Modi government needs to introduce wide-ranging security sector reforms. Writer and analyst Asma Khaled noted the same flaws of within intelligence infrastructure to intercept terror attacks:

"India is following the policy of presenting Kashmiri people as terrorists and Pakistan as a terrorist country. Nonetheless, the right of self-determination must not be coupled with terrorism. Pakistan should not withdraw from its principled stance of the right of Kashmiris for self-determination. So the question arises that in the renewed circumstances what should be Pakistan's course of action about Indian Occupied Jammu and Kashmir in the light of new developments? Another dimension of the issue is that India is following the policy of presenting Kashmiri people as terrorists and Pakistan as a terrorist country. Nonetheless, the right of self-determination must not be coupled with terrorism. Pakistan should not withdraw from its principled stance of the right of Kashmiris for self-determination. So the question arises that in the renewed circumstances what should be Pakistan's course of action about Indian Occupied Jammu and Kashmir in the light of new developments?"[22]

The West Bengal Chief Minister Mamata Banerjee warned that the terror attack in Jammu and Kashmir on a CRPF convoy at Pulwama which claimed 40 lives was due to "intelligence failure". "I demand 72 hours mourning for the ultimate sacrifice of the soldiers. Only one flag is not enough for it," she said. "It is most unfortunate but how did it happen? What was the National Security Advisor [Ajit Doval] doing? What has happened is wrong and we have a right to know," Mamata added.

Chapter 2

The Jaish-e-Mohammed, Lashkar-e-Taiba, and Pakistan's Intelligence War against India

The Jaish-e-Adl, an Iranian Baloch separatist group operating in the borderlands of Iran and Pakistan, attacked Iranian forces and killed 27 Revolutionary Guards, provoking an angry statement from the Iranian government against the US and its proxies. Prominent Pakistan Journalist and analyst Lal Khan argued that Massoud Azhar and other terrorist and war criminals being protected by the army that used them for personal interests and destabilization of the region:

> "After the attack, the Indian corporate media along with the politicians were quick to emphasize the Pakistani state's relations with Jaish-e-Mohammad, the group claiming responsibility for the attack. Jaish's leader is Masood Azhar, who was released from an Indian prison after Islamic terrorists had hijacked an Indian Airlines plane to Kandahar demanding his freedom in 1999. After release, Azhar set up this religious outfit involved in sectarian and proxy terrorist acts. According to some reports, Masood Azhar is protected by the Pakistani deep state. In 2016, he opened a new headquarters for this group in his hometown Bahawalpur. India's foreign ministry has issued a statement accusing the Pakistani regime of propping up Masood Azhar "to carry out attacks in India and elsewhere with impunity." At the same time, Pakistan's "close friend" China has obstructed Indian efforts to get Azhar included on the UN Security Council's

list of designated terrorists. However, the Pakistani foreign ministry spokesman condemned the attack but rejected 'insinuations' of any link to the Pakistani state. The mass movement that erupted in Kashmir in July 2016 openly defied the subjugation by the Indian state and its military – the fifth largest in the world. The upsurge also refuted the corporate media's portrayal of the movement as being religiously motivated. This struggle has been about the will and determination of Kashmir's oppressed people to achieve their national, social, economic and cultural emancipation".[1]

Membership of ISIS terrorist group in Afghanistan and Pakistan is in thousands, but keeping in view its sphere of influence and operations, experts fear that the group's fast growing cadre can spread across South Asia in a relatively short space of time. The Islamic State of Khorasan once approached extremist sectarian groups of Pakistan for support, and distributed leaflets and other propaganda material in Pashtu, Urdu, and Persian languages to invite young people from different communities. This group also threatened India and Russia, and became a consecutive headache for Afghanistan. The group has established its networks in South and North Waziristan, Jalalabad, Kunar, and Nooristan province. Analyst and writer Amira Jadoon in her recent article also warned that the Islamic State has infiltrated in Kashmir to recruit Muslim extremist groups:

"The presence of Islamic State in J&K progressed gradually during 2017, starting with reports of Islamic State flags being waved during rallies and protests around the valley. While this claim is still pending official verification, Islamic State's Amaq news agency claimed responsibility for an attack in Srinagar on November 17, 2017, which killed an Indian policeman. The militant killed in the attack, Mughees Ahmed Mir, is suspected to have been inspired by the Islamic State's online propaganda and was found wearing an Islamic State T-shirt at the time of the attack. For the most part, though, signs of ISJK's existence have largely been observed in the online realm alone. Since late 2017, the pro-Islamic State J&K-focused media group Al-Qaraar has engaged in a social media campaign, directing messages tailored to inspire a Kashmiri audience. In December 2017, a pro-Islamic State video in Urdu was shared via its Telegram channel, using the hashtag "Wilayat Kashmir," in which a masked man representing "Mijahididin in Kashmir" pledges allegiance to the Islamic State and specifically invites the al-Qaida-affiliated group Ansar Ghazwat-ul-Hind to join the caliphate. In addition, numerous posters and written documents encourage followers to target both the Indian and Pakistani armies and "those who disbelieve, fight in the cause of Al-taghoot." More recently, a poster with pictures of two purported "Islamic State Soldiers," in which brother Firdoos and brother Sameer are depicted as ISJK martyrs in Kashmir, was circulated".[2]

The full body of Islamic State machine is strong as its radio stations, photographic reports, and bulletins are being circulated in different languages. Internet is also the source of propaganda of the ISKP groups where experts of the group disseminate controversial information through videos and articles. Moreover, the group has challenged the presence of US and NATO forces in Afghanistan. Some members of Afghan parliament severely criticized the United States and its NATO allies for their support to the Islamic State. Amira Jadoon highlights activities of ISJK in the Indian Kashmir:

"Given the present limitations on data regarding actual ISJK followers, evaluating ISJK's online propaganda against the current ground realities in J&K suggests that the group's goals are ambitious at the very least. Given the complex political dynamics of J&K and the territory's symbolic value for both Pakistan and India, ISJK seeks to inspire its Kashmiri followers to take on a rather formidable task. Followers must not only favor pan-Islamism over nationalist goals, but also target both the Pakistani and Indian states and take a directly opposed position to APHC's leaders (groups seeking self-determination) and militant groups with connections to the Pakistani state".[3]

On 22 February 2019, Dawn reported Pakistan's Director General

(DG) Inter-Services Public Relations (ISPR), Maj Gen Asif Ghafoor's resentment against India on the Pulwama incident. The DG ISPR, while addressing a press conference in Rawalpindi, predominantly spoke about India's reaction following suicide blast in Indian Kashmir's Pulwama area, in which at least 40 Indian soldiers lost their lives. Maj Gen Ghafoor began by providing historical background and context about Pakistan-India ties dating back to Partition, saying that although it had been 70 years since then, "India still hasn't been able to accept it." "Whenever there is supposed to be an important event in Pakistan, or the country is moving towards stability, then there is always some sort of staged incident in either India or occupied Kashmir," the DG ISPR said, adding that such incidents also seem to occur when India is just months away from elections.[4]

On 26 Feb 2019 India launched air strikes against militants in Pakistani territory, in a major escalation of tensions between the two countries, but unfortunately the site Indian air force targeted was closed in 2005. The government said strikes targeted a training camp of the Jaish-e-Mohammad (JeM) group in Balakot. India accused Pakistan of allowing militant groups to operate on its territory and said Pakistani security agencies played a role in the 14 February attack claimed by JeM. Pakistan denied any role and said it did not provide safe haven to militants. Indian Foreign Secretary Vijay Gokhale told a news conference that the strikes had killed a "large number" of militants, including commanders, and had avoided civilian casualties.[5]

The News International on 02 March 2019 reported the release of an Indian Pilot Abhinandan Varthaman by Prime Minister Imran Khan as good step: "The effort for peace was also pushed forward strongly by Prime Minister Imran Khan's decision to release captured pilot Wing Commander Abhinandan Varthaman. Abhinandan, who has already gained huge publicity in both countries through the social and mainstream media, returned across the Wagah border on Friday. India's continued viciousness following this gesture, with Prime Minister Modi hinting that more action may follow means that sadly tensions may remain high in the region"[6].

Moreover, Indian security expert Prakash Katoch admitted that air strike of Indian air force was humiliated far worse than the US strike against Osama bin Laden in Abbotabad. Mr. Katoch argued that Jaish-e Mohammad inflicted scores of casualties in India through different actions:

> "The Indian air strikes were humiliating and probably far worse than America's Abbottabad raid to kill Osama bin Laden, considering that India has been Pakistan's traditional rival. But while JeM has inflicted scores of casualties in India through multiple terror attacks, India must proportion some of the blame for releasing Maulana Masood Azhar, the JeM founder, in 1999. Indian capitulated to the hijackers who held nearly 200 passengers hostage on an Indian Airlines flight..... Pakistan has always used the threat of nuclear war to deter a conventional retaliation by India. But this time Pakistan seems to have miscalculated. Imran Khan chaired a meeting of the National Command Authority, apparently to signal the threat of a nuclear attack. Or perhaps this was meant to attract foreign intervention to defuse the crisis. The Karachi Stock Exchange had plummeted by 8% in two days"[7]

Pakistan's Foreign Minister, Shah Mahmood Qureshi, told a media briefing that Pakistan was planning its response. "This is an aggression against Pakistan and Pakistan will respond," he said. Islamabad released pictures on social media showing uprooted trees and cratered soil, which it claimed was the extent of the damage from the Indian bombing. The Indian military action was foretold after the Pulwama suicide bomb attack on a paramilitary convoy that killed over 40 Indian personnel in Kashmir. In the context of a war between two nuclear-armed states, the consequences can be far more severe. The repercussions of nuclear war between India and Pakistan would have to borne by the entire region, if not the whole world.

Meanwhile, in a series of press conferences, authorities in Islamabad warned that the army would respond on multiple fronts: political, diplomatic and military. In 2016, after the Uri attacks, India claimed to have conducted 'surgical strikes' inside Pakistani territory. However, after Pulwama, India once again bombed terrorist nests in Pakistan. The incident immediately led to increased hype in both countries. Nationalist feelings had already been running high following the Pulwama attack and its aftermath. The Indian media, in particular, continued its virulent attacks on Pakistan. In this, it was backed by the Indian government. While the sentiments of people were obviously emotional at that time, it was imperative that calm and restraint needed to be demonstrated.

On 27 February, 2019, the Hindu Newspaper in its editorial comment reported the resolve of the Indian government: "The government said all other options had been exhausted in making Islamabad keep its commitments since 2004 on curbing the activities of groups like the JeM. There is no denying the fact that the decision to send Mirage jets across the Line of Control (LoC) to fire missiles 70 km inside Pakistan represents a major shift. During the Kargil war in 1999, Prime Minister Atal Bihari Vajpayee had drawn a red line over the IAF crossing the LoC, to avoid international recrimination. This strike was carried out in Pakistani territory, not in Pakistan-occupied Kashmir, the theatre for retaliatory action in the past. It is still to be determined how far the JeM has been set back, but the strikes mark a new chapter with New Delhi's willingness to push the war against terror into Pakistan territory. The government has judged, perhaps correctly, that global opinion has shifted and there is little tolerance today for terror groups that continue to find shelter on Pakistan soil".[8] The Soviet withdrawal from Afghanistan was forced by the ISI and CIA. ISI was "an army within an army" with weapons, financial resources, access to current technology, and unparalleled authority. The CIA help made ISI more powerful. Former President Pervez Musharraf observed:

> "We helped created the mujahedeen, fired them with religious zeal in seminaries, armed them, paid them, fed them, and sent them to a jihad against the Soviet Union in Afghanistan. We did not stop to think how we would divert them to productive life after the jihad was won. This mistake cost Afghanistan and Pakistan more dearly than any other country. Neither did the United States realize what a rich, educated person like Osama bin Laden might later do with

the organization that we all had enabled him to establish".[9] General Musharraf's position was also at stake; his personal security and coup attempt possibilities made his country instable. In 01 October 2001, Pakistani intelligence attacked the Kashmiri legislature in Srinagar that killed 38 peopple[10].

On 13 December, 2001, Lashkar-e-Taiba attacked Indian parliament. Lashkar-e-Taiba (LeT), is known as an Army of the Pure or Army of the Righteous, is a terrorist organization based in Pakistan. It was founded in 1990 by professor Hafiz Mohammed Saeed. In 1990s, this group started targeting Hindus in Kashmir. In 20 March 2000 it carried our attacks in Chattisinghpora. On 13 December 2001, the Lashkar attacked Indian Parliament, and November 2008, the Lashkar attacked Mumbai.[11]

Security expert, and former Secretary of Research and Analysis Wing (RAW), Government of India, (Nov 17, 2016) Mr.Vikram Sood argued that clarity in intelligence operation is a must in a democratic system: "In a democratic system, it is desirable to have a measure of clarity in the working of intelligence agencies, both to define purpose and to ensure that tasks assigned are performed within the charter. Therefore, while on the one hand accountability of intelligence may be considered essential, it is meaningless without a legalized existence, a legalized charter, empowerment and then accountability. Legislation, therefore, has to be an aid to intelligence and not an impediment; it should encourage performance, risk taking and not stifle initiative and make the organization risk-averse. There must be a clear demarcation of responsibilities allowing for the necessary overlap. Each intelligence organization must have a clearly defined legalized charter. Previous attempts at a bill were expectedly thrown out because it was designed to run the intelligence apparatus as a human rights organization. The private member's bill, 'The Intelligence Services (Powers and Regulation) Bill, 2011', did not make any progress in the Lok Sabha as it was far too stifling in its endeavour to provide accountability without flexibility and empowerment. All the various extensive controls suggested would have killed any intelligence organisation".[12]

Having painting a picture of Indian intelligence, we normally come across several security and intelligence reports passed by Indian

Parliament after the failure of RAW and IB in several occasions. From Mumbai attacks to the recent Pulwama incident, we came to understand that Indian intelligence agencies are living in the past, and they are operation in old manner. Mr. SD Pradham has noted some important cases of intelligence failure in his analytical review article:

"Recent arrests of three wanted terrorists namely Abdul Karim Tunda, Yasin Bhatkal and Assadullah Akhtar alias Haddi indeed reflected success of intelligence agencies, yet there are several other cases that raise serious questions about the efficacy of the intelligence system. These include cases pertaining to Irshat Jahan, Samjhauta Express and the goof up in preparing the list of 50 terrorists that was sent to Pakistan as also circulation of photographs of two Pakistani citizens as those of terrorists who had penetrated into India. The list does end here. There were other important cases which include 26/11 attacks in Mumbai, Kargil intrusions and failures to provide warning on several occasions of bomb attacks. A task force appointed by the Institute of Defence studies and Analysis on the need for intelligence reforms had pointed out 14 important incidents, which reflected the "failure of the intelligence agencies". These did not include some of the cases, which occurred after the submission of report and were considered not so important. The four cases, mentioned above reflect systemic weaknesses of the intelligence system and need to be studied with a view to improve the intelligence system". Indian intelligence system needs urgent reforms. SD Pradhan.[13]

There are several committees established by successive India governments to investigate the failure of Indian intelligence agencies and fix the clefts of so called professional security approach. The lack of coordination, lack of high quality information gathering, and lack of professional approach caused their failure. The Mumbai, Pathankot and Pulwama terrorist incidents show inculcate us about the weak security approach of RAW and IB. Mr. SD Pradhan also estimates the level of intelligence failure in India:

"More embarrassing case was of sending the names of 50

terrorists to Pakistan, out of which two were in India- Feroze Abdul Rashid Khan, an accused of 1993 Mumbai blasts, was in jail since 2010 and Wazhul Kamar Khan, an accused of 2003 Malad blasts, was in Thane on bail. This reflected lackadaisical attitude of intelligence agencies as also the Ministry of Home Affairs. It is clear that the list was not subjected to thorough examination, which should have been done. While the list was sent by the Ministry of Home Affairs, it is well known that such lists are prepared by central intelligence agencies, reflecting lack of supervision at higher levels. Another case also equally embarrassing was the circulation of photographs of two Pakistani citizens as of terrorists who had infiltrated into Mumbai. It is well known that rival intelligence agencies indulge in operations involving supplying of wrong inputs. The checks must have been made before circulation of such inputs. This also reflects lackadaisical approach of agencies and lack of effective system of filters. The above cases highlight serious flaws in the system". Indian intelligence system needs urgent reforms. - SD Pradhan.[14]

Chapter 3

India's Intelligence Agencies: In Need of Reform and Oversight[1]

Manoj Joshi and Pushan Das

Introduction

The national security threats that India confronts today are much more diverse and complex than ever before. These threats range from nuclear-armed adversaries like China and Pakistan, to Maoists, and militancy and terrorism arising from within its borders and beyond. The question that we must ask is whether the country has a strategic measure of these challenges and the willingness and ability to confront them and, if required, pre-empt them. The tasks before India's intelligence community are similar to those that are confronted by their counterparts across the world:

They relate to strategic intelligence, anticipatory intelligence, current operations, cyber intelligence, and counterterrorism, counter proliferation and counter intelligence. The objectives require integrated mission and enterprise management, and innovation.[1] They are contingent upon the security challenges faced by a nation at a given time and necessitate reform and reorientation to meet evolving threats. Historically, intelligence agencies have been forced to reform and restructure because of failure. In India, too, reforms in intelligence agencies have occurred, primarily after wars and crises. This report shall highlight the tasks before

---

1   This article was first published in *Issue Brief - July 2015, Observer Research Foundation.* This paper has been reproduced here with special permission of the Observer Research Foundation.

the Indian intelligence agencies in implementing reforms and restructuring. It will seek to highlight the lack of political guidance and, in this regard, examine why recommendations made by previous task forces and committees have not been implemented.

The Conference

The report draws considerably from the conference on The Future Challenges to India's Intelligence System, organized by the Observer Research Foundation on 24 February 2015, which featured discussions involving serving and former Intelligence officers, research scholars and specialists interested in intelligence affairs. The discussions at ORF were divided into three broad themes: External intelligence; internal intelligence; and technical intelligence. The key issues that emerged from the discussions are the following:

- Co-ordination and tasking in need of improvement amongst intelligence agencies and between state and central agencies

- Intelligence collection is ad-hoc in the absence of clear-cut requirements from the consumers of intelligence

- Poor cadre management and inability to recruit qualified language specialists and technical skills result in a shortage of personnel

- Lack of intellectual capacity and investment in education system exacerbate recruitment shortfalls in intelligence agencies. Engaging private players for specialist tasks is therefore necessary.

- Agencies suffer from chronic shortage of military expertise big data analytics capabilities need to be commissioned and customized for the Indian context

- Special Forces capabilities need to be ramped up and their concept of use 'married' with the capabilities of intelligence agencies

- China's growth and the multiplication of its capabilities

requires a more focused effort in TECHINT (Technical Intelligence) and HUMINT (Human Intelligence)

- Parliamentary statute is the key for creating accountability in intelligence agencies

- Lack of political attention and effective guidance has prevented reform and optimal functioning of the intelligence system.

An Overview

There are currently 14 intelligence agencies operating in India with different and sometimes overlapping mandates. Most of these 14 intelligence agencies have come into being as a response to changing strategic environment and shortcomings in the intelligence framework on several occasions. Following the debacle of the 1962 war with China, the Directorate General of Security (DGS) was set up within the Intelligence Bureau (IB), with its operational unit, the Aviation Research Centre (ARC), tasked with obtaining intelligence on China.

Following the failure of IB in the 1965 war against Pakistan, the government decided to hive off external intelligence under a new agency, the Research & Analysis Wing (R&AW) and linked the DGS with it. Though there were various measures of internal reorganization and restructuring, the next wave of reforms came after the 1999 Kargil war, when there was a colossal failure on the part of various security agencies in detecting Pakistani incursions across the Line of Control (LOC).

The Defence Intelligence Agency (DIA) was set up in 2002 and tasked to collect, collate and evaluate intelligence from other service directorates and other agencies. The DIA was to control inter-service technical intelligence (TECHINT) assets primarily in Signals Intelligence (SIGINT) and Imagery Intelligence (IMINT). In 2004, the National Technical Research Organization (NTRO) was set up to be the premier TECHINT agency of the country with the mandate to collect communications intelligence (COMINT), Electronic Intelligence (ELINT), IMINT and cyber intelligence.

The NTRO's mandate created quite a storm, since it was given tasks already being done by other intelligence services, resulting in inter-agency turf battles that led to problems in its functioning for nearly a decade. The biggest problem has been the lack of co-ordination amongst the intelligence community in India. Each agency looks out for itself and guards its turf zealously. There is need for strict guidance and supervision to ensure that there is cooperation and coordination.

Former Union Home Minister P. Chidambaram enforced co-ordination at the apex level after the Mumbai attacks of 2008, but after his departure, the new Home Minister has not kept up the process. Since the Home Minister has a vast repertoire of responsibilities, there is need for a Director National Intelligence, or a Minister, to arbitrate between agencies and promote greater collaboration between them.

The question of accountability in the Indian context is no less important. Hardly anyone, if at all, is held accountable for serious failures on the security front—the inability to assess Chinese intentions during the 1959-1962 period, to pinpoint Pakistan's additional armored division in 1965, or the plans for Operation Gibraltar, the LTTE's reaction to the India-Sri Lanka Accord of 1987, the Kargil incursion, or the Mumbai attacks of 2008.

This has led to a culture where no person or agency is held responsible for major intelligence failures and hence the intelligence agencies have had little or no accountability. This is only partly due to excessive secrecy within which intelligence organizations and processes work. It is more part of a systemic flaw where authority and accountability do not go together. The Mumbai attacks in 2008 resulted in the implementation of further reforms at apex level coordination. The attack, while not a failure of intelligence gathering, was a failure of timely action and co-ordination. However, the Indian experience of reform and restructuring has, till now, been visited by only limited success. The reasons for this have been many and will be laid out in the conclusion.

Internal Intelligence

India's internal security environment is fraught with a number of challenges. They range from cross border terrorism, a Maoist rebellion, insurgencies in North-east India, violent Islamic extremism, communal and sectarian violence, as well as illegal migration, human trafficking, narcotics smuggling and money laundering. Such a wide gamut of threats requires a multi-pronged approach to intelligence gathering which would be beyond the remit of a single agency.

The Indian intelligence system emerged as an extension of the police system to track and counter the Indian national movement during British rule. This is a legacy and structure that it has not quite broken out of to meet the challenges of modern intelligence-gathering. It carries the burden of an intellectual infrastructure that has failed to build competencies essential to intelligence operations in a vastly different environment than the pre-Independence era. The lack of a dedicated intelligence cadre and the continuing practice of staffing intelligence agencies with police officers have resulted in agencies playing down the importance of language specialists, social scientists, technical specialists and cyber analysts.

The IB has over the years become a reporting arm of the government, often treated as an appendage of the Ministry of Home Affairs (MHA). Its location at the MHA, meant for convenience of administration, has resulted in supervision of the IB by the Home Ministry. The tight political control by the MHA made IB focus more on domestic and political matters at the expense of other security challenges. The agency also has responsibility over local police functions in the form of verifications and background checks, which further ties down its already-limited manpower.

All these factors put together have drastically compromised the IB's capabilities especially in the area of counterintelligence, which is one of its primary mandates, to begin with. In 2001, a Group of Ministers (GoM) had recommended an end to this practice and sought to confer the rank of Secretary to the Director of IB, on par with the status of the R&AW counterpart. On the GoM advice, the IB was designated as the premier Counter-Terrorism agency and authorized to create Multi-Agency Centre (MAC) and Subsidiary Multi-Agency Centers (SMACs) to collate and process intelligence inputs from various sources. These were to be located in state headquarters comprising representatives from various agencies from the state and the centre.

External Intelligence

The R&AW is the sole agency tasked to gather external intelligence. The organization was created by an executive order and not by parliamentary statute. It was interpreted, at the time of the R&AW's creation in 1968, that it would provide HUMINT and TECHINT to fulfill its mandate. Over the years there has been criticism that the R&AW relies too much on TECHINT and Open Source Intelligence (OSINT), and does not pay enough attention towards developing human intelligence (HUMINT). The blame for this deficiency should be shared equally, if not more, by the political leadership which, often, chose to limit R&AW's critical operational mandates.

The R&AW is faced with a number of challenges which have constrained its ability to deliver external intelligence in a rapidly evolving world. The organization often works under embassy cover which limits its ability in generating human intelligence. The Aviation Research Centre (ARC) gathers signals and image intelligence on China, a task which overlaps with the mandate of the National Technical Research Organization and the Defence Intelligence Agency. The IB too has recently set up a China Desk, though its functions are not quite clear but presumably relate to counter-intelligence.

While overlapping of mandates is natural, there is a need to clearly articulate the principal focus of each of the agencies to yield optimal output and avoid failures. Recruitment to the R&AW is still dependent on deputations from other central agencies especially the Indian Police Service. Its intake of scientists, cyber analysts and linguists is below required levels. The lack of lateral entry options reduces the agency's ability to recruit off the market. Elsewhere, intelligence agencies have moved much faster and much further in recruiting experts from private sector and academia to support intelligence operations.

Over the years, R&AW's efforts towards seeking 'outside's expertise have been few and erratic, at best. The agency is also faced with intelligence requirements being framed in an ad-hoc manner. Consumers are reluctant to clearly spell out their requirements, in part because they have not applied their minds to the task and in some measure because they have not worked out just how intelligence can be applied to enhance their own effectiveness. There is need for a better mechanism for tasking and fusion of intelligence with policy. Both the Joint Intelligence Committee (JIC) and the National Security Council with a well-staffed secretariat are mandated to fill this very gap, have not measured up to expectations, particularly in dealing with asymmetric threats like the Mumbai attacks of 2008.

Technical Intelligence

In view of the significant role of technology in intelligence collection, analysis and dissemination, an important development was the creation of the National Technical Research Organization (NTRO). The NTRO's mandate was to plan, design, and set up and operate major new TECHINT facilities. It was tasked with the establishment of secured digital networks to disseminate TECHINT to all the agencies as well as to enable information flow between agencies. As part of this, the NTRO is to host a common database of information so that it could be easily and quickly disseminated to other agencies.

The agency is tasked with monitoring missile launches in countries of interest and responsible for defensive and offensive cyber operations. Another agency that was created was the tri-Service Defence Intelligence Agency (DIA). It controls the TECHINT assets of the three armed services, primarily the Army's erstwhile Signals Intelligence Directorate and the Defence Image Processing Analysis Centre (DIPAC) in Delhi and the Defence Satellite Control Centre (DSSC) in Bhopal. There have been issues between DIA and NTRO over space-based assets and their control.

The creation of a new agency in the form of the NTRO resulted in predictable resistance, especially since it was given tasks which were being done by others. Creating facilities anew would have been an expensive proposition, and so, the obvious way was to transfer assets being held by the others. Strangely enough, this problem was not anticipated and addressed by the government. Subsequently, a committee was set up by the National Security Advisor (NSA) to come up with proposals and the NTRO came up only in April 2004, though its Chairman, former ARC head RS Bedi, had been appointed a year earlier. Another issue has been the overlap between NTRO and the ARC.

This has created a situation where NTRO controls high-resolution satellites and is responsible for space- and ground-based COMINT, while the ARC is responsible for collecting IMINT and COMINT through aircraft mounted sensors. The notification establishing the NTRO stated that its task was to gather COMINT, ELINT, IMINT and cyber intelligence and termed it as the premier technical intelligence agency of the country. There was some criticism that the agency's task was to merely collate and make the information available to other agencies, but when it was set up, it was clearly given an analysis role as well. Poor management and turf battles have, however, led to the agency over-exceeding its capacity and thereby failing to meet some important target areas.

Issues for reform

First and foremost, the Indian government needs to decide what challenges must be addressed by its contemporary agencies. What kind of an intelligence system would best serve internal and external security requirements? How best to strike a balance between traditional politico-military intelligence operations in target countries and working on pre-empting and containing non-state actors? How much emphasis should be laid on economic, commercial and scientific intelligence? Second, specialization is important in the modern era and multiplicity of agencies is inevitable. Quite often, the issue of turf war is over-blown. In fact, a certain level of redundancy among intelligence agencies can prevent a systemic failure in one outfit from becoming a catastrophic, all-round failure.

Oversight

Amongst democracies, India alone lacks any oversight of its intelligence agencies. As previously mentioned, its agencies do not have any constitutional authority. The problems with oversight and accountability are many. Intelligence agencies are reluctant to submit to any oversight as it is. In addition, intelligence agencies are equally concerned with the level of inexperience and ignorance among the political class with matters relating to security. The agencies have to contend with the very real worry of information leak if every action of theirs becomes subject to parliamentary scrutiny.

However, given the fact that there are several senior politicians who have served government in key ministries, it should not be too difficult to construct an oversight mechanism comprising a mix of former members of the Cabinet Committee for Security (CCS) and serving ministers. Alternatively a small ministerial committee, aided by external experts, could monitor issues related to performance, finance and privacy. Successive governments have historically been reluctant to create oversight mechanism for intelligence agencies. One reason could be the manner in which the governments use the Intelligence Bureau in domestic political espionage—in clearer terms, spying on political rivals. This is a widely known fact, yet politicians conveniently overlook it when they take charge of the government.

However, there is another kind of oversight which can be introduced—an office of the Inspector General who could be from the intelligence services or a security professional reporting to the top intelligence coordinator or the National Security Advisor. For the present, however, the more practical method seems to be the oversight provided by the National Intelligence Board (NIntB) comprising of the NSA (Chair), the Principal Secretary to the Prime Minister and the Cabinet Secretary who in their own way separately report to the PM as well.

Apex level management

At present, presumably this is being done by the NIntB, and the Chairman Joint Intelligence Committee (JIC) functions as the member-secretary of the unit. But the question that repeatedly comes up is whether the NSA, Cabinet Secretary and the Principal Secretary to the PM have the necessary time and attention span to provide the kind of supervision and leadership needed for the task of high-level direction to the intelligence apparatus—oversight, apex level tasking, supervision of agency and coordination between agencies. The government could consider a full-time intelligence adviser to do so or even appoint a Director National Intelligence to do the task and place him under the NSA and make him a member of the NIntB.

Coordination and Tasking

Coordination between the Centre and the states, and within states at district and *thana* (local police station) level remains deficient even after setting up new mechanisms like Multi Agency Centers (MAC) and Subsidiary Multi Agency Centers (SMAC), to enable intelligence sharing and coordination amongst multiple agencies. There is need for higher level coordination which involves the Home and Police departments working together with their Central counterparts. This is unlikely to come through an administrative fiat, and would need to be subject to legislation.

The Defence Intelligence Agency (DIA) offers an apt illustration. Its principal infirmity is the absence of the person or position at the top of the pyramid—the Chief of Defence Staff. This has created several problems for the organization which was otherwise robust and has potential. The experiment with annual tasking done through the NSCS came to a halt in 2008, after two cycles. Thereafter, the agencies have been doing "self tasking" based on their respective charters. Given the complexity of the security environment facing the country, single-point tasking is neither adequate nor reliable.

Self-tasking has its own problems since it puts the agency in policy-makers role, which is not an ideal solution. It is up to the consumers and policy-makers to decide what they want from an intelligence agency and, for coordination purposes; this should be mediated at the apex level by the NintB and at a lower level by the JIC or NSCS. There is need for a sharper look at the Intelligence Cycle which moves from tasking and planning, collection, processing, analysis in terms of original tasking, and dissemination back to the original task giver. The system needs to be sharply defined and degrees of separation need to be maintained between collection and analysis.

Shortage of personnel and recruitment

One of the major problems with all intelligence and specialized agencies in government is the challenge of addressing personnel issues. Some of the personnel shortage arises from the inability to recruit the right kind of people for specific tasks—technically skilled staff or linguists for instance. Equally important is the issue of cadre management—ensuring that the personnel are able to progress through the bureaucratic system in an orderly and productive manner and that no moral issues crop up because there is bunching of ranks at a particular level.[3]

Intelligence agencies also suffer from a chronic shortage of military expertise. While a system of deputation exists, military officers are reluctant to be posted to these agencies. In the absence of equivalent rank in the agencies, the military officers are compelled to work at a level which is often lower than their Service rank. Persistent staff shortages have raised a debate about a distinct cadre for the intelligence agencies with independent recruitment and promotion system similar to the civilian bureaucracy.

The obvious answer for technical issues is for the agencies to think in terms of getting private contractors to work for them. But India has no system for providing non-government personnel security clearances that would be required for such work. In the current framework, for there to be meaningful and long-term reform there needs to longer tenures for key personnel and chiefs like they have in western nations. There needs to be discussion on the time periods required to implement institutional reforms.

Open Source Intelligence

The internet has ushered in an information revolution beyond the traditional mediums of open source information like newspapers and television. At present the NTRO handles Open Source, mainly through the monitoring of TV and radio channels. It has often been indicated that the R&AW too draws a lot of information from open sources. Open source information now emanates not only from traditional media sources but also social media and other internet-based applications apart from professional journals and technical literature. The internet has also become one of the primary sources of communication all over the world for governments and non-state actors and people. There is a need for one agency to focus on open source information and internet-based communications which will cover all mediums, including newspapers, radio, the internet and social media sites like Twitter and Face book.

Legislation

There are two reasons why the intelligence agencies need to be governed by laws framed by the Parliament. First is the need to strengthen their accountability. The Indian agencies function outside the purview of any legislation, making it difficult to implement administrative, operational or financial accountability. The IB was established by the British in December 1887 as a part of the Indian Special Branch, but it has no legislative authorisation. The other agencies have come up through executive orders as well. Given the enormous power these agencies wield, it is important to legalize their functions and provide for means to guarantee the citizens against their misuse.

The second reason is the need for clarity in the functioning of various agencies. By definition, legislation is precise because its words have legal implications. The enormous powers provided to the agencies should be carefully spelt out in a legislative format to ensure that they are viewed with all the seriousness they deserve. There should be no room for misinterpreting authority or tasks of the agencies.

A quick look at the US Intelligence Reform and Terrorism Prevention Act of 2004 will reveal precise and detailed wording, spelling out duties, responsibilities and authority. In March 2011, Manish Teary, who also subsequently served as a minister in the UPA government introduced a Private Member's Bill "to regulate the manner of functioning and exercise of powers of Indian Intelligence Agencies".

The Bill will have authority within the country and outside of it, and aimed at providing "for the coordination, control and oversight of such agencies." One of the aims of the Bill was to provide legislative authority for the functioning of the agencies, another was to ensure against the misuse of their powers. The section "authorisation and procedures" specified that any kind of interception of communication or break-in could be conducted without a warrant issued by a designated authority.

The Bill also provided for a National Intelligence and Security Oversight Committee headed by the Chairman of Rajya Sabha, Speaker of the Lok Sabha, the PM, Home Minister, Leader of the Opposition in the two Houses of Parliament, and two MPs nominated by the Chairman RS and Speaker LS. The Cabinet Secretary would be the secretary of the Committee. This Committee would draw up and table an annual report, appoint an Intelligence Ombudsman to deal with staff grievances and administrative issues of the agencies and constitute a National Intelligence Tribunal to investigate complaints against the agencies. The Bill remains in the long queue of legislations waiting to be put to vote.

HUMINT and TECHINT

The world is going through a proliferation of information. Big data analysis in India is still in its infancy, but clearly it is the trend of the future. Documents that came out about the Boundless Informant programme of the US' NSA indicated that the agency collected almost 3 billion bits of intelligence from US computer networks, and 97 billion worldwide, in a 30-day period in 2013.[4]

According to a report, India's Central Monitoring System and National Cyber Coordination Centre will, between them, enable government to access all phone calls and internet-related data 24x7 and on a real time basis.[5] Some of the physical elements of these systems are already in place, but there is, as yet, no legislative authorisation for this large-scale invasion of privacy, penalties against the misuse of data thus obtained, or any guarantees against misuse.

The challenge of HUMINT remains, as intelligence agencies face critical shortages of skilled manpower. This is as much a problem of the lack of manpower as of the tendency to take the easy way out and rely on TECHINT to do the needful. The non-availability of personnel with the requisite language skills or aptitude for

41

intelligence work is of serious concern. The system of time-bound deputation from the police and armed forces and the lack of an intelligence cadre make it tough for organizations to create and retain skill required for such specialized work. Military expertise in intelligence agencies needs to be improved by implementing a policy of giving equivalent rank to military personnel vis-a-vis their civilian counterparts.

Counter-Terrorism and Counter-Insurgency

The issue of an effective counter-terrorism and counter-insurgency system remains. The failure to create the National Counter-terrorism Centre (NCTC) is one aspect of it. The government has to think hard and see how such a system can come up, even while meeting the requirements of federalism. In the wake of the 2008 Mumbai attacks, the government was able to push through legislation that created the National Investigation Agency (NIA) dedicated to investigating terrorism cases.

Under the law the Agency can be invited by a state to investigate a case, or the Centre can direct it to investigate one. However, given the nature of power-sharing, it has inevitably come into conflict with state police systems. The best example is the conflicting claims and actions of the Maharashtra state police and the NIA on the German Bakery blast case.[6]

The Burdwan blasts in 2014 in West Bengal saw similar conflicts between the state police and the NIA.[7] The big issue in counter-terrorism is the capacity of the various states to deal with terrorism, not only in terms of intelligence, but also dealing with a terror strike, as was evident during the Mumbai attack, besides investigation and prosecution of the case. The Centre has made great efforts to deal with the issue such as the creation of SMACs though proposals for fusion centers have yet to take root. The real problem is the extremely poor capacity of state police organizations to cope with even ordinary crimes, leave alone terror strikes. A lot of states also suffer from insurgencies of varying magnitude. The inability of state and central police forces to deal with these insurgencies reflects the poor state of policing in the country.

The problem of secrecy prevents us from assessing the effectiveness of counter-terrorism or counterinsurgency activities of Indian agencies. Agencies routinely claim that they have foiled several terrorist conspiracies and many arrests do indeed take place and are reported in the media. However, the gold standard—where the prosecution can actually obtain a conviction of those arrested— had not been achieved.

China

The rise of China poses all kinds of challenges to India. The opacity of the Chinese system makes it difficult for us to fathom its capabilities and intentions. China's military capabilities have shown an exponential growth. In the last five years, China has astonished the world with the advances it has made in aerospace and missile capabilities. Its prowess in cyber-space is considerably advanced.

India's focus on China till now was primarily on the border, gathering military intelligence with regard to the potential threat of Peoples Liberation Army (PLA) forces in Tibet and Xinjiang. But China is making inroads into the Indian Ocean Region and reports of the PLA Navy operating and visiting regions around India are becoming all too frequent. As China expands across into the Indian Ocean and establishes strong economic and arms transfer relationships in the South Asian region, the dimensions of the challenge will change. This requires a much more focused effort—through TECHINT and HUMINT to gather intelligence on Chinese military capabilities, scientific-technical capacities, politics, trade and economics. In turn, this requires the pooling together of specialist manpower—with requisite language and technical skills—and their effective utilization. It also requires huge investments in TECHINT and cyber capabilities.

Conclusion

The Indian experience of reform and restructuring of intelligence agencies has, till now, revealed only limited success. The reasons for this have been many. Primary among them has been the lack of political guidance for the reform process. Task forces and committees come up with recommendations for reform, but implementing them requires the process to go through the bureaucratic maze and that is where resistance often happens. To overcome this requires political attention and leadership which is attuned to the security needs of the country, as well as possessing a nuanced understanding of the ways of bureaucracy.

Both internal and external intelligence agencies continue to face critical manpower shortages. The lack of a separate intelligence cadre and the lack of language and technical specialists have blunted the effectiveness of the Indian intelligence community. Agencies in India have not been able to keep up with the technical revolution that has taken place in collecting and analyzing data. Indian public sector has not been able to meet the demands of systems that can handle big data. There exists a necessity to co-opt the private sector in intelligence work to make up for the shortfall.

India has in recent years become more adept at gathering and using IMINT gathered through satellites and aircraft. The Defence Image Processing & Analysis Centre (DIPAC) has acquired the capability to transfer imagery real-time over secure networks. The recent launch of the GSAT-7 satellite for the Indian Navy was another step in the same direction. A second satellite, GSAT-7A, is already in the pipeline.

There has been, over the years, a duplication of resources and capabilities, mainly because of ineffective coordination. The R&AW and the Aviation Research Centre (ARC) both are gathering electronic intelligence on China albeit on different platforms. The NTRO is now designated as the nodal agency for technical intelligence, but it is yet to gain control of all or acquire assets for other agencies to carry out its mandate. While there exists a necessity to create additional capabilities, duplication of assets and capabilities must be rationalized given the economic costs.

It is imperative those intelligence agencies and the armed forces develop the capacity to deal with unpredictable threats. This calls for urgent and comprehensive reform and restructuring of the intelligence apparatus. The initiative must come from the political leadership committed to secure the country's strategic interests in the face of phenomenal and often unexpected challenges.

Courtesy: "Issue Brief. July 2015. India's Intelligence Agencies: In Need of Reform and Oversight. Observer Research Foundation is a public policy think tank that aims to influence formulation of policies for building a strong and prosperous India". Manoj Joshi is a Distinguished Fellow at ORF. Pushan Das is a Research Assistant with ORF's National Security Initiative. www.orfonline.org. July 2015. This paper has been taken with a special permission of the Observer Research Foundation.

Chapter 4

Why Intelligence Fails[1]

Janani Krishnaswamy

Abstract

In this policy report, Ms. Janani Krishnaswamy examines the repeated failures of India's secret intelligence agencies through the lens of a broad 'reform failure'. She asserts that intelligence failures predominantly arise from reform makers' inability to make sensible reforms, than an analyst's failure to make imaginative analysis. After interacting with numerous former intelligence personnel and analyzing two major intelligence review committee reports published in the aftermath of Kargil 1999 and Mumbai 26/11, she argues that insufficient theorization in the field of intelligence studies and a few mistaken perceptions about intelligence failure among intelligence consumers have led to weak intelligence reforms.

At the heart of the policy report is a theoretical framework for cataloguing failures. She has created four categories of failure such as 'intelligence failure' or failure to produce accurate intelligence, 'policy failure' or failure to act on intelligence, 'adaptation failure' or failure to implement reforms, and 'reform failure' or failure to implement sensible reforms. As policy decisions are often guided by political perceptions about policy issues, she identifies that the apparent indifference towards and lack of knowledge of intelligence and security matters among political leaders is the reason behind the lack of a cohesive and coherent counter-terrorism

---

1   This article was first published as Policy Report No. 3 by the The Hindu Centre for Politics and Public Policy. The original article was supported and published by The Hindu Centre for Politics and Public Policy. This paper has been reproduced here with special permission of the author.

and intelligence policy. Asserting the importance of establishing definitional clarity in intelligence studies, Ms. Krishnaswamy aims at improving the quality of intelligence review committees in the country and enabling a better system of checks and balances to appraise the failures of the intelligence community through the theoretical framework developed in this paper.

Sub-Chapter 1

Introduction and Statement of Problem

"An intelligence failure or an inability to pre-empt an attack will easily get publicized because of the proportion of damage caused by the terrorist attack. On the other hand, the number of times bombs you (an intelligence agency) might have diffused never gets publicized."

–Information and Broadcasting Minister, Manish Tewari[1]

The Indian government has been spending a substantial amount of money for strengthening its intelligence apparatus.[2] Yet, the country has been witnessing numerous instances of terrorist attacks. India has now become prone to more terrorist attacks since 26/11 than the United States has since 9/11. While the recent Boston bombing was a major case of publicized intelligence failure in the US after 9/11, several Indian states have been constant prey to terrorist groups in the aftermath of 26/11. The intelligence agencies in several Indian states have been frequently coming under the scanner for perceived ignorance and incompetence in countering terrorism.

The central intelligence agencies have earned the wrath of the government for failing to sufficiently warn local agencies. Why do our secret intelligence agencies fail repeatedly? Is it because of (a) lack of adequate intelligence, (b) dearth of trained manpower in the intelligence sector, (c) failure to apply latest sophisticated technology in surveillance, (d) lack of proper intelligence sharing between the Centre and the states, (e) lack of action on available intelligence, (f) the current state of political instability or (g) the lack of sensible intelligence reforms? In the aftermath of the terrorist attack at Dilsukhnagar in Hyderabad, India's secret intelligence agencies were subject to an intense inspection. Heated political debates over the construction of the National Counter Terrorism Centre (NCTC), a controversial anti-terror hub that was proposed in the aftermath of 26/11 attacks, was stirred up after five years.

Are such organizational reforms sufficient to fix the problems of the intelligence community? Intelligence review committees and politicians constantly assess the performance of intelligence agencies and underline numerous failures within the intelligence system. As a result, they have reinforced the need for several reforms. Indian intelligence scholars, for the most part, are interested in subjects such as the legal framework for intelligence agencies and mechanisms for oversight. However, no one has questioned the state of intelligence theorization in the country or the level of knowledge of politicians and reform makers — about intelligence and intelligence failures. The main research question addressed in this paper is what do we (producers and consumers of intelligence) know about intelligence failures and what do we do about them?

Taking the cases of failure to prevent 26/11 and the Kargil conflict of 1999, this paper analyses the current state of intelligence reform making and addresses some of the most pressing issues relating to the Indian intelligence scene. The paper questions whether (a) the lack of sufficient understanding—of national security and intelligence issues —of a few politicians, (b) the current state of intelligence reform making or (c) gaps in intelligence sharing have led to the increasing number of terrorist attacks in the country. The policy paper calls for a theory to explain intelligence failures and advances two strong arguments relating to theory building. First, it argues that there is a lacuna in theory-driven academic treatises in intelligence studies in India.

Second, it makes the case that a theory developed with a better understanding of the culture and bureaucratic functioning of the intelligence agencies in India can be helpful in understanding why secret intelligence fails.

Aims and Objectives

The policy paper aims at analyzing why India's secret intelligence agencies fail repeatedly and find out what we do about them. Its objectives are:

1. To study the state of affairs of intelligence studies in India;

2. To examine what we know and what we do about intelligence failures;

3. To analyze the state of intelligence reform making in the country;

4. To identify the need for theorization on the subject;

5. To bring more definitional clarity to intelligence studies; and

6. To develop a theoretical framework towards a theory explaining intelligence failures.

Research Design

A mix of qualitative analysis and in-depth interviewing has been used to gain scholarly awareness of all the activities of the intelligence community at large, i.e. better knowledge about and less misunderstanding of the nature of the intelligence business in the country.

Qualitative Analysis

First, the paper will analyze the failure to prevent 26/11 by taking an in-depth look at the report of the Ram Pradhan Committee—the High-Level Enquiry Committee (HLEC) on 26/11—appointed by the Maharashtra Government on December 30, 2008, to probe the intelligence and law enforcement response to the 2008 Mumbai attacks. After this, the consequent reforms and the influence of American intelligence reforms in fixing the problems of the Indian intelligence community will be studied. Next, the report of the Kargil Review Committee, which was set up after the Kargil intrusions in 1999, will be analyzed. Later, the two aforementioned reports will be compared to determine the nature of intelligence reviewing and reform building in the country.

The analysis of the Kargil Review Committee report will be restricted to the intelligence-related problems identified by the Committee and the recommendations published in the Group of Ministers (GoM) report. Later, the paper will study what recommendations have been made in the post 26/11 era and identify how many of them have been implemented.

Second, it will review a few popular political perceptions about intelligence failure. After this, the paper will analyze the state of intelligence studies in India and later, look to several intelligence scholars in the international community to find some theoretical direction. I have had the desire to study the most significant and most recent material in the field as I hope such a literary review will illustrate the different theoretical standpoints.

I have managed to get some insight into the extent of theorizing in the West. As a starting point, I utilized *Intelligence theory: Key questions and debates*. This collection of essays has offered an excellent idea about the principal debates in the field. A survey report on the state of intelligence studies by Loch K. Johnson and Allison M. Shelton has also presented greater insight. However, I referred to several other works assessing several instances of intelligence failures spread across the history of the West. Such an inquiry into intelligence debates in the West is very useful because the Indian intelligence set-up is 'heavily modeled on its British and American counterparts.'[3]

In-depth Interviews

The paper gains awareness into the hidden problems of the intelligence community through in-depth interactions with several former intelligence personnel, government officials, terrorism experts, erudite scholars and journalists. Interviews were conducted over seven days in New Delhi and Mumbai. To understand the intelligence producer's perspective on intelligence failures, I had some in-depth interactions with a handful of former members of the intelligence community, including a recently retired director of the Intelligence Bureau[4], former R&AW director Vikram Sood, former additional secretary, Cabinet Secretariat and R&AW, Jayadeva Ranade, former IB deputy director and director, Central Bureau of Investigation, R.K. Raghavan, former special director, Central Bureau of Investigation, D.R. Karthikeyan, and former additional director, K.V. Thomas. Former home secretary, Gopal Krishna Pillai, and present Information & Broadcasting Minister & Congress MP, Manish Tewari, offered interesting insights into the intelligence consumer's perspectives.

As the paper looks into 26/11 in an in-depth manner, I interviewed the co-author of the Ram Pradhan Committee report, V. Balachandran, who pinned down the main problem of the intelligence community, and former Mumbai police commissioner and commissioner of intelligence, D. Sivanandan. Several others who offered great insight into the functioning of intelligence agencies included defence analyst Manoj Joshi, terrorism studies experts Ajai Sahni and Srinath Raghavan, and journalists from The Hindu Vinay Kumar and Sandeep Joshi. The interviewees were selected based on snowball sampling.

Justification for Selection of Case Studies

The reason behind selecting the case studies of Kargil 1999 and 26/11 is that the country's two major intelligence review committees have been set up in the aftermath of these attacks. The first major effort for internal security reform in the country was the setting up of a Review Committee on July 29, 1999 in the aftermath of the Pakistan intrusion in Kargil. The Kargil Committee submitted report on Dec 15, 1999.

A Group of Ministers (GoM) was formed on April 17, 2000 to re-examine the problems—of security and intelligence —raised in the report, and consequently set up Task Forces for (1) Intelligence (2) Internal Security (3) Border Management and (4) Defence. The GoM forwarded their recommendations to the Prime Minister on Feb 19, 2001. However, nothing much was done either by the NDA or by the UPA government till the 26/11 attacks. This was when former home minister P. Chidambaram codified the National Investigation Agency Bill (2008) within 19 days. Immediately after the attacks, he set up the Ram Pradhan Committee to review the intelligence and security lapses that caused the attack. Moreover, the 26/11 terrorist attacks provide a good case for greater understanding of (a) the influence of, or lack of influence of intelligence analysis on policy makers, (b) the influence of intelligence reforms in preventing future terrorist attacks, and (c) the influence of US intelligence reform making to tackle India's intelligence problems.

Organization of Chapters

In the chapters that follow, I will highlight the need for theorization in the field of intelligence studies in India. The introductory chapter will clearly state the research problem and explain how the paper will deal with the subject of intelligence failure. In the second chapter, I will clearly describe the problem in the different approaches of evaluating intelligence failures, analyze the shortcomings of the past research agenda and explain why there needs to be a theory to explain the repeated failures of the intelligence community. It will include a short review of past studies on intelligence failures and intelligence reforms and also set the mood for an elaborate investigation into why secret intelligence fails.

In the third chapter, I will discuss some of the important challenges faced by intelligence studies in the country. Here, I will make an inquiry into the nature of national security information that is available for intelligence scholars. This kind of inquiry is essential because the understanding of the nature and working of intelligence agencies and the repeated failures of the community is limited due to the unavailability of certain types of information. I introduce this section as I believe we should know far more about the activities and processes within intelligence agencies to be able to offer valuable policy insights and make useful policy recommendations.

Chapter four will try to gather evidence to justify the need for rigorous theorization in the field of intelligence studies in India. In this, I will make some imperative review of literature essential to have a clear understanding about the state of intelligence studies in the country. Next, I will analyze the perceptions of intelligence producers and consumers about what constitutes intelligence and intelligence failures. Here, I will also analyze a few theories explaining intelligence failures in the West. In chapter five, I will focus on making a critical analysis of two intelligence review committees taken for analysis— the Ram Pradhan Committee and the Kargil Review Committee. Later, I will compare the two to understand the state of intelligence inquiry and reform making in the country.

In the next two chapters that follow, I will try to bring some definitional clarity to a few concepts in intelligence studies and develop a framework for building a theory that can explain intelligence failures. I will test the theoretical framework developed in the earlier chapter by re-evaluating the failure to prevent 26/11 attacks. Chapter eight will make a conclusive note and highlight the need for India's secret intelligence agencies to strike a balance between sharing and secrecy. In this chapter, I will particularly explain how the intelligence agencies and policy makers can help intelligence scholars build a theory to explain intelligence failures. In the final chapter, I will recommend a set of intelligence reforms — which I think can help intelligence agencies avert future failures.

Limitations of the Study

There are some important limitations to this paper, as with any study. First, it is highly impractical to comprehensively catalogue in public the IB's or R&AW's record of failed judgments, the allegations aimed at them, and their responses in the way of remedial action. Second, the inferences made and recommendations advanced in the paper, therefore, are restricted by the limited exposure to classified and declassified documents on intelligence and the very secretive nature of national security intelligence that doesn't offer any scope to build definitive theories and doctrines on intelligence. Finally, a lack of sufficient evidence on intelligence working itself might also "lead to over-theorization", which has remained a major setback for intelligence scholars across the globe.[5] Moreover, the trouble in discerning the true intentions of the intelligence personnel in producing intelligence or that of a policy maker in carrying out reforms makes it tough to identify where the problem exactly lies. While it is not within the current research agenda to analyze why democratic governments are so tight-fisted in sharing even non-sensitive national security information with scholars, this is by far the biggest limitation of the paper.

Sub-Chapter 2

A Rationale for Theorizing

The story of 26/11 is one replete with allegations of failure[6]-failure to effectively process available intelligence, failure to share intelligence within agencies, failure to take strategic warnings seriously, neglect of open source intelligence, failure to strengthen sea patrolling, failure to understand the structure of anti-terror squads (ATS), failure to sensitize agencies about new terrorism, and failures to deal with lack of arms and ammunition, acute shortage of automatic weapons, non-availability of naval layout plans, and poorly equipped ATS. The biggest of them all was the failure to prevent Pakistani terrorists from making an amphibious landing onto the quayside of Mumbai on the night of November 26, 2008. Three days of siege followed as the world watched on television sets. The attacks quickly changed the security priorities of the country, like none other, and set in motion several intelligence and police modernization reforms that were in the pipeline.

I

The Mumbai attacks unveiled a number of innovations in terrorist tactics. Numerous monographs, media reports and interviews assessing the causes and outcome of the failure to prevent 26/11 have exposed several other shortcomings within the Indian internal security architecture at the state and federal levels. Several Western academicians called the 26/11 attacks India's experience of 9/11. Given the colossal reforms brought about following the attack, there is nothing wrong about the reference.

However, the description of 26/11 as an intelligence failure is totally misplaced. The Indian intelligence community had uncovered numerous "red flags" prior to the 26/11 attack with dozens of alerts about the possibility of a *fidayeen* (suicide) attack, multiple sea-borne attacks and commando operations. However, such strategic intelligence warning did not lead to effective and speedy strategic response. In that case, is the 26/11 terrorist attack a failure of policy and not of strategic intelligence?

What do we know about intelligence failures? How often do we identify a failure to prevent a terrorist attack as an intelligence failure? Yet, how many terrorist attacks really happen because of a failure to produce sufficient intelligence? Are counter-terrorism failures, failures of intelligence or failures to act on intelligence? As Prem Mahadevan points out in his book *Politics of Counterterrorism in India –Strategic intelligence and national security in South Asia,* "intelligence failure is a cliché that needs to be employed with great circumspection". This lack of definitional clarity is solely because of one of the inherent weaknesses of the Indian intelligence community in not disclosing the nature of intelligence that was on hand, prior to an attack.[7]

Scholars analyzing the failures of the intelligence community tend to advance several controversial arguments about the functioning of Indian intelligence agencies. For instance, the case that the "reluctance, and even refusal, to share information among intelligence and security agencies"[8] being identified as the most weakening factor of Indian intelligence agencies is unsettled. Wilson John, a senior fellow at Observer Research Foundation, noted that this reluctance has been highlighted in a recent case where the IB failed to help the Karnataka police identify how Riyazuddin Nasir, a motorcycle thief in Karnataka, could expose a HuJI network. This is probably a rare case that has exposed how spy circles in India continue to be reluctant to share such inputs. On the other hand, some others have argued that the tendency of a few intelligence agencies in resorting to shortcuts in assessments and the Indian government's trend to fake security preparedness have led to repeated failures.

Although the causes pinpointed in the above arguments are not explicitly linked to repeated failures of the intelligence community, academics and journalists are inclined to associate a failure to prevent a terrorist or militancy attack with improper sharing and coordination mechanisms in intelligence agencies. Such references tend to arise predominantly because "changing a culture of 'need to know' to 'need to share' does not come easily in spy circles".[9]

In fact, ever since the 9/11 Committee report has been made public; there has been a general trend to correlate terrorist attacks with failures of the intelligence community to adequately share information. The 'connecting the dots' metaphor is one we can find in every public debate in the US about a failure to avert a terrorist attack. The failure to avoid the Boston bombing from happening was also described in an analogous manner. Therefore, is it a valid argument to make in relation to what we call India's experience of 9/11 or for that matter any counter-terrorist failure? In my opinion, the answer is no.

First, the use of the metaphor is thoroughly misplaced. This one is not appropriate in explaining intelligence failures, because it is not as simple as it may sound. It is legitimately impossible to discover how many potential 'dots' the IB, R&AW or let's say the NIA and the other agencies gather. Moreover, these dots are scattered everywhere, including a variety of intelligence databases, files and folders, e-mails and also inside different people's brains. While it is extremely simple to work backwards and observe loopholes in the system by analyzing obvious warning signs, it is enormously difficult to analyze the millions of important and not-so important dots of information to uncover terrorist plans.[10]

Second, as American cryptographer Bruce Schneier points out in a debate on why the FBI and CIA failed during the Boston bombings, "Focusing on it (the failure to 'connect the dots') will only make us implement 'useless' reforms."[11] This is because intelligence failures are essentially not just a failure to connect the dots. In any case, individual cases of failure to prevent terrorist attacks are neither a failure of intelligence nor a failure of policy, but a failure of intelligence networks to penetrate into terrorist outfits that plan such attacks.[12]

When a terrorist plot succeeds occasionally, it is not automatically because the intelligence machinery failed. Beyond a shadow of a doubt, the efficiency of the intelligence apparatus of a country also plays a role in determining its rise or fall. However, we also have to take into consideration that the risk of terrorism will remain in spite of how strong our intelligence and law enforcement agencies are.

II

The problem lies with how we approach the subject of counter-terrorist failures. Terrorist attacks in India, for the most part, have been examined as either strategic or tactical intelligence failures. Seldom has there been any attention paid to the policy failures that precede them, or reform failures that follow them. The reason why failures of the intelligence community prolong even after systematic reform building is simply because studies on intelligence failures are fraught with questionable assumptions. The paper, therefore, attempts to address the lack of definitional clarity in intelligence studies by answering a few enduring questions: What are intelligence failures and why are there so many of them? What do we do about them? Whenever a terrorist attack happens, faulty or inadequate intelligence is cited as a major cause, regardless of whether there happen to be policy failures. However, there are a few exceptions.[13]

As a consequence of linking terrorist attacks with inadequate intelligence, the argument of an existing intelligence system not being capable of dealing with immediate threats arises all the time. This unbalanced approach of routinely establishing a strong link between intelligence and counter-terrorism policy is due to the assumption that intelligence analysis normally influences policy decisions leading to a natural deduction that the availability of good intelligence can only lead to effective policies and vice versa. However, this is not to dismiss the need for more capable intelligence machinery.

The model inaccurately links flawed counter-terrorist policies to insufficient or erroneous intelligence. The helplessness of the intelligence community to defend any allegations of failure has only reinforced the claim made above.[14] Such an unsound analysis will lead to questions such as why or how policy makers overlook available intelligence. Similar arguments followed the recent Bodh Gaya serial blasts of July 2013,[15] which add to the overwhelming majority of failures that arose from the state's inability to process or unwillingness to follow up such intelligence warnings from the centre. The failure to 'connect the dots' has overwhelmed Indian intelligence agencies since the 1962 border conflict, the 1999 Kargil intrusion and the failure to prevent 26/11. Yet, have we learnt any intelligent lessons from the crises of yesteryears?

The principal debate among Indian intelligence scholars starts with the assumption that counter-terrorist decision making is influenced by intelligence analysis. This approach of studying a failure of the intelligence community involves evaluating the accuracy of the intelligence analysis and critiquing either the intelligence producer or policy maker for not providing or not acting upon provided intelligence. Though intelligence agencies do play a vital role in policy making, pursuing this kind of a research agenda can be extremely difficult given the secretive environment of national security intelligence. Further, it cannot offer holistic solutions to the problems of the community. Instead, as Henry Kissinger explains in his article on intelligence failures, "Resetting the priorities of intelligence and adapting to the new realities of terrorism must start with an understanding of the problems requiring solution."[16]

Besides shoddy tradecraft and problems arising from intelligence analysis, sources of intelligence failures may stem from a variety of factors, including (a) misunderstanding about what the intelligence community can reasonably provide and what some decision makers or journalists expect, (b) organizational flaws within the community, and/or (c) implementation of faulty reforms.

III

The answer as to why there is very less definitional clarity — within intelligence studies in India—is evident from the lack of methodology-driven studies that address the real dilemmas of the intelligence community and theory-driven discourses that explain the intelligence failures. Several studies focusing on intelligence reforms have emphasized the need for the intelligence community to interact with citizens at multiple levels[17], the need to provide for adequate whistleblower protection mechanisms for those who report orders perceived as illegal and the need for effective legal and parliamentary oversight systems to monitor the performance of intelligence agencies.[18]

The Indian intelligence system suffers from a lack of checks and balances and the consumer hardly gets the required intelligence product. The politicization of some of the agencies has led to reduction of their efficiency. At times, intelligence agencies even tend to take upon themselves the task of decision-making rather than restricting themselves to the advisory role. "The bane of intelligence agencies has been the lack of focus and direction, turf-battles, poor coordination, uncorroborated reports and the lack of professionalism and motivation."[19]

Looking at intelligence oversight structures in three countries, the US, UK and Australia, an issue brief by Danish Sheikh has outlined four levels within which effective oversight should operate in a democratic framework, namely the internal level, executive oversight, parliamentary oversight, and accountability by external review bodies. It indicated how the 'intelligence community' conceptualized by former R&AW chief Girish Chandra Saxena, can be fully realized only when internal organization and their 'tasking' are managed in a thoroughly professional basis—their smooth coordination with minimal overlap ensured through the formulation of formal charters."[20]

It called for 'a holistic approach to an intelligence policy which, while recognizing the indubitable need for intelligence gathering....also highlighted the other factors that should comprise a worthwhile policy'.[21]

A workshop on *Intelligence failures in the US, UK and Russia* organized by Observer Research Foundation offered several lessons to deal with the failures of the Indian intelligence community. IDSA recently took an in-depth look at the problems facing the intelligence community and suggested a wide-ranging set of reforms to better equip the system to respond to the new threats of terrorism. Looking for a reason for stalled reforms, the Task Force report noted that 'rigid and stodgy bureaucracy may have stood in the way of developing or enhancing the desired core competence in the field of intelligence analysis and operations'.

It identifies three factors that have worked against developing imaginative and unconventional intelligence reforms: (a) conflicting motivations of those considering reforms, (b) environmental challenges at initiation of reform, and (c) failure of leadership. To this, let me add (a) the lack of definitional clarity, (b) the failure to recognize the unspoken failures of the intelligence community and (c) the lack of sufficient theorization in the field.

IV

The topic of India's unfinished internal security reforms has been repeatedly studied by several scholars in the aftermath of every major terrorist attack or intelligence review committee.[22]

However, rarely has there been any study to evaluate why this has been 'unfinished'. The 26/11 terrorist attacks prompted a huge security outcry and revealed the often ignored problems of security and intelligence. However, reforms advanced in the aftermath of the attacks did not stop another major terrorist attack from happening. Several papers looking at the counter-terrorist failure of 26/11 have focused on the terrorist innovations witnessed during the attack, studied the immediate security response and analyzed the continuing infirmities in the Indian security system. Often, it is surprising how the 26/11 attacks stirred up such huge proportions of intelligence reform whereas previous deadlier attacks did not. As a result, some scholars have examined the important strides in internal security reform since the 26/11 attack and analyzed several factors that explain why it triggered more reforms than earlier attacks.[23]

A study that addresses the cause-and-effect relationships between repeated counterterrorist failures and the other malfunctions within the intelligence community is necessary to draw the right intelligence lessons. The first step towards achieving this is to look at different failures of the intelligence community as failures to produce (and analyze), adapt, reform and execute.

Very often, theories explaining intelligence failures advanced by politicians and intelligence review committees are weak, ambiguous and fail to address one core hiccup of the intelligence community. This failure to add causal weight to the several hypothesized variables often compels them into building too many recommendations for intelligence reforms. These reforms either don't get executed or get put into operation only in parts.[24]

For instance, the Group of Ministers (GoM), which was formed in the immediate aftermath of the Kargil intrusions by Pakistan in 1999, made 300 recommendations, including the setting up of a marine police force for coastal states. Several scholars have often established a causal link between the non-implementation of that one recommendation and a failure to prevent 26/11. Though several other proposals for reforms made by the Kargil Review Committee were implemented prior to 26/11, the failure could not be averted. The problem practically lies with the approach towards intelligence failures. Over the past couple of decades, reform makers have endlessly resorted to 'meta-institutional reforms', which are initiated based on the premise that there is an intelligence coordination failure.[25]

In fact, politicians, while arguing for or against such a reform to make an organizational change, are often driven by certain not-so-important power equations. There is hardly any debate in the nation about whether or not making wide changes in intelligence organization can make any difference. This failure of intelligence review committees and political leaders to sufficiently explain failures and appropriately make proposals for intelligence reforms have been routinely overlooked as a possible cause for repeated failures of the intelligence community.

In revisiting the intelligence failures—and the consequent reforms—of the past, including the failures to prevent the 1962 border conflict, the 1999 Kargil intrusions and the 26/11 attacks[26], the paper assesses the troubles in understanding the real problems of the intelligence community. Intelligence reforms are hardly intelligent.

V

The following paper looks at counter-terrorist failures through the lens of reform failure. I assert that there is sufficient reason to believe that certain causal elements of alleged intelligence failures reside more in the failure of the reform makers to make sensible reforms and in the failure of policy makers to implement them, than in the collection and analysis domain of the intelligence tradecraft. The perils of shallow theorizing of intelligence failures by certain intelligence review committees are evident in the sweeping 'meta-institutional reforms'[27] made over the past decades and the persistent failures of counter-terrorism and intelligence. This paper advances three major arguments:

First, the proposed reforms of the past are insufficient[28] or overambitious[29], if not unrelated to the hypothesized causes of failure. The intelligence community influenced by a set of mindless politicians has continuously focused all its efforts in "prettifying the apex without bothering about the ground"—what with its meta-institutional reforms. The state of reform building in the country is beset with "imitative solutions looking at irrelevant models of the West"[30.]

There is no shortage of schemes of reorganization: the Kargil 1999, Ram Pradhan Committee of 2008 and Pradhan-Haldar-Narsimhan Committee of 2009 have all made plenty of proposals for such reforms. However, what is required at the present moment is a "pause for reflection" as rightly pointed out by Henry Kissinger in his article entitled *Lessons from four major failures*, published in Washington Post in 2004.

After every major perceived intelligence failure, there are several debates about revamping the intelligence apparatus. Structural reforms get implemented very often. However, systemic and fundamental change does happens very often.[31] Second, no reforms have been made towards addressing the main predicament of the community, which clearly lies in its inability to recruit, retain and adequately train resilient minds to cope with the changing scene of transnational terrorism.[32]

Third, a major source of intelligence failures stems from a misunderstanding between what the intelligence community can legitimately provide and what policy makers or journalists expect from them. The patterns that emerge from the failures of 1962 and 1999, as some academicians point out, largely exist at the intelligence analysis level. As Richard J. Heuer points out in his CIA publication *Psychology of Intelligence Analysis*, the inherent psychology of intelligence analysis can lead to unimaginative inductive reasoning. However, neither is deductive reasoning an appropriate method for intelligence analysis. "Sensitizing intelligence professionals to social sciences methodology and cognitive barriers" may put an end to failures in analysis of intelligence and facilitate better anticipation of security threats.[33]

Though faulty intelligence analysis could be the main causal factor relating to a failure to produce sufficient intelligence, it is not the only reason for repeated failures within the intelligence community. This research paper, therefore, tries to address the systemic failures of the intelligence community, including the failures to produce, execute, adapt and reform, with an intention to provide a direction towards meaningful reforms that should address both producers and consumers of intelligence.

Keeping in mind the limitations of the past research agenda, this policy paper will:

1. Examine the mission and constraints of the intelligence community,

2. Review the dominant discourses of intelligence failures of the past,

3. Analyze the practicability of certain recommendations for intelligence reforms in the past and present,

4. Study several other unspoken failures of the intelligence community, and

5. Offer a theoretical framework for a descriptive theory to explain how the Indian intelligence agencies make mistakes—of production, analysis, assessment and reform.

The long list of intelligence failures across the world offers ample motivation to believe that no matter how affluent a nation is, sporadic cases of counter-terrorist and intelligence failures are inevitable. Though secret intelligence fails no matter how prepared a country is, nations that have experimented with procedures of accountability tend to be better equipped than the rest. The US and the UK offer excellent examples to show how intelligence review committees influence major national security decisions. Nations that have politicians and scholars with a clear understanding of what certain national security and intelligence terminology mean are certainly better-qualified to assess such failures. While the need for a legal and parliamentary oversight in the country is widely discussed elsewhere, this paper looks for evidence to validate the latter argument.

By arguing the need for theorizing, the paper is not urging for a binding doctrine on intelligence. In fact, it is fully conscious that the prospect of developing all-encompassing theory on/for intelligence is unworkable. On the other hand, the paper is only urging for a debate on how to analyze the failures of the intelligence community and therefore tries to deal with the problem of definitional clarity—a precursor to any theorizing in the field.

Sub-Chapter 3

Challenges Facing Intelligence Studies in India

Knowledgeable public debate on national security issues is often a casualty due to the lack of declassified documents on secretive or non-secretive information about the functioning and failings of intelligence agencies. In fact, the Indian government's policy of keeping most of such information permanently classified or declassifying only parts of such information has consistently resulted in a situation in which no authentic account of national security management can be presented. Routine declassification of such information in several Western countries has facilitated public debates in the subject and is clearly the motivation behind the rigor with which intelligence failures are analyzed elsewhere. The sparing nature of the Indian government in sharing such information not only restricts serious scholarship in the subject, but also indirectly permits intelligence agencies to function without sufficient accountability.

However, the history of the Indian intelligence is full of alleged or demonstrated shortages. Routine intelligence review committees have taken place after every major perceived failure of the intelligence apparatus in the country, including the Henderson-Brooks Committee (Indo-China border war of 1962), B.S.Raghavan IAS Committee (Indo-Pak war of 1965 and Mizo revolt of 1966), L.P. Singh Committee investigating Emergency between 1975 and 1977, K. Shankaran Nair Committee constituted in early 1980s, Kargil Review Committee (Pak intrusion of 1999) and the Ram Pradhan Committee (Mumbai attack of 2008). Several reports have been developed to press forward proposals for intelligence reforms, including ones by the Pradhan- Haldar-Narsimhan task force and the FICCI task force of 1999.

Towards addressing the deficiencies highlighted by the Kargil Review Committee Report, the Government of India constituted a Group of Ministers (GoM) to review the entire internal security scenario in the aftermath of the attack. The GoM was assisted by four Task Forces to focus on strengthening internal security, intelligence apparatus, border management and coastal security. The Task Force constituted to study and suggest improvement in the intelligence apparatus, led by Girish Chandra Saxena, made a variety of imperative recommendations, which were classified and have since been deleted.

The report of G.C. Saxena Special Task Force, set-up as part of the Kargil Review process, habitually identified as the "most enlightened document ever written on reforming India's intelligence apparatus", continues to remain classified. As strategic affairs expert Praveen Swami points out in an article entitled *Stalled Reforms,* published in Frontline, "the 244-page paper called on India's intelligence establishment to take an honest and in-depth stock of their ...challenges and problems." When an attempt was made to find out the 'status of classification' of the report, the Ministry of External Affairs (MEA) had no information on it. There was neither any further response from MEA nor could former intelligence personnel help. However, the recommendations relating to intelligence put forth in the Group of Ministers (GoM) report gives a clear picture of the state of reform-making in the country.

Given the lack of transparency about intelligence activities, successes and failures in the country, it is astounding how at least parts of the report on the 1999 Kargil Review Committee and the High-level enquiry Committee (HLEC) on 26/11 are available in the public domain. Kargil was a significant blow to India's perception of external security, similar to what 26/11 did to the internal security scene. Several high-level military leaders and politicians have time and again described the Kargil disaster as India's Pearl Harbor and the horrendous 26/11 attacks in Mumbai as India's 9/11. Such academic understanding and comparison of these failures are good enough reason why this paper should consider these as case studies.

The lack of availability of some of the aforementioned reports has without doubt blurred the national security (and intelligence) management image of the country. Moreover, failures of the intelligence community are often more publicized than intelligence successes in the country. The latest and most hyped intelligence coup is the one relating to the arrest of Yasin Bhatkal, who made bombs for a majority of the attacks orchestrated by Indian Mujahideen.[34]

A former director of the IB says information relating to success stories is often not accessible to the public, because "there is a certain ethical constraint which restricts an intelligence official from revealing too much about an operation".[35] Another former director of R&AW, Vikram Sood, elaborated the significance of "source bias and operational loyalty".[36] Moreover, India's central intelligence agencies, the IB or R&AW, do not reveal any figures about rates of successes or failures, even in the face of serious allegations. Sood clearly explains the actual predicament. "If the intelligence agencies were to say there were twelve operations of which ten were successful and two were not; questions about which two or which ten will arise." Likewise, several other questions relating to why the ninth operation, for instance, was a failure or how the eleventh one was a success might arise. "Intelligence agencies often avoid such debates simply because this might require a revelation of operational details that even the Prime Minister doesn't want to know."[37]

This makes it unfeasible for scholars to ask questions relating to the performance of intelligence services, such as what is the proportion of intelligence failures to successes, what their performance rate is or how the 'sporadic yet broadcasted' failures measure up to the actual current performance of intelligence services. In addition, former or serving intelligence personnel are extremely wary of revealing the real troubles of the intelligence community. Pursuing a research agenda to address the lack of sufficient dialogue between the producers and consumers of intelligence was a particularly challenging task. For instance, I found it particularly tricky to gather any evidence for one of my core research questions at the start of the project:

Are interagency rivalries and failure to align thinking among intelligence agencies the reason behind repeated counterterrorist surprises? The Ram Pradhan Committee report revealed that the inherent flaw arose from the lack of a centralized sharing mechanism; due to which key information was either lost in transit or officials failed to 'connect the dots'. Yet, such evidence is not adequate to claim that the lack of such a mechanism for sharing arises from an inter-agency rivalry. Likewise, it was exceptionally tough to find proof to confirm that alleged intelligence failures reside more in the failure of the producers and consumers of intelligence to engage in a continuous dialogue than in the collection and analysis domain of the intelligence tradecraft.

We need to urgently ask why the government and intelligence professionals do not provide the kind of data that might be useful in addressing a lot of problems within the intelligence community. As rightly pointed out by Professor Anthony Glees from the University of Buckingham, "The greatest challenge for intelligence studies is to surmount intellectual isolation by working together more systematically and less hierarchically — more workshops, more study groups, fewer large showcasing conferences."[38]

Despite such limitations within the literature pertaining to the functioning of intelligence agencies, a closer look into the functioning and reporting of the intelligence review committees of 1999 and 2008 can throw light on the state of intelligence reform building and security management, albeit to a limited extent. However, in-depth interactions with former intelligence personnel, academicians and politicians proved extremely useful in understanding why secret intelligence fails, repeatedly.

Sub-Chapter 4

What Do We Know About Intelligence Failures? Historical Background of India's Intelligence Agencies

I. Historical Background of India's Intelligence Agencies

There are two central intelligence agencies in India—the Intelligence Bureau and the Research & Analysis Wing. Both agencies play a large part in keeping the country secure—from internal and external (and military) threats. Before the reorganization of intelligence agencies in 1968, the Intelligence Bureau was responsible for both internal and external intelligence. The need for an effective intelligence network in India did not emerge until the Indo-China border conflict of 1962. It is only since the birth of Research and Analysis Wing in 1968 that the Intelligence Bureau was expected to collect intelligence within the country. It is henceforth identified as the premier agency for counter intelligence. On the other hand, "it is widely appreciated that the primary responsibility for collecting external intelligence, including that relating to a potential adversary's military deployment, is vested with the Research & Analysis Wing".[39] However, both agencies play a major role in producing intelligence relating to counterterrorism. Regrettably, the performance of both these agencies has been affected hugely by different sets of 'unreasonable expectations' from intelligence consumers in political, military and other circles.

The Intelligence Bureau has its roots in the policing system created by the British during their colonial rule and has 'a mixed reputation' among several Western intelligence agencies and their own consumers in India. While it has earned praise from their Western counterparts, the agency routinely comes under the scanner whenever there is a terrorist attack in the country, or when a major internal security threat goes unpredicted. Unfortunately, it is often considered as political machinery used to spy on opposition politicians rather than national security machinery to predict genuine security threats.

Intelligence agencies have faced routine allegations of intelligence failures and are regularly under the regulatory scanner for outdated surveillance equipment, lack of efficient online surveillance in the light of increasing technical sophistication of terrorists, lack of infrastructure and severe shortages in terms of trained manpower. The headquarters of the Intelligence Bureau's operations in New Delhi, the main part of the counter-jihadist wing of India's agencies, is poorly staffed with a reportedly meager set of 30 analysts and field personnel. It was only in 2009 that former home minister P. Chidambaram authorized the hiring of 6,000 intelligence personnel, which barely covers the number of personnel who retire every year.

II. Traditional View of Intelligence Failure

The Indian roots of intelligence, statecraft and espionage date back to the Vedas and the Upanishads. The great epics of Indian mythology, the Ramayana and the Mahabharata, provide an excellent introduction to the world of spying and offer numerous case studies of successes and failures of intelligence, and specifically, of spying. Although theories of intelligence might have existed in one form or another since the birth of the subject itself, it was not until Kautilya's *Arthashastra*—which had a unique influence over the rise of Chandra Gupta Maurya—that there was any written work on the art of collection of intelligence. In fact, a systematic translation of the ancient Indian treatise on statecraft, dating back to the 4th century BC, can provide a new direction for theory building in intelligence studies. However, there hasn't been any major effort towards that direction in India.

The study of intelligence failures dates back to several eras and is by far the most advanced field within intelligence studies. Many scholars have studied intelligence failures and surprises and developed theories to explain disasters—ranging from Pearl Harbor to Cuban missile crisis of 1962 to the 9/11 and the recent Boston bombing. However, the systematic study of security lapses and intelligence failures in India existed only over the past two or three decades. Several books and research papers have been written to explain India's failures to prevent China's military intrusion of 1962 and Pak intrusion in 1999.[40] Several generations of scholars have laboured to extract what happened in the past, yet we don't seem to have learnt the right lessons.[41]

A failure to learn from the past failures is by far the biggest failure of the intelligence community. Up until now, barely has there been any full-fledged effort to use earlier literature on intelligence failure to understand the current terrorist threat, except a few essays that try to learn from the surprise attacks of the past.[42] Studies like these are probably few and far between predominantly because of the lack of open-source information relating to the working and functioning of intelligence agencies. This is pretty obvious from the current problems faced within the intelligence community. Looking back at the Chinese intrusion of 1962, the main cause of the failure to prevent the border conflict was identified as "limited military intelligence, which led to the flawed threat assessment and the corresponding levels of security preparedness".[43]

However, between April and October 2012, the Intelligence Bureau, which was responsible for providing external and internal intelligence during that time, reportedly produced regular assessments of the Chinese disposition. IB's own report of May 1962 allegedly indicated having learnt about Beijing's intention to forcefully remove Indian posts in Ladakh.[44] Further, IB argued that another report of September 1961 confirming occupation of Chinese posts along their 1960 claim line was not followed up.[45] Almost 50 years later, the Kargil conflict once again exposed a similar failure of the intelligence community — that of insufficient intelligence, analysis of available intelligence inputs, timely sharing of intelligence and corresponding follow-up by security forces.

In the months preceding the Kargil intrusion, several intelligence reports were circulated about a possible intrusion in the Kargil sector. In June 1998, the IB allegedly warned of increased activities along the border and reported 'increased movement' of Pakistan Army opposite the Kargil sector. However, this piece of intelligence was shared exclusively with the home minister and the director general of military intelligence, bypassing the Joint Intelligence

Committee (JIC) and the Research & Analysis Wing.

The inputs were consistent with the military intelligence available in the aftermath of the nuclear tests of May 1998. R&AW foresaw a limited offensive threat as Pakistan was bent upon interdicting the Dras-Kargil highway by means of increased shelling. However, neither R&AW nor JIC were in a position to make any further clarifications. After the Kargil intrusion in 1999, enquiries by Kargil Review Committee identified that 'the critical failure in intelligence was related to the absence of any information on the induction and de-induction of battalions and the lack of accurate data on the identity of battalions in the area opposite Kargil during 1998'.[46]

As former intelligence personnel and strategic affairs expert B.Raman noted in his paper entitled *Dimensions of Intelligence Operations* that there is an "unfortunate awareness" among the general public that "the Kargil conflict of 1999 was a case of intelligence failure by the R&AW. It was not". As he highlights, a careful reading of the Kargil Review Committee report shows that there has been no reference of the term 'intelligence failure'; however, the report has "drawn attention to serious deficiencies at various levels in the intelligence and operations process".

Ever since the Kargil Review Committee report has been made public, intelligence failure has been linked to a failure to produce adequate intelligence, failure to process available analysis and failure to initiate follow-up action even on limited intelligence that was available. Much emphasis was placed on the tactical 'failure to connect the dots'. However, the Kargil debate also focused on redefining the role and responsibilities of some intelligence agencies over the other, and consequently called attention to the 'turf wars' between these organizations. But, is it the most significant 'intelligence' lesson we can learn about the failure to prevent the Kargil intrusion?

III. Intelligence Failures: The Consumers' Perspective

Politicians of ruling parties have often faced the brunt of most failures of counterterrorism than anybody else in the country, because of the conventional view that intelligence analysis is influenced by political leaders in power. Debates relating to terrorism and intelligence arise all the time, and predictably, politicians often tend to protect the intelligence agencies in such a discussion. In recent years, the following acts of terror have been conducted on Indian soil: Mumbai 26/11, 2009 Guwahati bombing, 2010 Pune bombing, 2010 Varanasi bombing, 2011 Mumbai bomb blasts, the Delhi bombing of 2011, 2012 Pune terror attack, 2013 Dilsukhnagar blasts, 2013 Bangalore blasts and the most recent 2013 Bodhgaya blasts.

A review of political responses to these attacks shows that there has been a general trend among politicians to correlate intelligence failures with the reluctance of intelligence agencies to share information or investigate further, or the failure of the state government to implement or act on the intelligence that was made available by central agencies.[47] This has been the case ever since the Ram Pradhan Committee report was made public. It is unfortunate to note "that the political discourse in the country is extremely irresponsible when everybody jumps the gun".[48]

However, despite what the hypothesized cause of failure is, debates relating to organizational reforms take place all the time. This trend was pretty evident in the aftermath of the 2011 Mumbai attacks, when the debate on reorganizing the national intelligence structure in the country was rekindled. It is understandable because the city of Mumbai witnessed a major incident of terror despite the rapid overhaul of the intelligence and security apparatus in the country. Predictably, several politicians hypothesized the delay in implementing the NCTC as a major causal factor for the failure to prevent the 2011 terror attacks. However, it was not identified as an intelligence failure. Former home minister P. Chidambaram said there was "no failure of intelligence, because there was no intelligence". In a media response, he confirmed that "having no intelligence in this case, however, does not mean that there was a failure on part of the intelligence agencies".[49]

His argument partly was in agreement with the philosophical case made by Richard K. Betts, a recognized American scholar specializing in national security issues, in saying 'intelligence failures are not only inevitable, they are natural'. However, P.

Chidambaram did not have any case in the first place, as he did not hold anyone accountable for the attack. This sort of lack of definitional clarity is probably one of the major obstacles in making useful and realistic proposals for reforming the intelligence apparatus.

Terrorism studies expert Ajai Sahni conflicted with the former home minister's comments in an interview with Karan Thapar. He noted that the case of 2011 clearly manifests "the failure to create an intelligence network across the country, which would be able to penetrate and dismantle the networks that are creating these incidents". Responding to the unacceptable approach to failures of intelligence, he emphasized the need to evaluate an instance of intelligence failure "in terms of intelligence capabilities and mandate".[50]

Barring the 2010 Pune blasts, roughly all other counter-terrorist failures were viewed as cases of inadequate intelligence or improper sharing and coordination of intelligence. Dismissing allegations of intelligence failure in the Pune blasts, P. Chidambaram noted that the attack was not a case of intelligence failure. He said that because intelligence inputs were taken seriously, the police had been sensitized about the likelihood of the attack and security measures were in place. The attack was, therefore, characterized as a case of 'an insidious planting of a bomb' which made it impossible for the intelligence agencies to predict accurately.

Ever since the Ram Pradhan Committee report was made public, the political rhetoric on counter-terrorist failures routinely avoided the reference of 'intelligence failure'; and when it did, it constantly identified the intelligence failure as a tactical failure of state intelligence agencies 'to connect the dots'. The Indian government identifies most cases of counter-terrorist attacks not as a failure to collect intelligence, but as a failure to integrate and understand available intelligence. This approach is extremely biased, as it ignores other possibilities. On the other hand, there are a set of well-informed politicians who understand the constraints within which intelligence agencies operate.

I spoke to former home secretary, Gopal Krishna Pillai, and the present Information and Broadcasting minister, Manish Tewari, to get a better perspective of some 'pro-intelligence' politicians. Speaking to Tewari was of particular significance because he presented the Intelligence Services (Powers and Regulation) Bill in the Lok Sabha in 2011 "to regulate the functioning and use of power by the Indian intelligence agencies within and outside India and to provide for the coordination, control and oversight of such agencies". Pillai was extremely insightful as he took over as Officer on Special Duty (OSD) in the Ministry of Home Affairs in 2009, in the aftermath of the 26/11 attacks.

Tewari says, "Intelligence is neither a perfect nor an imperfect science." Noting that intelligence is all about a 'preponderance of probabilities', he explains the tricky circumstances that intelligence personnel have to deal with during a pre-warning stage. "At times, you are able to lay your hands on an input which you can develop that can tangibly lead to pre-emption. At times, you are not able to develop inputs which can lead to intelligence. At several other times, you are caught up in the dark. You have no prior information of something that is going to happen for the simple reason that a conspiracy to create a criminal act by its very nature is conceived in darkness and implemented in secrecy. It is that opacity that you are trying to pierce."

Calling for a need to understand the "asymmetry" with which the intelligence community has to operate, he says that intelligence production and analysis is a very challenging task. Instead of routinely accusing intelligence agencies for alleged failures, "what we really need to focus on is how to build their capacity and to establish a modicum of accountability for the functioning of these agencies". Both Tewari and Pillai sympathized with the unfortunate plight of India's secret intelligence agencies and noted that it is only at times when the intelligence agency slips that we get to know about it.

According to Pillai, the repeated failures of the intelligence community (he likes to call it lapses) are primarily because the number of intelligence personnel is extremely low and it takes several years to hire and whet personnel. He noted that it was only subsequent to the 26/11 attacks, that the government "found that we (Intelligence Bureau) were short of as much as 2,000 intelligence personnel". While the agency only has "a capacity to hire and train only up to 150 to 200 such personnel a year", he said each of them will have to undergo at least five to seven years of training before they are ready to be used in the field.

A politician's perception about intelligence is often influenced by media leaks about the nature of intelligence that was available to state or central governments prior to a terrorist attack. Political oversight of intelligence agencies can offer a clearer picture about the failures of the intelligence community. However, the lack of methodology-driven studies on intelligence and the absence of scholar-policy interactions in the field are the main reasons behind weak, unsubstantiated theories advanced by certain politicians.

IV. Political Debate about NCTC

Such inappropriate theorization of a few politicians has also led the debate about the setting up of NCTC to a totally different direction. In 2009, former home minister P. Chidambaram said the organization's goals will include "preventing a terrorist attack, containing a terrorist attack, and ...responding to terrorist attacks". According to the initial proposal, he wanted all agencies involved in counter-terrorism intelligence gathering to report to the proposed NCTC. According to the 2012 executive order, the NCTC was meant to work as an integral part of the Intelligence Bureau and was given powers of 'arrest, search and seizure'. However, the latest 'watered-down' draft of the NCTC said it will work directly under the Home Ministry and not the IB. Besides, when a terrorist or a terror group is identified or located, operations against them would be carried out through or in conjunction with state police.

In light of the Dilsukhnagar blasts in February 2013, the debate over the creation of NCTC was ignited. However, there is still no political consensus on the watered-down proposal of NCTC. According to several media reports, the government has decided not to go ahead with the proposed NCTC after facing strong opposition from Chief Ministers of several states, including those of West Bengal, Bihar, Tamil Nadu, Gujarat, Chhattisgarh, Madhya Pradesh, Maharashtra, Karnataka and Assam.[51] Immense support for NCTC came from the state of Andhra Pradesh in the aftermath of the Dilsukhnagar blast.

Though there was some anxiety about over-centralization of intelligence agencies initially, the organizational reform faced stiff hostility because states considered the NCTC as an encroachment upon their law and enforcement powers and in conflict with the federalism features enshrined in the Indian Constitution. Yet, none of these oppositions focus on the actual problem. This is primarily because security is still compartmentalized in India. However, the reason why there is no consensus among states is because there can be no security reform in an 'environment of mistrust' between the central and state governments. Past studies assessing the problems of NCTC have all uniformly highlighted the need for establishing a legal framework for intelligence agencies and the need for holding them accountable.

Going forward, political leaders ought to 'set aside their egos' and question the requisite for such organizational reforms. The most pressing question that must steer political debates in the future is whether such a sweeping reorganization of the intelligence community is required for fixing the problems of repeated failures. However, such informed debates relating to intelligence failures calls for a clear understanding of what intelligence and intelligence failures are in reality.

V. Intelligence Failure: The Producers' Perspectives

The source of intelligence failure resides not only within the boundaries of the intelligence producers but also in the inaction of policy makers to react on the intelligence made available, the intelligence community's inability to adapt to the changing faces of terror, and the reform maker's failure to make appropriate proposals of intelligence reforms. Yet, in the event of a counter-terrorist failure, the producer of intelligence is indicted for most of the failures, while they are the ones who barely get an opportunity to defend themselves. Contrary to the intelligence consumer's perspective highlighted in the above chapter, the reason for repeated failures within the intelligence community in reality is rather different.

As part of my fieldwork, I had an opportunity to interact with several former intelligence personnel, former and current government officials and a few academicians who openly shared some intriguing inside stories about the working of intelligence agencies and helped me understand why India's secret intelligence agencies fail repeatedly. A single strand of thought that emerged from most of my interactions is that India has "failed to implement any meaningful internal security reforms since 1947".[52]

The story of intelligence reform is far from complete. Even if some reforms were sensible in fixing a few troubles of the intelligence community, reform makers have not been able to mend the core predicaments of the community because of (a) a failure to make any post-event audits[53], (b) lack of professionalism and systematized functioning[54], (c) communication gap between producers and consumers of intelligence[55] and lack of protocol for engaging and de-engaging,[56] (d) failure to implement reforms to recruit and train intelligent personnel[57], (e) failure to improve the working of intelligence personnel and (f) failure to adequately strengthen local intelligence. In the pages that follow, I will discuss each of these failures independently, and consequently expose the dangers of constricted reform making.

VI. Failure to Implement Meaningful Reforms

India's agencies are facing two types of failures in relation to intelligence reforms—failure to make meaningful reforms addressing the urgent predicaments of the community and failure to implement useful reforms that were advanced as a result of past intelligence review committees. In an honest confession about the real problems of India's agencies, V.Balachandran, former Special Secretary, Cabinet Secretariat, and member of the Ram Pradhan Committee, setup in the immediate aftermath of 26/11, noted that "we have missed several opportunities to reform our internal security by studying the measures taken in other countries". Moreover, he said India has failed to implement any "meaningful reforms" since 1947. In specific, he pointed the following cases, where individual states played a role in the implementation failure in the past:

1. In 1972, the Intelligence Bureau had suggested that the anti-hijacking squads then being set up in several airports should be handed over to the Central Industrial Security Force (CISF). All the states turned down this suggestion till they were forced to hand over airport security to CISF in the wake of IC 814 hijacking in December 1999.

2. In 1974, the Rustamji Committee recommended a separate maritime force like BSF to guard our sea border. It is an open secret that 26/11 attacks could have been prevented had there been one such agency like in several other countries like Israel, the UK or even America.

3. It needed the assassination of our Prime Minister in 1984 to set up a special force to protect Prime Ministers, which were earlier inadequately carried out by the Intelligence Bureau, Delhi police and local police.

4. When the Railway Ministry suggested empowerment of the RPF to investigate cases on the railways, it was shot down by the MHA and the States although the highly fragmented State Railway police systems under 28 states often spar among themselves over jurisdiction.

While there has been delay in implementing several such reforms, what we continue to lack is level-headed intelligence reforms addressing ground-level problems. Several former intelligence personnel, including Vikram Sood, Jayadeva Ranade, K.V. Thomas and terrorism studies expert, Ajai Sahni, and another former IB director (name withheld) have amply provided evidence to prove the case.

VII. Failure to Address Problems at the Base

While V. Balachandran clearly highlighted the 'lack of sensible reform making' in the country, Sahni explained where the actual trouble lies. He noted that "the whole problem is with the approach" of certain reform makers. Over the past decade and a half, reform makers have focused on making 'meta-institutional reforms', which according to him are instigated on the premise that intelligence failures predominantly arise from coordination failures. Dismissing that a counter-terrorist failure emerges from an intelligence agency's failure to coordinate and share intelligence, he says: "Nobody in the intelligence business would offer an evidence of a case where a piece of intelligence input was not shared within intelligence agencies and the policing community – which is the essence of a coordination failure."

Observing the bad influence of American intelligence reforms, he says that Indian policy makers 'unfortunately pick these ideas from the Western experience'. The crisis in America, he notes, is "the overwhelming flow of intelligence and the inability to extract the most relevant information which will be operationally relevant and which will be able to be shared immediately". This, for certain is not our problem, in India. Our problem, he says, is "the absolute dearth of intelligence". What are we to coordinate when we don't have anything? Making an argument against the proposed NCTC, he notes "the core problems in India are to do with the capabilities at the ground level and are not anything to do with these institutional and organizational reforms".

VIII. Failure to Formulate Reasonable Expectations

Intelligence personnel often argue that allegations of intelligence failure predominantly arise because of the failure to establish what the intelligence producers can legitimately provide. It is due to a lack of understanding from the consumers of intelligence and the journalists that the intelligence community gets routinely blamed for every counter-terrorist failure. "It is unfair to expect all intelligence to be complete," exclaims Sood. He says it is particularly unreasonable "especially when we are dealing with immediate issues—such as terrorism". He explains that it might be easy to predict—from a geopolitical angle— about how China or India would react to its enemies ten years from now. However, it becomes "extremely difficult to gather intelligence about enemy action, especially when he is too near". When the enemy action is expected tomorrow, he notes that intelligence personnel at ground zero can only offer intelligence about enemy action based on mere observation. It gets difficult for someone to predict whether or not an enemy would start firing.

IX. Failure to Train and Recruit Resilient Minds

The numerous proposals for 'meta-institutional reforms' in the past, including NTRO, NATGRID, NCTC, have all exposed the improper approach of reform makers in constantly 'focusing on the apex and ignoring the ground-level'. In a country with a massive population like India, capacities for response and data generation are far more important and are the base of the pyramid. "Unless you have that, you cannot have the apex of the pyramid hanging in the air."[58] In reality, reforming the intelligence apparatus "does not (only) mean creating newer organizations or giving more money".[59] What we clearly lack are reforms that start at the bottom level. There have been barely any reforms that aim at "improving the intelligence curriculum, training, in-service improvement, hiring procedure or promotion policy".[60]

Unfortunately, even the intensity of training in certain intelligence agencies has deteriorated over time, as former R&AW official Ranade notes. "We are not intense right now — relating to the kind of people they are taking in and the kind of places they are taken from." Moreover, the handicap in a system like India is with whetting. It takes intelligence agencies (specifically, the R&AW) almost a year before they whet a person. In a span of one year, Ranade worries there might be a higher turnout. Further, intelligence services in India are rarely looked upon as organizations that lure individuals. Explaining the sad state of agencies in India, Ranade notes how working in secret agencies like the CIA or the MI6 is a badge of honour. But, the scenario is very different in India. He attributes a lot of this to old police colonial legacy. Moreover, he noted, "a lot of journalists and communists have a leftist attitude and have a negative view about the police". And, this is one reason why the image of intelligence agencies in India doesn't match up to their Western counterparts.

X. Inter-agency rivalry

As several earlier studies have highlighted, there is a serious 'cultural problem' within the Indian intelligence agencies. In a candid interaction, several former intelligence personnel agree that one of the main reasons for intelligence and counter-terrorism failures is the rivalry among intelligence agencies. A former intelligence personnel, S[61], said, "The same set of informers operate among different intelligence agencies—like BSF, military, army, navy, IB, R&AW—to infiltrate into the same terrorist outfits. All intelligence agencies focusing on counter-terrorism intelligence are all poaching into the same set of experts and, as a result, the same intelligence is peddled in different ways to the different agencies."

In fact, former chairman of the JIC, S.D. Pradhan, also highlighted a similar problem in his article entitled *Indian intelligence system needs urgent reforms*, published in the Times of India immediately after India's intelligence agencies publicized a huge success story relating to the arrest of three wanted terrorists, namely Abdul Karim Tunda, Yasin Bhatkal and Assadullah Akhtar. He noted that a situation where faulty intelligence is provided by all agencies raises the question whether "only one source was providing inputs to all agencies". Such a situation calls for serious examination of the functioning of intelligence agencies.[62]

In a country where credit snatching often influences intelligence analysis and dissemination and intelligence personnel suffer from a "crab mentality", i.e., there is no way to judge the accuracy of intelligence produced. Furthermore, as agencies believe that 'information is power', they rarely reveal their sources when they provide intelligence alerts or warnings. This often leads to questioning the authenticity of an intelligence warning. Further, the problem also lies in the intelligence culture, and more clearly in defining the function of intelligence in India. For instance, we are not a security state like the Americans, the Israelis or the British. While they view intelligence as an aid to state power, India does not.

Historically, in India, intelligence was a function of the empire. In free India, intelligence continued to primarily cover political opposition and communism. We (Indians) thought political opposition, like the British did, was important for the survival of the government. Unless the culture of intelligence is changed from a 'need to serve the government' to a 'need to serve the nation', there can be no real transformation.

XI. Dialogue Failure

While the inter-agency cultural rivalries remain to be addressed, the deeper reason for the repeated failures of the intelligence community is a failure to align thinking among different agencies. There is reason to believe that certain causal elements of counter-terrorist and intelligence failures reside in the "failure of the producers and consumers of intelligence to engage in a continuous dialogue", Ranade confirms. This failure was highlighted during the 26/11 attacks, he says. Generally, when an intelligence input relating to terrorism comes from an external source, it is generally procured by R&AW and then shared.

Two things happen. First, the piece of input is subject to analysis depending on the nature of the intelligence. Second, R&AW, like any other organization, or human—with an intention to be the first to share—immediately shares it with the MHA, and thereafter, with the Multi Agency Centre (MAC). Finally, the rest of the community evaluates it, after which the MAC decides whether or not it should send it to the state concerned. Often, there is no problem within MAC. However, sometimes, "MAC will not assess the criticality of the information — the value or importance of the information."[63]

Here's where the problem starts. Explaining how one can avert such failures in intelligence flow, Ranade says, "It is the responsibility of the intelligence organization which initially sourced the piece of information —which it thinks is sufficient to predict an attack—to send it to the targeted state, which MAC will probably do. But, they should follow it up. This is one area where there is laxity (in communication)." In his opinion, the intelligence agency should take up the responsibility to chase the states concerned and question follow-up action. This is particularly crucial because "if the importance of the piece of intelligence is not expressed during dissemination, there might be a tendency, (among law enforcement agencies) to act on it in a relaxed manner".

XII. Failure to Make Post-Event Audits

One of the major setbacks of intelligence agencies is its failure to do post-event audit and aftermath analysis. While most agencies do not subscribe to it, Ranade and D. Sivanandan argue for the need of such independent audits. "Though agencies often dismiss such failures by passing the buck towards insufficient manpower, it is essential to evaluate an agency's performance in preparing intelligence estimates prior to an attack," says Ranade.

For instance, when an X agency sends 300 threat warnings prior to an attack, it must sit back and get one of the intelligence personnel— not associated with the operation —to independently evaluate (1) how many of those 300 warnings have been shared with local intelligence agencies, (b) how many of those 300 warnings have been stopped at the level of MAC after initial scrutiny and (3) how many of those 300 warnings have been used to avert the attack. Such an approach will not only help the intelligence agency assess its own ability to gather and analyze accurate intelligence, but will also highlight any failure in sharing or coordination.

XIII. Failure to Build Capacity at Ground Level

One of the major findings of the Ram Pradhan Committee in the aftermath of the 26/11 attacks was the low capacity of trained manpower in IB and local intelligence agencies to analyze bits of intelligence scattered everywhere. The GoM set up by the Kargil Review Committee made several recommendations, including a proposal for a Joint Task Force on Intelligence (JTFI) whose primary role was to strengthen local intelligence. Most DGP conferences also routinely recommended that the state intelligence apparatus have to be strengthened to ensure an effective internal security apparatus. In line with its primary role to strengthen state intelligence apparatus, the JTFI planned to strengthen the state intelligence, albeit with a handful of training centers. However, as strategic affairs analyst Praveen Swami noted in an article entitled *stalled reforms,* the finance ministry shot down the request. In the post-26/11 era, as Swami observes, "The MAC at least has one office; the JTFI does not have even that." Had the intelligence community recognized such lack of trained analysts at state level, the 26/11 attacks could have been averted.

However, another problem relating to manpower trouble relates to the number of intelligence personnel gathering intelligence relating to counter-terrorism. The proportion of such personnel to ones gathering other kinds of intelligence, including political espionage, is extremely worrying. In fact, Sahni confirms: "While the IB has a total strength of 19,000 personnel, only a few hundred personnel are concerned with counterinsurgency and counterterrorism. Moreover, between 2008 and 2013, we have not strengthened the IB by even a few dozens. For a country of more than a billion, it is laughable!"[64]

One of the other main failures pointed out by the Ram Pradhan Committee related to the over-dependence on central agencies for intelligence relating to terrorism. Among the different levels of intelligence agencies in the country, "the best agency which can most effectively deal with the subject is the state intelligence set-up with grassroots level linkages and close connections with local police stations. On the other hand, IB and R&AW only have skeletal presence at the district levels, which are of no use."[65] However, our capacity of intelligence gathering in the ground has been systematically destroyed. "For decades, investments on policing have been regarded as non-developmental."[66]

XIV. State of Intelligence Studies in India

The difference in the perspectives discussed in the above chapters clearly indicates a producer-consumer divide about what constitutes intelligence and intelligence failures. However, the failure to establish a clear understanding of such terminology is also because intelligence within terrorism studies in India has occupied a marginal position in mainstream academic circles. Whatever has been published so far on the Indian intelligence community is either narrative or descriptive. Only a handful of academics in India have toiled away individually to address the problems faced by the intelligence community. Even in such cases, hardly has there been any methodological study advanced towards theorizing. On the other hand, the subject has been dealt in a more organized way in the West and our political leaders have several lessons to learn from Western scholars. In the next part, I make a short review of a few prominent debates in the West to find some direction towards intelligence theory building.

XV. State of intelligence theorizing in the West

Intelligence has been an academic discipline in the West for half a century,[67] and studies on intelligence failures have existed since Pearl Harbour days; however, the interest significantly increased in the aftermath of 9/11. It was not just because of the intensity of the attack, but also because of the controversial reforms that were made following it. The principal debate among Western intelligence scholars, for the most part, exists around what 'intelligence studies' actually is. However, beyond definitional issues, the question of intelligence failures has remained clearly important as a subject of interest within intelligence studies, which often explicitly claim that the 'failures reflect the poor performance of the intelligence agencies as a whole'.[68]

Roberta Wohlstetter's classic book *Pearl Harbor: Warning and Decision* attempted to explain how even one of the most capable intelligence systems in the world can encounter surprise attacks 'in spite of the vast increase in expenditures for collecting and analyzing intelligence data and advances in the art of machine decoding and machine translation'.[69] Several other scholars made several theories to explain other disasters, including but the American intelligence failures in Korea and the Israeli surprise in the 1973 Yom Kippur War. While a majority of literature related to strategic surprises have been extremely pessimistic in claiming that in the difficult task of intelligence, failures are inevitable.

However, modern theorists have identified several causal factors for intelligence failures. The predominant distinction among these theorists often lies in the question of what or who causes intelligence failure. While most writers tend to believe that the fault lies with decision makers at the policy level, a small set of academicians tend to assign the fault to the intelligence community while a few others look at the deception of the enemy as a cause for surprise. Richard K. Betts, for instance, made the case that few attacks can qualify 'as genuine bolts from the sky'. Most of them are preceded by some measure of pre-warning. Therefore, he wrote in one of his well-cited articles, 'Failures in intelligence are not only inevitable, they are natural.'[70]

Later, in his book *Surprise Attack,* Betts elaborated his point about responsibility of decision makers in averting an attack: he noted that 'the principal cause of surprise is not the failure of intelligence but the unwillingness of political leaders to believe intelligence or to react to it with sufficient dispatch'. He made an argument that policy makers are often responsible for failure, for not having taken the advice given by intelligence. The proponents of this school, including former CIA analyst Paul Pillar and former CIA operative Amos Kovacs, many 'intelligence failures' are not so much failures of intelligence per se, but rather failures to use intelligence.

On the other hand, the school of organizational failure, advanced by Amy Zegart in her book *Spying Blind,* identifies two organizational deficiencies as the main causes of counterterrorist failure: information sharing and strategic analysis—one of which has been the cornerstone of American intelligence reforms.

While both these causal factors—in the hypothesis of Betts and Zegart—are extremely useful in identifying the problems of the Indian intelligence community, "the reason for such failures in India is not caused by improper organizational management, but the unwillingness of the consumers of intelligence to take independent follow-up action".[71]

Further, the failure of the Indian intelligence community to adapt and make reforms is attributable to the bureaucratic nature of agencies and the self-interests of government bureaucrats, as Zegart rightly points out. Besides addressing the failures of the intelligence community, studies in the West have often focused on questions of intelligence acquisition[72], ethics in intelligence gathering[73], politicization of intelligence[74], organizational failures of intelligence agencies[75], the role and structure of intelligence oversight[76], and relationships between intelligence agencies and the state.[77] There have also been several studies relating to 'the intelligence cycle and how it might be modified'.[78] Besides all these, scholars in the US and UK have also expressed concern about the theory-policy divide and have remained critical about the strained relationship between intelligence academicians and practitioners.

In an article entitled *the future of intelligence studies,* Anthony

Glees noted, "The principal debates in intelligence studies in UK are currently concerned largely with the political accountability and oversight of secret intelligence agencies, their accountability and competence in terms of tradecraft, political skills and ethical values." Drawing lessons from recent examples in the UK, he noted that the UK currently faces big problems "in respect of making covert action accountable".[79]

On the other hand, questions about the role of theory and its opportunities come up all the time. Scholars often wonder if they should try to develop a grand overarching theory or simply focus 'to generate theoretical bases for key areas of inquiry'. The form of theorizing in the West that most closely approximates to the professional world of intelligence has been either explanatory or problem-solving, but rarely predictive.[80]

Theories answering empirical questions, such as why repeated failures happen or who is to be blamed for such failures, have been developed very often. Such a research agenda has led to a long and rich list of obstacles. For the most part, such kind of research helps arriving at similar causes for different cases. However, it will be useful to trace the specific effect of each of these causes of failure in order to facilitate better reforms — an issue this paper through its proposed model theory will seek to address.

Sub-Chapter 5

Critical Analysis of Intelligence Review Committees

I. Explaining the Failure of 26/11

Several scholars have dissected the 26/11 terrorist attacks to examine the performance of India's counter-terrorism intelligence agencies or to analyze the important strides in internal security reform. However, to my best knowledge, none have analyzed the reports of intelligence review Committees to study the level of understanding of the problems faced by the intelligence community. And they have overlooked the deadly weaknesses in repeated organizational and institutional reforms. An in-depth look at the Ram Pradhan Committee Report, which was generated in the aftermath of

26/11, can provide answers for why repeated counter-terrorist attacks happen in the country. By offering useful insight into the state of intelligence review committees and subsequent reform making in the country, the Report can —at several levels—help point and fix the dilemmas of the intelligence community. The theories advanced in the Ram Pradhan Committee Report and the subsequent reforms clearly point towards the failure to adequately assess its own problems.

II. Evaluating the 26/11 Ram Pradhan Committee Report

The Ram Pradhan Committee, a two-member High-level Committee headed by former Governor of Andhra Pradesh, R.D. Pradhan, and former special secretary, Cabinet Secretariat, V. Balachandran, was initiated in the aftermath of the 26/11 attacks to systematically evaluate the lapses in intelligence and law enforcement agencies and suggests measures to prevent events like 26/11 Mumbai attacks. It accurately identified that the following have jointly led to the inability to prevent Pakistani gunmen from attacking the Mumbai city:

1. A 'glaring systemic loop hole' in the way intelligence in processed and shared between central and state agencies, [81]

2. A confusion in processing intelligence alerts,

3. The Maharashtra state government's neglect of useful open-source intelligence, and

4. Insufficient interagency coordination.

Additionally, in pinpointing the mistakes of the law enforcement agencies, the Committee found that the Mumbai Police was not sufficiently armed with the required arms and ammunition to respond to the fully equipped *fidayeen*-style terrorists. The report also noted that the delay of the police modernization plan, the inflexible procurement rules for small and routine purchases of ammunition and the poorly equipped anti-terrorist squads (ATS) were all peripheral reasons for the failure. Fifteen days after the 26/11 attacks, numerous recommendations were advanced to give a face-lift to the country's defense and intelligence gathering mechanism.

It included proposals for setting up a National Investigation Agency (NIA), a federal agency to combat terror, a coastal military command, the INR 3,400-crore National Counter Terrorism Centre (NCTC), a controversial anti-terror hub that was modeled after the US namesake, and the National Intelligence Grid (NATGRID), an intelligence grid that aims to link several intelligence databases to help aggregate comprehensive patterns of intelligence that can be readily shared and accessed by the entire intelligence community. Proposals were also made to strengthen the Multi Agency Centre (MAC), which had not been fully set in motion during that time. Besides this, there were several proposals made to strengthen the security apparatus and equip the existing agencies with advanced technology to enable improved surveillance.

As a consequence, several improvements were made to make the security apparatus more effective. A number of regional hubs have been established for the rapid response NSG units as well as the creation of counter-terrorism schools. There has been an enhanced integrated approach between the Indian Navy and the Coast Guard, with a key achievement being the development of Joint Operation Centers under the control of Naval Commanders-in-Chief. To fulfill its expanding responsibilities, the Coast Guard has been strengthened with an additional 3,000 personnel at various levels. There has also been a marked improvement in capabilities, with a variety of fast patrol vehicles, interceptor boats, coastal surveillance aircraft and offshore patrol vehicles being procured.[82]

While the NIA was immediately established by Parliament with the enactment of the National Investigation Agency Act, 2008, the NATGRID and NCTC are yet to be made operational. Most of the failures pointed out in the report and the reforms suggested after the inquiry committee have focused on correcting organizational weaknesses. However, the intelligence agencies are still left with the same set of problems since the Kargil crisis of 1999. Problems of 'lack of focus and direction, turf-battles, poor coordination, uncorroborated reports and the lack of professionalism and motivation'[83] persist. Probably, these organizational reforms are not the most suitable solutions to end the problems faced by the intelligence community.

III. Arbitration and Analysis

The Ram Pradhan Committee found that the existing intelligence analysis mechanism was inadequate to make an overall assessment of available intelligence warnings prior to the attacks. This made it impossible for the analysts to gauge the threat accurately and the policymakers to react to it. More professionalism within the intelligence community with better abilities to process intelligence for enhanced ground action would have revealed a strong indication that some major terrorist action was being planned against the Mumbai city. In simple words, the Indian intelligence community was unable to 'connect the dots' because the apparatus was not sufficiently equipped to handle mass volumes of alerts.

The assumption of the Committee that a lack of capacity to process intelligence has made it impossible for the intelligence community to predict the 26/11 terrorist attack is probably correct. Former home minister's proposal to create a National Counter-terrorism Centre (NCTC) almost certainly emerges from this assumption. Although there were repeated warnings from several agencies about a possible attack in Mumbai, our anti-terrorism squads (ATS) failed to extract focused intelligence from a mass of information and did not take sufficient steps to guard against a surprise attack of such greatness. As the committee points out, "The mode of attack and targets were correctly conveyed without an exact date." Specifically, the committee found that the dual control of the ATS was not working well. Such incomplete intelligence creates "serious difficulties for ground personnel" and therefore calls for "better intelligence processing".[84]

What the Committee failed to point out, however, is the lack of sufficient conflict simulation and scenario building within our counter-terrorism intelligence agencies. The Indian intelligence community, for instance, does not sufficiently train its analysts to develop a deep analytical understanding of terrorist strategies to avoid failures of 'institutional imagination'. The Indian NCTC, however, might not put an end to all confusion in processing intelligence alerts in future. Like the US and the UK, India too handled problems in intelligence processing through its joint intelligence committees (JIC) during Kargil days. The US, under the Department of Homeland Security (DHS), created the NCTC in 2004 to do strategic operational planning to counter terrorism and assign roles to lead departments. Yet, it had no power to direct the execution of operations. Moreover, it communicated through 72 fusion centers, 27 of which were capable of directly receiving and circulating secret intelligence.

The Indian NCTC does not fully replicate its US counterpart. In India, the initial proposals on NCTC were made with an 'overarching responsibility to perform functions relating to intelligence, investigation and operations for preventing, containing and responding to terror attacks', which is awfully over-ambitious.[85] Though the proposal is extremely watered-down, it still might not serve as a practical reform to address the problem of analysis and 'intelligence arbitration'.[86] In fact, without rigorous hiring procedures and improved professional training programs, an institutional reform of such stature may not help get to the bottom of the problem.

Besides this, the committee also pointed out a problem in relation to who processes routine intelligence alerts. The Ram Pradhan Committee was told that 'under the "desk officer" system, intelligence circulars are directly received and processed by concerned "desk officer" who … may or may not keep the higher officials informed'. In other words, there is no procedure to properly analyze the intelligence received, formulate a plan and act on it immediately. Though the committee acknowledged it as a 'shocking revelation', it has not explicitly made any proposal to handle such failures within the community. If the intelligence community fails to address such organizational deficiencies, however trifling they may sound, repeated intelligence processing failures may never end.

IV. Sharing, Coordination and Integration

The Ram Pradhan Committee detailed a second theory of intelligence failure: that of failure of coordination and alignment in processing intelligence alerts at the state level. It observed a 'glaring systemic loophole in the way intelligence from central agencies is processed at the state level'. It also observed that counter-terrorism intelligence is handled by several officials leading to the problem of coordination and cohesion in thinking. The assumption of the committee that leadership weaknesses within the intelligence community have made it impossible for the system to make sound articulations is perhaps inadequately corroborated. The intelligence community was therefore unable to prevent the 26/11 terrorist attack not only because of an inability to process intelligence, but also because of a failure to develop a cohesive strategy between the agencies at the Centre and the state.

V. Over-dependence

The committee was careful to recognize that it would not be correct to conclude that the Mumbai police did not take available intelligence reports seriously. However, it pointed out that there is a tendency on part of local police to depend entirely on outside inputs for terrorism-related intelligence. As a matter of fact, it also indicated that the local police themselves are in a better position to collect local intelligence since they are in daily touch with their area. However, no reforms were advanced to strengthen local intelligence.

On a different note, the committee noted that the resources available with the Mumbai police weren't adequate to conduct sea patrolling so as to intercept the boat used by terrorists, because of which nothing perhaps could be done on receipt of intelligence alerts relating to seaborne attacks. Rigorous implementation of intelligence and coastal security reforms of the past would have put the intelligence and security agencies in a better position to promptly react and prepare for the upcoming attack.

Besides all these, the over-dependence on central agencies, clubbed with a disregard for open source intelligence jointly contributed to the Mumbai police's inability to avert the attack. In fact, the committee also noted that the Mumbai police failed to analyze the capacity building by the terrorist groups concerned and their implications for Mumbai's own security following the Kabul Serena Hotel attack (January 2008) or Islamabad Marriot attack (September 2008). This causal hypothesis in relation to the state government's neglect of open source intelligence was made with an understanding that open source intelligence acts as a valuable input for further tactical action and for drawing lessons. However, the committee did not dwell on the subject for too long and no reforms were made in this connection.

VI. Hits and Misses of the Ram Pradhan Committee

The 26/11 High Level Enquiry Committee (HLEC) is a little problematic on its own terms because of the gap between its weak theories and recommended reforms. The three main theories— of analysis, sharing and over-dependence—have all been poorly conceptualized. While the Committee accurately pointed out the intelligence community's lack of capacity to analyze, however, it failed to spot the root cause behind such a failure. Further, it is highly unlikely that any of the major changes, including the proposed NCTC and NATGRID, help generate the missing analytical imagination. And there is no reason to expect the organizational changes to stimulate imagination in the first place.

The theory of analysis and arbitration is especially unclear because it only mentioned that the community was unable to process numerous intelligence alerts because the intelligence analysis mechanism during that time was inadequate. However, it did not clearly define what it meant by adequacy or inadequacy at an analytical level. In this light, it becomes clear that the Ram Pradhan Committee left a few important questions unanswered: Is there something as adequate intelligence analysis mechanism? How much is enough? Have there been cases where the mechanism was adequate? In other words, when is an intelligence community analytically adequate? Such questions, if asked by the committee, could have led to the recognition of an importance of performance and accountability within the intelligence community. On the other hand, a root cause analysis into the failure of analysis could have prompted reforms relating to better training.

The limited exploration of the Committee almost certainly arises from the terms of reference that were extremely limited. What the intelligence community lacks is a full-fledged aftermath analysis after every major terrorist attack. The police and intelligence agencies rarely analyze—either alone or together — what they could have done better. It is not incorrect to assume that such review Committees are basically set-up to cover the repeated mistakes of the intelligence community to appraise its working and the failures of the policy makers to take any corrective action.

To make the argument that poor centralization was the cause of 26/11 requires answering a number of questions. Take for instance the committee's main example: Suppose perfect coordination existed and if the Mumbai police had watch-listed the terrorist groups and analyzed their capacity building, could they have averted 26/11? Further, the argument that the intelligence agencies should have done more to research the capacity building of a terrorist group without being asked for also reveals a misunderstanding of the role of specific agencies within the community. The 'adequacy' theory in relation to intelligence analysis, sea patrolling, ammunition and strength of anti-terrorism squads are also slightly flawed —in terms of definitional clarity.

In developing two or more theories of failure, the committee has attributed too many causes to the failure to prevent the attack. It neither highlighted one major dilemma nor did it sufficiently explain each causal factor. A more extensive theoretical treatment would have at least addressed the underlying tension between the hypothesized causes. However, such errors and omissions are not any new to review committees analyzing counter-terrorist failures. The Kargil Review Committee, which was initiated in the aftermath of Pakistan's aggression in Kargil in 1999, made similar mistakes in establishing causal links.

The Kargil and Ram Pradhan enquiry committees—which were initiated against the backdrop of a vigorous public discussion about the repeated failures of the intelligence community— provide a wealth of knowledge about the nature of theoretical underpinnings within the intelligence community and the state of intelligence reform in the country. A comparison of the two review committees not only serves the purpose mentioned above, but also offers useful insights about the problems within the intelligence community.

VII. Evaluating the Kargil Review Committee Report

The Kargil Review Committee, headed by K. Subramanyam, was appointed by the Government of India in the aftermath of the Kargil conflict in 1999 to systematically review the events leading to Pakistan aggression in Kargil district of Jammu & Kashmir, to evaluate the overall security scenario prior to the attack and to recommend measures as are considered necessary to safeguard the country against such attacks in the future. A special task force led by Girish Chandra Saxena, was constituted to analyze the lapses in intelligence operations prior to the intrusions and suggests measures to prevent occurrence of events like these in future. The committee drew attention to several deficiencies in the intelligence system relating to collection, reporting, collation and assessment of intelligence. The critical failures identified by the Committee related to:

1. Absence of information on the induction and de-induction of battalions and lack of accurate data on the identity of battalions,

2. Overload of background and unconfirmed information,

3. Lack of institutionalized process of interaction,

4. Flawed mechanism of intelligence gathering and

5. No system of checks and balances to assure that the intelligence consumer is getting all that he is due to get.

The G.C. Saxena Special Task Force made proposals for several organizational reforms, including the creation of Defense Intelligence Agency (DIA), empowered to conduct trans-border operations, the National Technical Research Organization (NTRO), modeled after the US National Security Agency, the Multi-Agency Centre (MAC), and a state-of-the-art mechanism to facilitate intelligence sharing between the central and state agencies. Most of the reforms advanced by the committee were implemented. However, a key component of the intelligence reform programme—the Joint Task Force on Intelligence (JTFI)—which was proposed "to liaise with the Special Branch of the state police and the officials of the Criminal Investigation Department, offering real-time information on terrorist groups" was not fully implemented before the 26/11 attacks.

The hypothesized failures indicate a clear understanding of the problems faced by the intelligence community; however, most of the subsequent reforms are somewhat isolated and fail to tackle the problems listed above in a holistic manner. As rightly pointed out by B. Raman, the Committee shows clarity in pointing out the deficiencies in the intelligence system. However, it 'suggested further enquiries' by the Government of India into such deficiencies 'as a prelude to corrective action'. Subsequent intelligence reforms listed above were suggested; however, no effort was made by the Group of Ministers (GoM) report to explain the relevance or significance of each of those reforms in addressing the deficiencies originally pointed out. It is because of this reason that the organizational reforms are questionable.

It will be incorrect to say that the DIA, NTRO or MAC has made no change in the functioning of intelligence agencies in the country. Yet, a majority of the problems highlighted by the Kargil Review Committee remain even after the implementation of reforms published in the GoM report, as I have highlighted in the evaluation of the Ram Pradhan Committee report made above.

VIII. Lack of Adequate Intelligence

The Kargil Review Committee made the assumption that the critical failure in intelligence was related to the absence of information on the induction and de-induction of battalions and the lack of accurate data on the identity of battalions in the area opposite Kargil during 1998. It indicated that the intelligence structure and the state of intelligence gathering were inadequate to assess available intelligence, manage the overload of unconfirmed background information or gather sufficient tactical intelligence to suitably warn the system. This, according to the committee, made it impossible for the intelligence agencies to make an assessment of the threat.

Further, the committee indicated that there were 'no specific indicators of a likely major attack in the Kargil sector, such as significant improvements in logistics and communication or a substantial force build-up or forward deployment of forces reported by any of the agencies'. While the committee continuously pinpointed the agencies for improper judgment and analysis, it barely recognized that the surprise attack arose predominantly from the enemy's capacity of deception rather than the intelligence analyst's failure of perception. This improper correlation between lack of adequate intelligence and the failure to prevent the intrusion is probably misplaced, because it is definitely "unreasonable to expect all intelligence to be complete".[87]

IX. Absence of Checks and Balances

The committee report rightly observed that the lack of (a) intelligence oversight and (b) a system of regular, periodic and comprehensive intelligence briefings were the predominant causes for the failure to avert the Pakistani intrusion in Kargil. Yet, no intelligence reform was implemented to put in place a system of checks and balances.

X. Coordination, Interaction and Dialogue

The committee report noted that 'the Indian Army did not share information about the intensity and its effect of its past firing with other agencies' in 1998. R&AW's inability to assess the significance of the enemy activities 'in terms of ammunition storage or construction of underground bunkers', were linked to the absence of this piece of information. The case was also identified as 'another example of lack of inter-agency coordination as lack of coordination between the Army and the agencies'. The Multi Agency Centre (MAC), which failed during 26/11, was set-up in the aftermath of Kargil to ensure better sharing and coordination. Yet, problems relating to coordination, interaction and dialogue persist. The Committee report noted that there is 'no institutionalized process whereby R&AW, IB, BSF and army intelligence officials interact periodically at levels below the JIC'. Yet, fourteen years later, there is still a lack of protocol for engagement and interaction. Furthermore, the Committee did not acknowledge it as a case of R&AW's overdependence on army inputs to make judgments about enemy action.

XI. State of Intelligence Review Committees and Reform Making

Both the Kargil Review Committee set-up after the Kargil conflict in 1999 and the Ram Pradhan Committee set-up in the aftermath of 26/11 attacks have their own share of problems. While the Kargil Committee reflected a clear understanding of the causes for such a failure, the reforms suggested by the Group of Ministers (GoM) did not clearly explain the practicability of these measures. Moreover, as the report created by the Girish Chandra Saxena Committee that was set-up by the GoM remains classified, it is inappropriate to say they were poorly developed. As former intelligence personnel and strategic affairs expert B. Raman noted in his paper entitled *Dimensions of Intelligence Operations,* the Kargil Review Committee drew attention to serious deficiencies at various levels in intelligence process. He also noted that the committee did not go to "the reasons for these deficiencies". Without making such an inquiry into the causal factors hypothesized in the report, "it had suggested further enquiries by the Government into these, as a prelude to corrective action".

It suggested a few corrective measures, including the creation of a Defense Intelligence Agency (DIA) and a separate agency for the collection of Technical Intelligence (TECHINT), patterned after the USA's National Security Agency (NSA). However, a more elaborate theoretical treatment to a few causal factors identified in the report would have led to more sensible reforms addressing problems relating to intelligence analysis. Both the committees have been influential in sparking debates relating to huge organizational changes in the intelligence community. Many of their recommendations were implemented. Yet, intelligence failures continue to happen, and for the same causes that were identified by the Kargil Review Committee. This exposes at least three problems in intelligence reviews: (1) a lack of understanding of what constitutes intelligence and intelligence failure, (2) the ambiguity in defining certain key terminology and (3) lack of sufficient analytical clarity in evaluating intelligence failures.

The theoretical framework created in the chapter below argues that a method to avert intelligence failures is the establishment of a clearer understanding of the expectations of the intelligence machinery and a sound conceptualization of what constitutes an intelligence failure and who needs to be held accountable for the different failures of the intelligence community.

Sub-Chapter 6

A Theoretical Framework for Explaining: Repeated Failures of the Intelligence Community

Popular literature analyzing intelligence failures in the West have little scholarly work explaining how intelligence failures should be assessed. Without such a theory to explain why secret intelligence agencies fail, what intelligence failures are, and how they are starkly different from other failures of the community, it becomes difficult for intelligence review committees and/or politicians to understand the problems of the intelligence community and make appropriate proposals for reform making. In this chapter, the paper presents a theoretical framework, which might be helpful in advancing a theory at a future date.

I. Need for a Theory for Analyzing Intelligence Failures

Is a counter-terrorist failure an unavoidable 'bolt from the blue' or the result of numerous failures of the intelligence community that are avoidable? Is it an inevitable disaster or a major blunder of warning? When can one call a counter-terrorist failure an intelligence failure? Often, intelligence review committees and politicians assume counter-terrorism policy making is influenced by intelligence analysis and come up with a long list of causal factors for what they tend to call 'intelligence failures'. Reform makers do not mark out the specific effect of each factor, and therefore, are unclear about which variables have more causal weight over the others.

Such an approach leads to long lists of proposals for reforms, which are rarely operationalized in full. Adding causal weight is especially significant since some causal factors can be remedied while several others can barely be overcome. The question of which factors causing intelligence failures are more vital ones in making intelligence reforms can provide useful answers to help make functional reforms, and as a result, prevent terror attacks arising from a failure of the producers or consumers of intelligence.

The literature review on the state of intelligence theorizing in the West has clearly documented the sharp differences among the various theoretical traditions of intelligence studies. While a majority of the Western theoretical discourses have focused on intelligence failures, each of them has approached intelligence failures differently and has consequently provided direction for intelligence reforms in relation to the hypothesized causes. Yet, no theory can be all encompassing and address all failures of the intelligence community. A majority of the causal factors identified in several Western theories advanced earlier are extremely useful in explaining intelligence failures, no matter where they happen. However, none—to my best knowledge—have dealt with the failure of intelligence review committees in advancing narrow theoretical treatments in explaining failures. Western scholars have formulated theories about what causes intelligence failures and also explain how to destroy these causes.

However, the root cause of the various failures of the intelligence community in India predominantly exists in the failure to sufficiently understand such causes. It is essential to create a theory to: (a) help intelligence review committees analyze intelligence failures with more clarity and rigor, (b) facilitate them—inquiry committees and policy makers—in determining which failures of the intelligence community are more urgent and (c) systematize the intelligence reform making process. The starting point in addressing the above failure, and subsequently, determining the weight of a certain causal factor in explaining an intelligence failure is a system for cataloguing the various failures of the intelligence community. An apparently simple, yet systematic questioning of the various failures—identified as causal factors for an intelligence failure—can be extremely helpful in this process.

In an attempt to build a theory of intelligence failure, it is essential to understand the nature of counter-terrorist failures. Traditionally, scholars note that there could be three types of intelligence failures: those pertaining to the collection of information, to its analysis, and to the response to the produced intelligence.[88] "While failures to collect adequate intelligence may be attributed to the agencies, failure to respond or analyze the intelligence made available to policy makers are considered failures of political-strategic leadership."[89]

Yet, calling all three failures an intelligence failure could be misleading and can often make the wrong stakeholders accountable. Therefore, I call for a different approach through this policy paper. I believe it is important to clearly make a distinction between the failure of the intelligence community to produce accurate strategic or tactical intelligence (intelligence failure), failure of policy makers to respond or process available intelligence (policy failure), failure of intelligence officials to adapt to the changing faces of transnational terrorism (adaptation failure) and failure to make sensible intelligence reforms to avert such failures (reform failure). Such an approach, I argue, is necessary because it makes it easier to hold someone accountable, be it intelligence agencies, policy makers or reform makers.

Any significant theoretical treatise in intelligence studies has to be either explanatory or problem solving. "The ability to explain is more important than the ability to predict," as IR scholar Kenneth Waltz points out as function of theory. Before getting to explaining what intelligence failures really are, we need some clarity in definition, especially as the term "intelligence" means different things to different people.

Key Terminology

For the purpose of this research paper, intelligence is conceptualized as a distinct activity aimed at increasing the understanding or influence of an opponent. The usage is adapted from Michael Warner who defines it as a "secret, state activity to understand or influence domestic or foreign entities",[90] and Thomas Troy who calls it "knowledge of the enemy".[91] While the 'secrecy' element of national security intelligence is often emphasized elsewhere, this paper looks at the several other perceived definitions from major discourse producers, including the intelligence producers and the consumers, i.e. policy makers, military, and several others. "To the intelligence community, it is perceived as a kind of information that helps to inform, instruct, and educate the policy world. However, it conjures different meanings for the policy makers. It might be considered a political asset or liability, depending on whether the information helps or hinders the fulfillment of political goals."[92]

Moreover, this paper also keeps in mind that intelligence is viewed differently across the globe. For instance, intelligence is differently conceptualized in countries like the US, the UK or Israel, which are 'security states'. In India, intelligence is still considered an activity to protect the security of the government, and this is evident from the proportion of counter-terrorism related intelligence personnel to the rest of them at the Intelligence Bureau. This is where we lack as a society in our understanding about what the intelligence function constitutes.[93]

Strategic vs. Tactical Intelligence

Basically, there are two different kinds of intelligence — strategic i.e. long-term intelligence of the threat that an opponent poses to national security & tactical i.e. highly perishable, short-term intelligence. Strategic intelligence is required to alert policy makers to any changes in the nature and trajectory of a terrorist threat, thus helping them formulate timely policy responses. In addition, it also provides a focus for tactical efforts. On the other hand, the primary purpose of tactical intelligence is to identify ground-level information on terrorist outfits, predominantly for the consumption of local police forces.

II. What is an Intelligence Failure?

> "They're not all intelligence failures. There is a failure to act, or a failure to appreciate intelligence. Or, there could be cases where the consumers — policy makers and law enforcement agencies—suffer from an inability or lack of capacity to act."
>
> *–Vikram Sood, former director, R&AW.*

Universally, it is accepted that intelligence failures arise only when analytic judgments of intelligence analysts turn out to be imprecise in a big way or when a major surprise occurs because of inadequate or imprecise intelligence warning. In other words, the production of accurate intelligence is understood as an important part of the process of preventing militancy or terrorist attacks. However, as collecting information relating to terrorist operation is an awfully complicated task; several stakeholders from the intelligence business strongly feel the community of intelligence agencies cannot be solely blamed for all terrorist attacks in the country.

Obviously, this calls for a different approach of categorizing such a failure. As American intelligence scholar Stephen Marrin explains in his article entitled *Preventing intelligence failures by learning from the past,* "Intelligence failure can lead to surprise when information is not collected or integrated effectively, and policy failure can lead to surprise if actions were not taken despite intelligence warnings. Nonetheless, exploring the role intelligence plays in preventing surprises can shed light on the ways that changes in intelligence process could prevent future surprises."[94]

Since the 9/11 Committee Report was made public, there has been a widespread tendency to equate intelligence failures to a 'failure to share information'. However, according to American non-conservative scholars Abram Shulsky and Gary Schmitt, intelligence failure is essentially "a misunderstanding of the situation that leads a government to take actions that are inappropriate and counterproductive to its own national interests". While the subject of 'intelligence failure' by itself can be very contentious, there needs to be greater caution in deducing whether a failure to prevent an attack is an intelligence failure. Therefore, in this paper, I insist that a few pertinent questions should be asked in order to determine—with certainty—that it is an intelligence failure.

To resolve a failure as one of inaccurate intelligence production, I suggest three questions should be asked and answered: [95] (1) Did the policy community have any strategic, tactical or generic intelligence about the likelihood of an attack? If so what? (2) Was there any pre-attack intelligence alerts—direct or indirect—from the central, state or any international intelligence agencies? (3) To what extent is the intelligence community equipped to detect or pre-empt attacks? Besides these questions, it is also essential to understand the knowledge gap between policy makers and intelligence officials about a perceived threat.[96]

In addition to the above, former director of R&AW Vikram Sood suggests asking two more questions to understand the quality of intelligence produced: Is the production of intelligence good per-se? If the intelligence input is poor, why is it so? Only if the intelligence produced is considered poor or inadequate to avert a surprise attack can it is confirmed as an 'intelligence failure', he says. Only if there is sufficient evidence to suggest that there was no intelligence available prior to the attack can it be categorized as an intelligence failure. As former intelligence personnel K.V. Thomas agreed: "Only a dearth of intelligence should be associated with failure of the intelligence community."

Contrary to the traditional approach of categorizing intelligence failures based on how much intelligence there was available, this approach would accommodate scenarios where there is limited intelligence within the failure of policy makers to act on general or strategic intelligence. However, specific answers to each of these questions can help make a thorough post-event analysis from which intelligence agencies can benefit.[97]

III. When do Intelligence Agencies Fail to Adapt?

Failures of intelligence can also be associated with a failure of the intelligence community to adapt itself based on the changing needs of the community. 'Adaptation failure', as intelligence scholar Amy Zegart puts it, is the intelligence community's failure to adapt itself based on the changing needs of the community. According to her, three factors tend to explain such adaptation failures. They are: "The nature of bureaucratic organizations, the self interest of presidents, legislators and government ....and the fragmented structure of the federal government."[98]

What exactly does it mean to say that an organization adapts or fails to adapt? For the purpose of this paper, the term 'adaptation' will mean a failure of the intelligence community to adjust to the changing faces of terrorism by implementing ingenious organizational reforms. In simple terms, it is a failure of intelligence policy makers to implement the organizational reforms or other intelligence reforms they originally thought were crucial in averting terrorist attacks in future.

Determining whether a counter-terrorist failure is a failure of the intelligence community to adapt necessitates answering a different set of questions: (1) did intelligence officials and policy makers recognize the gravity of the threat posed by terrorist outfits such as the Indian Mujahedeen or the LeT before the attacks? (2) Did they understand the connection between terrorist threat and the imperative for organizational change? (3) And to what extent did they achieve the organizational changes they believed were necessary? [99]

Answering such questions will not only help familiarize ourselves with the nature of reforms made to strengthen the intelligence apparatus prior to a terrorist attack, but also be of assistance in finding out which of these reforms were implemented and how a few political leaders validate the reforms they make.

IV. How do we recognize a Policy Failure?

'An intelligence agency is as good as its consumer. If the consumer is not going to consume the intelligence, it's pointless.

–Vikram Sood, former director, R&AW.

Even the best intelligence product can go waste if the policy maker fails to act on it at the appropriate time. Regardless of how well the intelligence community predicts flawlessly, intelligence failures can happen—either due to policy makers' neglect or due to unreasonable expectations about the function of intelligence. The conscientiousness of the intelligence agencies ends where intelligence is produced and disseminated. It's up to the policy makers —the consumers of intelligence — to either avert an attack or let a surprise happen, despite intelligence.

According to the Girish Chandra Saxena committee, which was set up after the Kargil conflict, if intelligence agencies are not given long-term and strategic priorities, then it may be attributed as a policy failure. However, for the purpose of this paper, failures of a policy maker to act on strategic or tactical intelligence produced by central intelligence agencies are called policy failures. As former

JIC director S.D. Pradhan points out in an article entitled *Indian intelligence system needs urgent reforms,* published in Times of India, "Failure to provide timely warning is considered a failure by the policy makers and other consumers."

To find out whether we are left with a case of policy failure, the best way is to analyze the influence of the intelligence community on decision makers.[100] This could be done by evaluating whether a certain intelligence warning would have made a difference in preventing an attack from happening. For this purpose, it is vital to recognize (1) the extent to which intelligence warnings are taken seriously, (2) whether government leaders understand the gravity of the threat alerts, and (3) whether they take any policy action to avert the threat.

If the intelligence community provided intelligence analysis that would have sufficiently warned the consumer of intelligence—in this case the policy maker—and if such intelligence has not been acted upon, it is appropriate to call it a policy failure. In India, the central government often passes the buck to the state governments for not acting on available intelligence. The intelligence community is often blamed for improper coordination. However, the question of whether the intelligence was 'actionable' and sufficient is often missed in the debate. However, it is not always the fault of the politician. In case of the 26/11 attack, Ranade pointed out that there was a counter-terrorist failure because "the system of crisis management did not function to its fullest extent, and the person at the helm of affairs believed that he knew better. He thought the 26/11 attack — before it happened — was not a terror attack; but simply gang violence".

V. When do we face a Reform Failure?

While all the above failures are more explicit, a reform failure is one, I think, that is the most hidden failure among them all. Indian intelligence review committees set up by the government after major attacks often do not make an exhaustive assessment of the problems of the intelligence community when a surprise attack happens. They tend to find too many reasons for a counter-terrorist failure and as a consequence make proposals for several reforms. In India, there is a general tendency to believe that all hypothesized causes can be corrected by 'meta-institutional' reforms. Reform makers are also prone to make several reforms to destroy the many causes identified initially. However, their failure to understand where the problem lies or who is accountable for a particular failure leads to ambiguous, if not totally irrelevant, reforms.

To establish whether a counter-terrorist failure is a reform failure, one has to undertake the kind of inquiry advanced in this paper so far. This involves making (a) a review of the state of intelligence theorization in the country that faces the failure, (b) analyze certain perceptions of intelligence failures among political leaders, and (c) assess the state of intelligence review committees in the country. Such an inquiry will show whether the failure is a result of past reform failures, i.e., a failure to make appropriate reforms that prevent several other failures listed above.

Intelligence review committees assessing the performance of intelligence agencies and policy makers in the aftermath of a counter-terrorist failure should preferably ask all the four sets of questions and gather evidence from central and state intelligence agencies, policy makers and the policing community. Such an approach to analyzing the causes for counter-terrorist failures will definitely offer different solutions—if not the most appropriate ones. Though getting the concepts right is fundamental to good reform making, the ability to make suitable reforms vests with the reformer's imaginative way of thinking.

The theoretical foundations advanced above are extremely rudimentary. While it focuses on a very broad picture, it fails to get to the details of any particular failure. Take for instance, an intelligence failure, which arises from a failure to produce intelligence, could be dealt in a different way. Failures to produce appropriate and accurate intelligence estimates may arise from factors such as (a) an intelligence analyst's inability to make assessments, (b) inadequate intelligence machinery in a country or (c) lack of professionalism in the community. Such an approach to intelligence failures might result in a theory of intelligence gathering and analysis.

Sub-Chapter 7

Re-interpreting the Failure to Prevent 26/11

"The approach of calling the 26/11 attacks an intelligence failure is not appropriate."

–D. Sivanandan, former Mumbai Police Commissioner.

As noted in several chapters above, the failure to prevent the 26/11 attack is not a failure of intelligence production. There is sufficient evidence to believe that there were numerous pieces of intelligence available for policy makers to act upon. The 26/11 attack was undoubtedly a failure of policy makers to act on available pieces of specific intelligence. Yet, the intelligence community's failure to adapt, i.e. implement past intelligence reforms, and the reform maker's failure to advance the appropriate reforms before the attack were more evident. However, in this concluding chapter of this policy paper, I will show how thinking differently about intelligence failures and having more definitional clarity can help in making a sound assessment of a counterterrorist failure.

In this chapter, I will first justify why the counter-terrorist failure of 26/11 is not an intelligence failure. Second, I will analyze whether the 26/11 terrorist attacks was the result of intelligence failure or policy failure. A closer look at the pre-26/11 intelligence architecture and estimates will help distinguish between the two. Third, I will question if the 26/11 attacks happened because of the failure of the intelligence community to adapt to the changing needs of new terrorist threats.

Finally, I will argue for calling the failure to prevent 26/11 a reform failure, and answer a few lingering questions such as: Why has the 26/11 stimulated intense levels of internal security reforms whereas previous—and more deadly attacks—have not? Why were the standards of intelligence collection, analysis and sharing not adequate prior to 26/11? What changes have been made to the intelligence apparatus in the post 26/11 era, and how are they adequate? What areas of improvement can be made in order to make the intelligence process more adequate to combat terrorist attacks of this kind?

I. Why 26/11 Was Not an Intelligence Failure

During 26/11, scattered pieces of intelligence were circulated relating to possibilities of sea-borne attack, multiple attacks, commando operation and *fidayeen* plans. Not all pre-attack estimates were taken seriously. The law enforcement and security agencies took a few precautionary measures. However, as the intelligence agencies did not get the dates right, a few security structures — like the detection doors — were dismantled two days before the attack took place. It is probably not right to argue that the attacks might have not taken place if the security structures were still in place. However, this only clarifies that there was sufficient intelligence to create such structures in the first place. On the other hand, "Central agencies received a series of intelligence alerts from 2006 that LeT was training teams for sea-borne attacks on multiple targets, including several luxury hotels."[101] Yet, because of several 'capacity issues', the government of Maharashtra could not strengthen the coastal security.

II. Is 26/11 a Case of Policy Failure?

The case of 26/11 is clearly a failure to act on intelligence that was available, rather than an intelligence failure. While some inputs were put to use and security measures were made stronger, some other vital pieces of information were ignored. Yet, it was not the failure of the politician alone, says Ranade answering to a question on 26/11. "The system of crisis management did not function to its fullest extent, because the person at the helm of affairs believed that he knew better. He thought the 26/11 attack— before it happened—was not a terror attack but simply gang violence. What a terrible mistake!"[102] The argument relating to 'policy failure' is also mistaken because the government leaders in power did not realize the 'gravity of the terrorist threat'.[103] Further, as the terrorist methodology used in 26/11 was extremely innovative, it is not accurate to hold the policy maker accountable for the failure.

III. Why 26/11 was a Failure of the Intelligence Machinery?

A co-author of the Ram Pradhan Committee report, V.

Balachandran highlighted in his paper entitled *Dealing with the aftermath of attacks: Lessons from Mumbai and elsewhere on what to do and what not to do*, that the Maharashtra state government failed to strengthen coastal security and neglected open-source intelligence. More than a failure of the 'government machinery', the 26/11 attacks were a failure of intelligence machinery. The Multi Agency Centre (MAC), which was set up after the Kargil conflict in 1999, failed to work. Answering a question about communication and sharing failures within the intelligence community during 26/11, Ranade noted that a crucial piece of intelligence, which was shared by R&AW—about a ship moving down the coastline—was shared through MAC.

"Unfortunately, the system failed to recognize the importance of the alert." R&AW subsequently passed it through the MAC; but the Coast Guard or Navy did not act upon the intelligence input. It is not correct to say that the attack could have been averted with this one piece of intelligence. However, this was clearly a failure, and that of adaptation, as the MAC, which set-up after Kargil Review Committee, was not fully operationalized before the 26/11 happened.

IV. Why 26/11 is Not Just a 'Failure to Connect the Dots'

As Roberta Wohlstetter once explained in her classic 1962 study, *Pearl Harbor: Warning and Decision*, "It is much easier after the event to sort the relevant signals from the irrelevant signals. After the event, of course, the signal is always crystal clear.... but, before the event, it is obscure and pregnant with conflicting meanings."Most writers of intelligence failure studying the 26/11 often note that the failure arose from the intelligence community's failure to 'connect the dots'. However, it is extremely challenging to sift through the noise to pick relevant pieces of intelligence. While supporters of NATGRID often feel the reform will end such failures, 'the vacuum cleaner approach is only suitable for big governments such as the US or China', [104] which are technically more superior.

The greater failure, of course, is that of changing the mentality of a few intelligence personnel. There is a greater necessity to redefine the sole purpose of intelligence from 'need to know' to 'need to share'. Organizational reforms such as the NCTC or NATGRID will happen only in such an environment, though political pressures still play a major role.

V. Why 26/11 is a Reform Failure

It is clear from the arguments made above that intelligence producers should not have been held responsible for such a failure. Policy makers should be criticized for the counterterrorism failure because of three reasons: (1) they failed to act on available intelligence in a timely manner, (2) they failed to implement the past intelligence reforms in full, which the earlier governments considered imperative, and (3) they failed to sufficiently educate themselves about new faces of terrorism. However, the blame for the failure should be partly shared by the intelligence producers themselves, for their failure to be imaginative. Nevertheless, what is clear is that 26/11 happened because of a poor intelligence apparatus, inadequate sharing mechanism, and lack of capacity, all of which could have been rectified through implementation of sensible reforms.

The very fact that the 26/11 attack stimulated intense levels of internal security reforms while previous attacks have not clearly points to a failure to recognize the need for such reforms in the past. There could be a few reasons for such failure: (1) Intelligence review committees do not do full-fledged aftermath analysis after every major attack. (2) Even if they do, they don't analyze all aspects of failure. Even in cases where they sufficiently analyze, intelligence reforms barely address the hypothesized causes. And, most such reforms tend to be meta-institutional. Intelligence review committees—the only way of governmental assessment of a counter-terrorist failure—lack a clear understanding of what constitutes and intelligence failure and what are the other failures faced by the intelligence community. This failure of the review committees and policy makers to clearly distinguish between the problems and make specific stakeholders accountable has led to the reform failure prior to the 26/11 attacks.

"Since 26/11, greater focus has been on sharing and coordinating actions on pieces of information available and then hoping to develop more leads on it."[105] One of the most important changes made to the intelligence apparatus was the strengthening of the Multi Agency Centre (MAC), which was created much earlier but had not been fully activated. The MAC brought together all the law enforcement and intelligence agencies on one table to share their pieces of information so that necessary action could be taken in consultation with the relevant agencies. State MACs (SMACs) were created to enable the local security agencies to share relevant information.

However, "MAC, like all other intelligence agencies, is under-staffed."[106] Though "MAC meets every day and SMACs do not meet every day", the efficiency of such an agency is affected because "there is no written protocol either for interaction, engagement or coordination".[107]The revamped intelligence architecture in the post 26/11 era failed miserably during the Mumbai 2011 attacks. "Even today, it is not in a position to make timely and holistic assessment and assist in swift and coordinated response."[108] It still lacks the teeth and unambiguous authority over Subsidiary Multi Agency Centers (SMACs) and state intelligence machinery. The story of intelligence reform is not over.

Sub-Chapter 8

The Golden Mean: Striking a balance between Secrecy and Sharing

I

In this policy paper, I argue that repeated failures of the intelligence community are a result of a failure to implement sensible intelligence reforms. Based on the several interactions I have had with producers and consumers of intelligence, I conclude that such a failure arises because of two reasons: (1) the inability of policy makers and reform makers to understand and appreciate what constitutes intelligence and intelligence failure and (2) the lack of rigorous academic investigation of the intelligence business. The paper, therefore, makes the claim that intelligence reforms in India are not sufficiently 'sensible' because of insufficient analysis into intelligence failures — both in policy and academic circles.[109]

Towards the end, I suggest that thinking differently about intelligence and intelligence failure can certainly help better appreciate the problems of the intelligence community, and as a result, can lead to sensible intelligence reforms. I also demonstrate how measuring the performance of intelligence reforms might be a useful way of finding where India is in the war against terrorism.

I diagnose failures in this manner and offer such a prescription as narrated above, because several intelligence reforms that have been advanced in the past have not been able to avert terrorist attacks in the future.[110] All evidence collected in the paper suggests that the intelligence reforms made in the past have not been very sensible and have barely addressed the problems at the root. The performance of intelligence reforms, as measured in the initial chapters of this policy paper, are purely based on (1) interactions with former intelligence personnel and academicians, (2) observations made from intelligence review committee reports and (3) deductions about counter-terrorist failures purely arising from intelligence failures. However, such reasoning might not be adequate to put together a theory or doctrine to explain such failures. Even before measuring the performance of intelligence reforms, what is more crucial is to measure the contribution of intelligence to counter-terrorism. Moreover, such measurements should be more standardized.

How can we measure the value of intelligence accurately to see if it is contributing to victory in the war on terror? How can we measure the progress in intelligence reform making? When is intelligence reform complete? Only intelligence agencies and the government—who are the custodians of secretive national security information—can answer. Though statistics about intelligence successes can reveal a lot about the success of an intelligence reform, Indian intelligence agencies hardly reveal such stories.

This concealment of such information makes it impossible for academicians to access seminal material about the functioning of intelligence agencies. As a result, it gets hard to make any strong arguments about the performance of intelligence agencies, or the performance of intelligence reforms. Though measuring consumer satisfaction is a helpful way of judging the performance of intelligence, policy makers hardly divulge the full nature of intelligence that was made available to them, as they are wary of debates that might follow. Some journalists covering intelligence issues tend to make biased judgments about the performance of agencies by looking into hundreds of faulty or useless intelligence alerts issued by intelligence agencies.

II

In such a scenario, where intelligence agencies and policy makers fail to offer such information, identifying a method to measure the value of intelligence and the performance of intelligence reform becomes extremely complicated. Without any doubts, legal or parliamentary oversight of intelligence agencies can provide the most appropriate mechanisms for measuring the performance of intelligence. However, given the complexity of creating such oversight mechanisms in the near future, here's what I think the producers and consumers of intelligence should consider doing to help intelligence scholars come up with solutions to avert the failures of the intelligence community in future.

1.   As a starting point, intelligence agencies should reveal—at least to a small group of "reliable[111] intelligence scholars"— information about the nature of intelligence that was shared via the Multi Agency Centre (MAC) prior to a terrorist attack. This could be particularly useful to assess a failure and identify who should be held accountable. Such a disclosure of information can also help scholars arrive at a trend chart about the kind the intelligence that has been produced and shared.[112]

2.   Though the intelligence community confirms the effective functioning of the MAC, politicians constantly correlate failures of intelligence to failures of coordination. To put an end to such wrong allegations made by a handful of

politicians, there has to be a mechanism where MAC should be held accountable to intelligence agencies if they fail to pass any pertinent piece of intelligence. Of course, it might be helpful to agencies if MAC returns the alerts it discards during its evaluation.

3. Useful statistics about the functioning of the MAC can help intelligence scholars rule out the likelihood of failures arising from intelligence sharing and coordination. After all, evaluating how well intelligence flows is an excellent metric to assess the performance of intelligence agencies.

4. Though intelligence agencies often tend to interact among themselves despite the invisible 'turf war' among themselves, sharing information about the source of an intelligence input can avoid duplications. This could particularly prove useful if the intelligence agencies are more concerned about the quality and precision of intelligence they produce. If such a quality-control mechanism was put in place, and if it was also made public, that can be a useful way of measuring intelligence accuracy.

5. The country's premier intelligence agencies—the IB and the R&AW—should reduce their levels of secrecy at least in divulging successful operations, like the recent story about the arrest of Bhatkal brothers. For instance, this particular story is an excellent case of successful coordination between Indian and Nepalese agencies, and between R&AW, the IB and the NIA.

III

Reducing the level of secrecy of intelligence agencies in sharing such information alone will not put an end to this problem. In order to help scholars identify a trend in intelligence failures or successes, policy makers or other consumers of intelligence, including the military or the navy, should be open to sharing some information about what they know. Here's the kind of information I think scholars would benefit from if shared by the consumers of intelligence. Such sharing can put an end to the 'buck-passing' that happens in the aftermath of every major counter-terrorist failure in the country.

1. The consumers of intelligence should regularly share information about the nature of intelligence that was made available prior to an attack. Such frankness will be appreciated as it will help scholars develop databases and also make agencies more accountable.

2. Even if they are wary of sharing such information, creating feedback mechanisms in public will be of some help. Though this could reveal huge misunderstandings about the producers and consumers of intelligence, it could be a useful way through which a handful of intelligence scholars can understand the intricacies of the producer-consumer divide.

3. On the contrary, if they are worried about making such feedback mechanisms public, they might want to share useful statistics about the successes of intelligence agencies as a useful way of boosting their morale. Scholars could also benefit from such statistics.

4. Another useful way is to establish a clear mandate for intelligence agencies in public and provide occasional metrics about how they perform.

Sub-Chapter 9

Direction for Future Intelligence Reforms

Several monographs relating to intelligence reforms have made the following recommendations:

1. A sound system of checks and balances is an absolute necessity in averting repeated intelligence failures. The intelligence agencies, Parliament, legislature and external review bodies should play independent roles in overseeing the workings of the intelligence community.[113]

2. As old-fashioned traditional military threats are overshadowed by new asymmetric threats, there is a need for reprioritization of national security objectives and for redefining the intelligence priorities of the country.[114]

3. As key intelligence experts in the US note, "Speed and agility is the key to war on terrorism, not more levels of bureaucracy."

4. There is a growing realization that the obsession with secrecy has prevented agencies from interacting with experts in the outside world where a good deal of knowledge and expertise exists. Advances in technology, and information revolution calls for a multidisciplinary approach to data analysis. An IDSA Task Force report on intelligence reforms noted that "there is a broad consensus shared by a wide section of Indian intelligence professionals and academicians about the need to enable better coordination amongst various agencies". Yet, the evidence I have gathered through frank discussions with several former intelligence personnel calls for a different direction towards intelligence reforms.

Summary of Recommendations

The absence of an independent body to monitor the performance of intelligence agencies, the lack of reasonable expectations from the intelligence community, coupled with a recruitment bias has hampered professionalism within intelligence agencies. This will be clearly addressed in the recommendations advanced below:

I. Towards building a theory to explain failures

Intelligence review committees in the country often take the wrong turn because the subject of intelligence failure is overloaded with questionable assumptions.

1. There is a need for more theorizing in the field to reduce the lack of definitional clarity, and to enable a better understanding of the problems faced by the intelligence community.

2. There's a need to develop a professional literature of intelligence studies which will contribute to the growth of a systematic body of knowledge about intelligence processes in the country.

II. Recruitment, Training & Recognition

1. The bureaucratic nature of intelligence agencies should not hamper recruitment and training. What agencies urgently require is a more open recruitment policy and a rigorous procedure of hiring the most flexible minds in the country.

2. Agencies should set high standards for recruiting and insist on special language or other interpretation skills from prospective candidates.

III. Capacity building & skill management

1. Out of the total intelligence personnel within IB, only a few hundreds of them have been specifically hired to gather and analyze intelligence relating to counter-terrorism. Therefore, both the manpower quality and quantity should be improved to effectively avert failures of intelligence.

2. Though a need for professionalizing the intelligence agencies has been highlighted in the past, no reform has been proposed to allow lateral entry and/or promote the use of interpersonal skills in gathering intelligence. For example, a banker will have a better grip on issues relating to money laundering than a normal intelligence analyst who is recruited without knowledge about the subject.

3. There is a need to relax the secretive nature of intelligence agencies and outsource experts from varied backgrounds to allow for creative analysis.

IV. Intelligence Analysis

1. Reforms relating to improving training for intelligence analysts should aim at reducing the time taken to whet an individual. Such reforms should also allow for inter-

agency training, which can provide an insight into how their counterparts in other agencies work.

2. The real challenge is to recruit and train intelligence analysts who are encouraged to think creatively. Scenario building and conflict simulations can certainly address the lack of imaginative intelligence reasoning of a handful of intelligence analysts and also provide a direction for future intelligence gathering.

3. Former intelligence personnel can be particularly helpful in building real-time scenarios and making conflict simulations.

V. Coordination and cohesion in working

1. Organizational reforms such as MAC can effectively function only if the community creates a clear communication protocol and establish a set of rules for engaging and de-engaging. NCTC or NATGRID are also likely to benefit from it when implemented.

2. What's more urgent is a change in the attitude of a few intelligence personnel and the need to change the culture of spy circles from 'need to know' to 'need to share'.

VI. Need for post-event audits

1. Creating mechanisms for intelligence oversight might not happen overnight. However, there is a need to do in-depth aftermath analysis within intelligence agencies. This will not only help them identify where they've gone wrong, but also provide direction for future intelligence operations.

VII. Intelligence reforms

1. Sweeping organizational reforms such as NCTC or NATGRID are not the only ways to make intelligence agencies work together. The cultural barriers that stop agencies from adequately sharing intelligence can be corrected using less severe measures.

2. The first step towards changing such a culture is

standardizing the rules for protecting information and relaxing certain ethical constraints relating to 'operational loyalty.'

3. Reforms should not only focus on creating newer capabilities, it should lay more importance on what obstacles are stopping existing capabilities from being efficient. Real reforms should try to change organizational culture instead of altering organizational charts.

This paper has been reproduced here with special permission of the author. Janani Krishnaswamy's research interests include intelligence, transatlantic security, information security, counter-radicalization and social media research. An International Relations postgraduate from King's College London, she has worked in two prominent public policy think tanks in London (Demos) and Washington (Hudson Institute) and a global security firm, G4S Risk Management in London. As a student at King's, she specialised in Conflict Simulation and has simulated a two-player wargame simulating the Allied Reconquest of Burma. In the near future, she intends to develop a wargame simulating the War of Kurukshetra.

Chapter 5

Pakistan's Secret Agencies, Miltablishment, Talibanization and the Tug-of-War

"Pakistan, and then China will be conquered. Hind, Sindh, i.e. Pakistan and China too will be conquered. This whole region will be conquered by the army of Mahdi, and Indian rulers will be tied up in chains, and they will be presented before the throne of Hazrat Mahdi in Jerusalem."

YouTube Video of Dr. Tahirul Qadri

Pakistani intelligence agencies are dancing to different political and regional tangos within the rim of controversial counterterrorism and national security approach, which evinced the country in the eyes of international community as an irresponsible state that support terrorist groups and proxies in neighboring states. After 9/11, Pakistani agencies vacillated between continued sponsorship of extremist groups and cracking down on radical anti-ISI groups within Pakistan. This perception of protecting national security interests becomes controversial when the army began training jihadists to destabilize Afghanistan. Pakistan never promised to destroy terrorist groups, instead hoping to nurture them and use them in the future against Pakistan's regional rival, India. In Afghanistan, Pakistan's primary goal is to prevent India from gaining ground and obtaining too much influence.

On 04 March 2019, Dawn reported the FATF warning to deliver on its commitments to curb terror financing and money laundering risks to the global financial system. Pakistan banned Jamat-ud-Dawa (JuD) and Falah-e-Insanyat Foundation to partially address the concerns rose by India that Pakistan supported these and six similar organizations, including Jaish-e-Mohammad (JeM) or at least considered them low-risk entities. JeM reportedly claimed responsibility for the recent Pulwama attack in which 44 Indian security forces personnel died. In Pakistan, ISI sits at the core of the Pakistani state, and challenging democratic governments and hampered Pakistan's democratic progress. Its networks in Afghanistan and India's neighboring states caused pain and irksomeness. Indian research scholar Animesh Roul (2014) has elucidates the ISI networks against India:

> "India's intelligence agencies have been investigating an espionage network reportedly run by Pakistan's external intelligence agency, the Inter-Services Intelligence (ISI), from Sri Lankan soil. The ISI uses legitimate government structures like the Pakistani High Commission and Consulate located in Colombo and Kandy, respectively, as staging grounds for anti-India activity. Pakistan has long used neighboring South Asian countries like Nepal, Bangladesh and the Maldives as bases from which to surreptitiously surveil or possibly attack India. Of late, Pakistan's ISI seems to have expanded its network among Sri Lanka's Muslim minorities and disenfranchised Tamil community by exploiting the existing trust between the Sri Lankan and Pakistani governments".[1]

Expanding the theatre of their illegal business of torture and forced-disappearance to cover major foreign and domestic policy areas, the agencies have assumed more controversial proportions than ever before. Normally, the prime task of intelligence agencies is to lead policy makers on right direction, but the case here in Pakistan is different[2]. The agencies are misleading political leadership and policy makers on wrong direction, and making alliances of radicalized elements in support of miltablishment's business of forced disappearances and torture of civilians.[3] In all previous democratic governments of the country, even Cabinet Minister never stumped out to question secret agencies about their illegal prisons, and kidnapping for ransom. Those who dared to ask generals and spy masters about the wrecking they inflicted on the country were retired, killed, or transferred to remote regions[4]. Civilian and military intelligence agencies in Pakistan face numerous challenges, including widespread lack of civilian support, faith in oneself, sectarian and political affiliations, and the war in Waziristan, and Baluchistan where their circumference of intelligence information collection has shrunken[5].

In most parts of the country, intelligence information collection faces numerous difficulties since the Taliban and other militant groups controlled important strategic locations. Having failed to defeat insurgent forces in Baluchistan and Waziristan, the agencies started translating their anger into the killing and kidnapping innocent civilians with impunity. In 1980s, the real journey of the ISI, Intelligence and Bureau (IB), began when they tightened their belts to challenge the KGB and other European intelligence networks in Afghanistan[6]. They learned intelligence operations in war zones, and tried to professionalize their ranks and file, but sectarian policies of General Zai-ul Haq evaporated their hopes. Thus, intelligence infrastructure became deeply radicalized, ethnicized and sectarianized, and its members physically participated in Afghan jihad. During the Zia military regime, the process of radicalization began in military barracks, and intelligence infrastructure, and a major change occurred when Zia-ul-Haq instructed military and intelligence units to take on combatant mullahs with them to the frontline. Soldiers and officers were also required to attend Tablighi Jamaat classes. The purpose was to indoctrinate young officers[7].

All military, civilian and policing agencies have been participating in Tablighi congregation regularly to purify their soul for the Afghan and Kashmir jihad. With the Afghan war came to an end, and jihadists returned to Pakistan, a new wave of terrorism and radicalization challenged authority of the state, and weaken resolve of secret agencies. The Inter-Services Intelligence (ISI) never tried to intercept their violent actions against civilian and military installations. The ISI's intransigence and remorselessness to cooperate with civilian intelligence agencies on national security issues often prompted internal tug-of-war. The ISI never extended hand of cooperation to civilian intelligence agencies, or even considering Intelligence Bureau as an older civilian brother during the last two decades. This unending tug-of-war forced former Prime Minister Nawaz Sharif to restructure the IB and make it more effective to counter ISI's influence in political institutions. The greatest challenge Prime Minister Nawaz Sharif faced was on national security front1. The miltablishment was not happy with his national security approach and his silence over the arrest of Indian spy Kulbhushan Yadav[8].

The Intelligence Bureau is the country's main civilian agency that functions under the direct control of the Prime Minister-tackling terrorism, insurgency and extremism. The way military intelligence has operated in the past was not a traditional or cultural way. Inter-Services Intelligence, Military Intelligence and other units mostly concentrated on countering democratic forces, instead of tackling national security challenges[9]. When intelligence war among military and civilian agencies intensified, the blame-game became the main nucleation of literary debates in newspapers and electronic media that these jihadists make thing worse. Democratic forces stood behind civilian intelligence agencies, while pro-establishment supported ISI and its undemocratic business. Journalist F.M Shakil (04 Oct 2017), has depicted a congenial picture of secret war between the MI, ISI and the IB:

> The civilian watch-dog under instruction from a ruling Pakistan Muslim League-N whose grip on power looked ever more shaky-had been carrying out round-the-clock surveillance of judiciary, opposition parties, and military intelligence for some times. It is known the officials from the military's Inter Services Intelligence (ISI) agency had their phone calls listened to at the height of civil-military tension in 2014, following an attempt on the life on the Geo-TV anchor Hamid Mir, who said he suspected ISI involvement. The bubbling rivalry between the IB and ISI boiled over in June 2017 when a joint investigation team IJIT) probing alleged money-laundering by the Sharif family made a written complaint to the Supreme Court that the IB was Wiretapping JIT members, including ISI and military intelligence personnel. The JIT further reported that the IB was hampering its inquiries, adding that military-led

intelligence agencies were not in "good terms" with the IB. It said that IB had collected intelligence on members of the JIT from the National Database and Registration authority (NADRA) and presented it to Nawaz to use it against them[10].

All civilian and military agencies follow a specific mindset. Their sectarian affiliation and dearth of electronically trained manpower, lack of professional surveillance approach, and lack of proper intelligence sharing culture, raised serious questions about their credibility, and weak national security approach[11]. These and other things also caused the failure of National Counter Terrorism Authority (NACTA), to effectively counter exponentially growing radicalization and extremism in Pakistan[12].

Military and civilian intelligence agencies did not cooperate with NACTA in its war against radicalized forces. As a matter of fact, NACTA established a Joint Intelligence Directorate and appointed 413 competent officers from ISI, MI, IB, and policing agencies to help democratic government in dealing with extremism and Talibanization in four provinces, but neither government paid long-term attention to support it financially, nor military establishment helped it to trains its operational managers.

Under the NACTA Act, the agency was entrusted to the board of governors (BOG).The Prime Minister is its chairman, while defense, finance, and foreign Ministers, law Minister, members of senate and national assembly, Chief Ministers of four provinces, Prime Minister of Kashmir, Interior Secretary, Director General Federal Investigation Agency (FIA), all chiefs of intelligence agencies, and chiefs of police department from all provinces were given membership of National Counter Terrorism Authority (NACTA). On 25 September 2018, Prime Minister Imran Khan chaired first meeting of the board of governor of NACTA. Mr. Khan expressed dissatisfaction over the performance of NACTA, and ordered the establishment of a special committee to oversee its performance and make it competent.

Journalist and expert Imad Zafar painted a hard-featured and ominous image of the army deep state in his all-inclusive article. He mainly focuses on the army political and bureaucratic role in state institutions: "As per the constitution of Pakistan every democratic government is answerable to the people of Pakistan. But in reality they are actually answerable to the GHQ............ Every single Prime Minister in Pakistan can only do their job smoothly if they completely surrender in the matter of defense, interior strategic decisions and foreign policy. It means the rule for civilian governments are already decided and they have been told to go by the book, not to cross the red-lines defined by the defense establishment. This makes it a "state within a state" that instead of ruling the country from the front prefers to politicians and civilian governments to implement its decision and exercise power"[13].

In 2017, Prime Minister Nawaz Sharif tried to take control of foreign and internal policy of the country, but disqualified by the Supreme Court. He desired to lead Pakistan's India and Afghan policy on right direction; but he was intercepted, humiliated, and his movements were salami-sliced[22]. Retrospectively, former President Asif Ali Zardari tried to bring ISI under democratic control; he met eyeball-to-eyeball and faced the same fate. He was pushed around that his crippled and torturous body would be shifted to hospital by an army ambulance. The consecutive militarization and Talibanization of society, and instability led to the catastrophe of disintegration and failure of the state, while most part of these challenges was further inflamed by the US war on terrorism, and international military involvement in Afghanistan.[23] Pakistan's weak and unprofessional diplomatic approach towards Afghanistan prompted deep crisis, including the closure of trade routes and diplomatic impasse[14.]

To punish Afghanistan's National Army, Pakistan's intelligence agencies provided with sophisticated weapons to Taliban and other extremist organizations to make the war in Afghanistan disastrous and unfavorable since 2001. Military establishment of the country continues to train, arm, and transport terrorist groups inside Afghanistan to target civilian and military installations, and make lives of women and children vulnerable. The ISI has often been accused by Afghan army of playing a role in major terrorist attacks. Pakistan (Vanda Felbab Brown, 5, 01 2018) has long been a strenuous and troublesome state to Afghanistan struggling to limit political influence of India there, and organize radical to create war like situation in Kashmir[15].

The war brought instability, hater, disparities and destruction due to regional rivalries. Peace is far away dream in Afghanistan. Robert Kaplan (2012) warned in his book that if Taliban control Afghanistan, radicalization will get strong and Pakistan's sphere of influence will expand from India's border to Central Asia: "An Afghanistan that falls to Taliban sway threatens to create a succession of radicalized Islamic societies from the Indian-Pakistani border to Central Asia. This would be, in effect, a greater Pakistan, giving Pakistan's Inter Services Intelligence the ability to create a clandestine empire composed of the likes of Haqqani and the Lashkar-e-Taiba[16.]

Moreover, Afghans understand that Pakistan army pursued its own agenda in Afghanistan in ways the country purveys funds and sanctuaries to Taliban on its soil. Its support to Haqqani networks, and the ISIS, prolonged the Afghan war that caused catastrophe[17]. These and other misgivings and premonition caused great diplomatic and foreign policy challenges. Today, the country's leadership feels isolated, and no one likes to dance to its tango. These and other afflictions and suffering forced civilian leadership to recalibrate foreign policy of the country. On 28 February 2018, Dawn reported the country's National Security Committee (NSC) decision of recalibrating foreign policy to make it more effective and regionally focused[18]. Pakistan's nuclear marketing across the globe also caused embarrassment, mortification, and shame[19].

In February 2019, Pakistan apex court made public verdict against the 2017 Fakirabad sit-in, in which Tehreek-i-Labbaik Pakistan, had play a dangerous role. This Barelvi militant group was established by Pakistan army to pressure PTI government to for its share. According to Muhammad Zain's analysis the court warned intelligence agencies and the army to operate within their mandate. In the conclusion, Zain noted that the court directed the federal and provincial governments to monitor and prosecute those advocating hate, extremism and terrorism: "The judgment said the Inter-Services Intelligence, the Intelligence Bureau, Military Intelligence and the Inter-Services Public Relations "must not exceed their respective mandates". "They cannot curtail freedom of speech and expression and do not have the authority to interfere with broadcasts and publications, in the management of broadcasters/publishers and in the distribution of newspapers. The intelligence agencies "should monitor activities of all those who threaten the territorial integrity of the country, and all those who undermine the security of the people and the state by resorting to or inciting violence."[20]

Both of Pakistan's neighbors, India and Afghanistan, have suffered the results of the former's devices, recent examples being Mumbai, Samba, Pathankot, Kabul, Kandahar, Mazar-e-Sharif and Herat. It is well known that, in 2010, it was one of them, at the behest of Pakistan, who prevented the ban by the UN of the JeM and its terrorist leader Masood Azhar. In fact, it is also time for these so called benefactors to take a call. Do they want to help stop the freefall or do they want to speed it along? [21]

On 18 March 2018, Dawn reported Major General Asif Ghafoor, the Director General of the Inter-Services Public Relations (ISPR), interview with Gulf News. In his interview, General Ghafoor warned: "India is busy in fomenting unrest through terrorism using Afghan soil," he told Gulf News, mentioning Kulbhushan Jadhav—an Indian spy currently in Pakistan's custody—as an example. "So we are not having any let-up in safeguarding against Indian threat. While threat remains from India, both in conventional and sub-conventional domain, our biggest challenge is to maintain this stability with the threat still residing inside Afghanistan coupled with economic difficulties."[22] Pakistani scholar and Professor Pervez Hoodbhoy in his research paper uncovered the clandestine support of armed forces to sectarian religious groups against democratic governments:

> "For three decades Pakistan's military establishment has stoutly denied supporting violent religious groups irrespective of whether a group's target lay across national borders or, instead, its goal was to achieve specific political objectives within Pakistan. But today the military's attitude is more ambivalent. Both serving and retired senior army officers are now openly expressing support for some groups.

These include the newly emerged religious parties opposed to the PML-N government, notably Hafiz Saeed's Milli Muslim League (MML) and Khadim Hussain Rizvi's Tehreek Labbaik Ya Rasool Allah (TLYRA). Religious groups have already made their debut on the national scene and their initial successes—as in the NA-120 by-elections—are considerable. In a video that went viral, the serving DG of the Punjab Rangers, Maj-Gen Azhar Naveed, can be seen handing out coupons of Rs1000 to TLYRA demonstrators while assuring them support—"kya hum bhi aap kay saath nahin hain?" On 25 December 2017, Afghan Minister of Interior, Wais Ahmad Barmak warned that Daesh in Afghanistan receive support from Pakistan and majority of the fighters belong to Afridi and Orakzai tribes based in Pakistan[23].

South Asian intelligence review in its Pakistan: Assessment (2018) argued that Pakistan's consecutive policy of supporting terrorist groups created an environment of consternation where numerous individuals and groups engage in terrorism. On 07 April, 2018, more than 134 individuals and 23 entities with Pakistani connections were included in the Consolidated United Nations Security Council Sanctions List:

"Many of these individuals and entities continue to enjoy a free run in Pakistan. Hafiz Muhammad Saeed, who masterminded the 26/11 Mumbai terrorist attacks and carries a bounty of USD 10 million on his head, is the most 'prominent' among them. Saeed heads both the Lashkar-e-Taiba (LeT) and Jamaat-ud-Dawa (JuD) (both listed entities), but continues to enjoy open support from all sections of the Pakistani establishment. For instance, in a statement released on December 30, 2017, the Pakistan Foreign Office (FO) justified Hafiz Saeed's participation in a pro-Palestine rally, also attended by the Palestinian Ambassador to Pakistan, Walid Abu Ali in Rawalpindi on December 29, 2017. Interestingly, the Lahore High Court on April 3, 2018, ordered the Governments – Provincial and Federal – not to 'harass' Hafiz Saeed and to allow him to continue his 'social welfare activities' until further orders. The Court was hearing a petition filed by JuD against Governmental obstructions curtailing JuD's 'social welfare activities".[24]

South Asia Intelligence Review in its assessment of 2018 noted that on 29 November 2017, the Islamabad police submitted a 9 page report to the Supreme Court that the November 25 protest was caused irksome to the religious sentiments of security forces with their inflammatory speeches:

"Radicalized groups across Pakistan have received further encouragement from recent events, when the Federal Government bowed down before violent Islamist protesters. On October 2, 2017, the National Assembly passed the 'Election Bill 2017', making changes in the Khatm-e-Nabuwat [finality of Prophet-hood] clause of its earlier Bill. Soon after, countrywide protests led by the Tehreek-e-Labbaik ya Rasool Allah Pakistan (TLP), an Islamist party, erupted against the change. Other pro-Muslim parties, such as the Pakistan Sunni Tehreek and Tehreek-e-Khatme Nabuwwat (Movement for the Finality of Prophet-hood) also lent their support, demanding the resignation of Law Minister Zahid Hamid and the removal of the offending clause which, according to these groups undermined Islamic beliefs and amounted to blasphemy. Mounting pressure, the protestors began camping at Islamabad's Faizabad Traffic Interchange from November 6, 2017. The Government restored the original clause on November 17, 2017, but the Islamists continued with their protest. Eventually, on November 25, 2017, bloody clashes took place just outside Islamabad in which at least six people were killed and another 200 were injured. Speaking from the site of the clashes, TLP 'spokesman' Ejaz Ashrafi declared, "We are in our thousands. We will not leave. We will fight until end." Clashes also took place elsewhere in the country and continued on November 26 as well".[25]

The National Action Plan, 2014, signed at an All Parties Conference, highlighted the importance of this step as the sixth point of the Plan and called for choking financing of terrorist and terrorist organizations. Prior to this, several laws were addressing the financing of terrorist outfits including the Anti-Terrorism Act of 1997 and the Anti-Money Laundering Act of 2010, but there was no coordinated strategy. Terrorist outfits in Pakistan can collect funds through a number of sources, including criminal means, charitable donations, legitimate businesses, animal hides and philanthropic organizations. The Miltablishment and its secret agencies have been using jihadists in Kashmir and Afghanistan to achieve strategic goal since 2001. In Afghanistan, Pakistan backed Taliban are fighting to control natural resources sites in different province of the country in order to support the ailing economy. Pakistan army has already constructed a road from Chitral to Badakhshan province spick and span to make access easy to natural resources extracting sites. Expert Mr. Sanjeeb Kumar Mohanty and Jinendra Nath Mahanty in their research paper picked an argument on the military-Mullah Alliance, and their business of jihad in South Asia:

"The military-madrassa-mullah nexus has deliberately manipulated and encouraged jihadism by preferring a tactical deployment of jihadi groups in Kashmir and Afghanistan for expansion of regional influence......The internal situation in Pakistan has also deteriorated throughout these decades because of its focus on building up the militancy and grooming Islamic extremist groups as weapons in its eternal obsessive struggle against India. The military-militant cabal is the main problem of Pakistan today. The Abbottabad raid and the Mehran Naval Base attack in May this year were strong enough pointers in this direction. The two incidents were symptomatic of a large malaise that has been eroding the army's professionalism for quite some time. The signs of this malaise could be seen in the army leadership's obstinate hatred towards India, which has been driven primarily by paranoia and self interests."[26]

Pakistan's support to Taliban is for two reasons; to establish its political and military influence in Afghanistan, and push India back to the borderline of South Asia.[27] Pakistan is freethinking that India supports Baloch militants in Baluchistan, and its good Taliban are those who fight against Afghanistan and India, while it's bad Taliban are those who fight against its own army. This criterion for the identification of good and bad Taliban by miltablishment and the ISI is viewed by military experts as a left-handed game[28]. On 27 November 2013, Prime Minister Nawaz Sharif appointed war criminal General Raheel Sharif as a Chief of Pakistan Army, who later on resisted his government pressure to introduce security and intelligence sector reforms.[29] This change of face didn't make effective war against Taliban. War criminal General Raheel's mission of killing innocent Pashtuns in Waziristan failed to eradicate militancy.

Pakistan's involvement and its support to jihadist groups have threatened national security of Afghanistan. The Haqqani and Lashkar-e-Toiba terrorist networks have been fighting against the National Security Forces of Afghanistan since 2002-killing innocent civilians and destroying national critical infrastructure. These groups receive military and financial support from Pakistan army in order to further its foreign policy objectives in the country. Pakistan also supports Kashmiri jihadist group and Lashkar-e-Toiba to create environment of consternation in India. Research scholar, Seth G. Jones in his well-written paper has noted Pakistan's involvement in India and Afghanistan and sanctuaries of Haqqani and Lashkar-e-Toiba groups in the country:

"A continuing failure to curb the Taliban and Haqqani Network's sanctuary in Pakistan will undermine Washington's ability to achieve even limited goals in Afghanistan—including a peace settlement. The historical record is bleak. Insurgent groups like the Taliban that retain a sanctuary in neighbouring states, particularly a safe haven for their leadership, either win insurgencies or successfully drag them out over years and even decades. If the United States is serious about reaching a negotiated settlement with the Taliban—or even the unlikely goal of defeating the Taliban on the battlefield—it needs to quickly change its strategy and put pressure on the Taliban leadership in Pakistan. At the moment, the Taliban likely believes it is winning. A review of past peace negotiations suggests that insurgent groups usually negotiate a settlement when they believe they can't win on the battlefield. Until Taliban leaders in Pakistan begin to feel some heat, the war will likely persist. The Taliban and Haqqani Network's sanctuary in Pakistan and state support from organizations like ISI have been essential to their war effort, and the U.S. failure to undermine this safe haven may be Washington's most significant mistake of the

17-year-old war.[30]

After the terror attack on Pakistan army school in Peshawar in 2014, Prime Minister Nawaz Sharif ordered NACTA to monitor the exponentially growing militant power in the country. The 20 Agenda Items of National Action Plan were set to make the plan more effective:

1. Implementation of death sentence of those convicted in cases of terrorism.

2. Special trial courts under the supervision of Army. The duration of these courts would be two years.

3. Militant outfits and armed gangs will not be allowed to operate in the country.

4. NACTA, the anti-terrorism institution will be strengthened.

5. Strict action against the literature, newspapers and magazines promoting hatred, extremism, sectarianism and intolerance.

6. Choking financing for terrorist and terrorist organizations.

7. Ensuring against re-emergence of proscribed organizations.

8. Establishing and deploying a dedicated counter-terrorism force.

9. Taking effective steps against religious persecution.

10. Registration and regulation of religious seminaries.

11. Ban on glorification of terrorists and terrorist organizations through print and electronic media.

12. Administrative and development reforms in FATA with immediate focus on repatriation of IDPs.

13. Communication network of terrorists will be dismantled completely.

14. Measures against abuse of internet and social media for terrorism.

15. Zero tolerance for militancy in Punjab.

16. Ongoing operation in Karachi will be taken to its logical end.

17. Baluchistan government to be fully empowered for political reconciliation with complete ownership by all stakeholders.

18. Dealing firmly with sectarian terrorists.

19. Formulation of a comprehensive policy to deal with the issue of Afghan refugees, beginning with registration of all refugees.

20. Revamping and reforming the criminal justice system.

From National Internal Security Policy to National Action Plan, all strategies failed due to the army interference in policy making process. The NAP was a swift reaction to the Peshawar school attack, but the army targeted innocent women and children in North Waziristan, and bombed their house and market. The army forced thousands residents to leave the area, and killed 20 Truck drivers of the Dawar tribe (Wall Street Journal). Analyst and scholar Farhan Zahid in his report (2016) has described deficiencies and flaws of National Internal Security Policy and National Action Plan:

> "The first was the National Internal Security Policy (NISP) 2014-18 presented to parliament in May 2014, and the second was the National Action Plan (NAP) presented in December 2014. The NAP in particular, was a swift policy reaction to the tragic terrorist attack at the Army Public School in Peshawar in 2014. Technically speaking however, both the NISP and the NAP are not 'counter-terrorism policies' per se, rather these policies are surface rearrangements of security measures amid growing terrorist threats, developed in reaction to public outcry. No concrete or broad policy guidelines ¬- coupled with rules of engagement – were adopted. Concrete counter-terrorism strategies, such as the United Kingdom's Counter-Terrorism Strategy (CONTEST), provide security and law enforcement agencies with an exact set of measures

alongside categorically defined enemies of the state. These requirements of a counter-terrorism police are found neither in the NAP nor the NISP".[31]

Chapter 6

Intelligence Agencies, Sectarian Mafia Groups, Army, and the Culture of Jihadism

In 2014, Warlord General Raheel Sharif ordered his forces into North Waziristan to implement the kill and dump policy of miltablishment. The army killed thousands children and women with impunity-did not allowed national and international media to report its criminal business. Analyst Mr. Zeeshan Salahuddin (2016) in his article documented important facts about the actual function of National Action Plan, and military courts in Pakistan:

"Proscribed outfits in Pakistan have several points in the NAP dedicated to the mitigation and curtailment of their operations, communication networks, and funding sources. The government maintains a list of 63 banned organizations, but this list has been around since well before the NAP, and only the Islamic State (ISIS) has been added to it since the NAP went into effect in the first year. Two additional organizations were added this year, Jamat Ul Ahrar (JuA) and Lashkar-e-Jhangvi Al Alim (LeJA). However, being a proscribed organization has little meaning, as there are consistent reports of their members moving freely, holding rallies and public gatherings, openly inciting hatred and bigotry, and being given airtime. Schedule IV should go into effect, restricting their movements and communications, but it is rarely applied. As proof, the country was shocked by the victory in a by-election of Masroor Nawaz Jhangvi, a veritable person of interest under the fourth schedule, a son of the founder of one of the most violent sectarian groups in the country. But even this fails in comparison to reports of the Interior Minister Chaudhary Nisar meeting with the heads of banned organizations in the country".[1]

Moreover, a large number of his army officers and soldiers refused to fight against civilian population. War criminal Sharif refused to negotiate with tribal leaders, and refused to respect parliament and democratic norms. He himself designed the policy of kill and shot for Waziristan; killed women and children with impunity, and kidnapped tribal elders[2]. The army failed to develop a true ethnic representation process or motivate Baloch and Sindhis to join the ranks of armed forces, but gained a good experience in killing of innocent civilians. In Baluchistan, thousands Balochs men and women disappeared in a so called military operations during the last 15 years, while bodies of thousands of missing persons began turning up on roadsides. Since the killing of Akbar Bugti in 2006, more than 35,000 Balochs men were kidnapped or forcefully disappeared by Pakistani intelligence agencies and the police, in which of them 1500 were students and teachers. Mr. Dhruv C. Katoch explains operational mechanism of Pakistan's backed jihadists and their involvement in neighbouring states:

"The integration of "terror" into military concept of war and strategy and involvement of civilians in a total holy war naturally led to evaluation of the idea of non-state players who could be acting in connection with military as part of their pre-action preparation, including striking "terror" in the heart of the enemy. The launching of various civilian militant groups during Zia-ul Haq's time could be traced to the evolution of this military doctrine. Sipah-e-Sahaba Pakistan (SSP) and its militant wing the Lashkar-e-Jhangvi were floated to quell Shiite and Christian opposition to pro-Sunni Islamization measures and the promulgation of Blasphemy Law, respectively. Pretty soon this doctrine of "terror" was married to 1976 Whitepaper on Kashmir brought out by Z.A Bhutto regime and Kashmir specific terror groups were launched, beginning with JKLF and then JI floated Hizb-ul Mujahedeen and others"[3].

The miltablishment and the ISI view Afghan Taliban as a good Taliban, and perceive their fight against Afghanistan as a welcome development. The army also perceive the Quetta Shura as a strategic asset, according to a recent interview of former army Chief General Musharaf (13 February 2015): "Hafiz Saeed, Haqqani, Osama Bin Laden, Al-Jawahiri our heroes"[4]. In his most explosive interview with India Today Magazine (11 Feb 2016), former Pakistan president Pervez Musharraf pointed straight at the Inter-Services Intelligence for training Lashkar-e-Tayyeba and Jaish terrorists. "Inter-Services Intelligence (ISI) trains Jaish-e-Mohammad (JeM) and Lashkar-e-Taiba (LeT) terrorists," said Musharraf.[5] The issue of good and bad Taliban and their fight against Afghanistan and has been investigated and elucidated by Mr. Dhruv C Katoch in his research paper:

"The Pakistan army views Afghan groups such as the Quetta Shura located in Quetta, Baluchistan and the Haqqani network located in North Waziristan, as "strategic assets". The Afghan Taliban is supported by the ISI to maintain influence over Afghanistan post an American drawdown of forces from the area as many Pakistan's military establishment continue to think of the Afghanistan landmass as the backyard of Pakistan and an area which will provide them strategic depth in the event of hostilities with India. Pakistan has also encouraged and promoted terrorist organizations such as the LeT, JuM, and HuM which it views as strategic assets to be used against India. These terrorist groups have been waging a proxy war against India over the past two decades in Kashmir at very little cost to Pakistan-a policy of bleeding India with a thousand cuts-but keeping the conflict below perceived Indian threshold levels. While the army is concerned and active in addressing the Pakistan Taliban, it actively aids and abets the Afghan Taliban and the terrorist groups created by it to be used against India"[6].

However, Warlord General Raheel shifted Afghan Taliban commanders to safe houses. The challenge to Pakistan's sovereignty in Swat and Buner was addressed with brute force only after the Taliban appeared to be on a triumphant march to Islamabad. The insurgency in South Waziristan was tackled on a war footing after years of procrastination, but the writ of the Tehrik-e-Taliban Pakistan still runs in North Waziristan. The issue of ethnic representation within the armed forces also raised serious concerns. Some experts say this is not a national army and view it as the club of Punjabi generals. Lashkar-e-Taiba is a salafi jihadist organization that fights Indian army in Kashmir to further Pakistan's foreign policy objectives. Its broader objectives include librating Kashmir, and engaging Indian army in a long and an unending war. The Lashkar-e-Taiba was established in 1989 in Kunar province of Afghanistan as the military wing of the Pakistan-based Islamist fundamentalist movement Markaz al-Dawa wal Irshad. The LeT maintained several charities such as Falah-e-Insaniyat Foundation; Idara Khidmat-e-Khalq; Jamaat al-Dawa; Jamaat-i-Dawat; Jamaat Daawa, Paasban-e-Ahle-Hadis, and Milli Muslim League. In South Asia expert Ashley J. Tellis (2012) has viewed leT with different perspective:

"Thought the international community first began taking notice of the terrorist group Lashkar-e-Taiba (LeT) after its spectacular coordinated bombing and shooting attacks in Mumbai, India, in November 2008. The group was established in 1987 at a time when Pakistan was in the throes of Islamic ferment. Then, LeT had access to a steady supply of volunteers, funding and-most important of all—concerted state support. Long bolstered by Pakistan's Inter Services Directorate, this Wahhabi group promotes the vision of a universal Islamic caliphate through tableegh and jihad—preaching and armed struggle.⁷"

Lashkar-e-Taiba follows salafi faith. The only trained extremist organizations that fight against India in Kashmir receive military training from Pakistan army. Terrorist organizations like al Qaeda, LeT, Taliban, and Arab extremists and Takfiri jihadists in Pakistan and Afghanistan are posing a threat to regional security. They train suicide bombers across Asia and the Middle East. Religious and political vendettas are being settled by using suicide bombers against rival groups or families in Pakistan. This generation of fear and panic is controlled by extremist elements and non-state actors in Waziristan, Kabul and Quetta. Pakistan is also an epicenter of terrorism. Terrorists are being trained by Pakistan to further its foreign policy agendas in India and Afghanistan. But sometimes, these groups turn their weapons on the armed forces of Pakistan. This controversial, but faith based connection between Pakistan army has now weaken after the kill and dump policy of the rogue army in FATA and Waziristan regions. Mr. Alok Bansal, (28 June 2001) has highlighted some aspects of this regular business of Pakistan army with jihadist militias:

"Despite the denial of the Pakistani state, there have been clear pointers to the presence of sympathizers and collaborators of Islamic radical organizations within all three armed forces of Pakistan. Every single attack on a military installation bore clear marks of collusion by elements from within. Many Pakistan Air Force (PAF) and army personnel including six officers were convicted for attempts on General Pervez Mushrraf in December 2003, when he was the President. An army soldier, Abdul Islam Siddiqui, was hanged on August 20 2005 after an in camera Court Martial for triggering an explosion to target Musharraf in Rawalpindi. On another occasion, an anti aircraft gun was discovered on the flight path of General Musharraf's plane, when he was taking off from Rawalpindi Air base on a pitch dark night. In 2010, two former army officers along with two serving officers including a colonel were convicted by a court martial for planning an attack on the Shamsi airbase, which is used by the Americans to fly their drones. Even before Brigadier Khan, two serving army officers were court-martialled for links with Hizb-ut-Tahrir."[8]

On 14 February 2019, India warned that it would ensure the "complete isolation" of Pakistan after a suicide bomber killed 46 paramilitary police in Indian-administered Kashmir. The country claimed to have "incontrovertible evidence" of its neighbor's involvement in it, but Pakistan denies any role in the attack by militant group Jaish-e-Mohammad. Federal Minister Arun Jaitley said India would take "all possible diplomatic steps" to cut Pakistan off from the international community. The bomber used a vehicle packed with explosives to ram a convoy of 78 buses carrying Indian security forces on the heavily guarded Srinagar-Jammu highway about 20km (12 miles) from the capital, Srinagar.[9] Analyst Rajeev Agarwal (2019) argued that this attack caused shock and consternation:

"As the news of a suicide car bomb attack on a convoy of security forces on Srinagar–Jammu Highway on 14 February 2019 started filtering in, a sense of shock, dismay and outrage slowly took over the entire nation. In one of the most horrific terror attacks in the history of three-decade-old militancy in Jammu & Kashmir, 43 soldiers of CRPF travelling in a bus within the convoy were hit by an SUV laden with over 300 Kg of explosives at around 3.30 PM. The impact of the explosion was so massive that the bus was reduced to a twisted mangle of metal in no time. Other vehicles in close proximity too suffered severe damages. The attack has led to unanimous condemnation within the country as also across the globe. While Israel, Russia, UN and most of India's neighbours and Arab countries have condemned the terror attack, the US has been more categorical in its stance singling out Pakistan".[10]

Two years ago, Indian air force carried out surgical strike in Pakistan to undermine terrorist networks within the country, but couldn't succeed to target training centres of all terrorist and extremist groups inside Pakistan-occupied Kashmir. n the wake of the Pulwama terror attack, US National Security Adviser John Bolton told his Indian counterpart Ajit Doval that America supports India's right to self-defence as both sides vowed to work together to ensure that Pakistan ceases to be a safe haven for JeM and other terror groups.[11] The Greater Kashmir newspaper reported that militant group Jaish-e-Mohammed claimed responsibility. A pre-recorded video circulated on social media sites showed the purported attacker in combat clothes and surrounded by guns and grenades. US Today on 15 February 2019 reported the Doval and Bolton telephonic conversation during which they resolved to hold Pakistan to account for its obligations under the UN resolutions and remove all obstacles to designate Jaish-e-Mohammad (JeM) leader Masood Azhar as a global terrorist, the External Affairs Ministry (EAM) said in New Delhi.[12]

The 42 officers of Indian paramilitary Central Reserve Police Force and the teenager who drove the explosive laden vehicle into the convoy were merely the latest victims of the madness that continues in the Valley. The Daily Times editorial (16 February 2019) painted a different picture of the situation in Palwama: "The Pulwama attack must serve as a moment for reflection. On the Indian side, it should be acknowledged that there is widespread unrest among the Muslim population of the state, and that it has to do with the fact that a new generation of Kashmiris that has come of age amidst violence perpetrated by Indian forces does not accept New Delhi as a legitimate authority. This generation is on the frontline of the ongoing wave of the Kashmiri liberation struggle".[13]

Former Pakistani diplomat, Mr. Asif Durrani (2019) scrupulously noted in his column that the attacker came from the area where Jaishi-e-Muhammad maintains its terrorist army. Mr. Durrani also criticized Indian operation in Kashmir and argued that people of Kashmir have completely alienated from the state: "It is being claimed that Jaish-e-Mohammad (JeM) has accepted the responsibility of the suicide attack conducted through an explosive laden vehicle. The attacker reportedly hailed from the area which the Indian commentators view as growing influence of the JeM in the occupied valley. If this is true that the Kashmiri youth are now attracted towards taking ultimate steps to register their protest, it should ring alarm bells for the Indian leaders who have been feeding the population on misconstrued fallacies of 'Kashmir Bharat ka Atoot Ang hai' (Kashmir is an integral part of India). ....In Pakistan, while taking Indian government's threats seriously, there is a level of confidence within the State apparatus because of the ground situation in IHK where there is complete alienation. Indian attempts to pressurize Pakistan through the use of Afghan territory and support to the Tehrik-e-Taliban Pakistan (TTP) have by and large been neutralized while neighbours of Afghanistan have joined Pakistan to stabilize the region through dialogue. Major protagonists–US and Taliban–are also engaged in a meaningful dialogue".[14]

On 15 February 2019, former Afghan President condemned terrorist attacks in India and Iran. A suicide attack hit Indian-administered Jammu and Kashmir region in which more than 40 were killed: "I have repeatedly emphasized that foreign hands are keep the war aflame in Afghanistan to reach their goals," Karzai said Friday in a statement. "If the regional countries do not cooperate with each other to fight terrorism and extremism, such problems will finally catch them. Unfortunately, we see today that negative impacts of terrorism are facing them." Karzai said.[15] However, Indian media also criticized the attack and Pakistan's support to Jaish-e-Muhammad - a terrorist organization that fights for the freedom of Kashmir. Some newspapers published articles of Pakistan critics and some painted quite different picture of the JEM terrorist activities in Kashmir valley. The Hindu newspaper on 16 February 2019 noted some aspects of the incident in its editorial comment:

"There is no question that Pakistan bears the onus to explain why Masood Azhar, the leader of the Jaish-e-Mohammed, enjoys such freedoms on its territory, if not outright support from the establishment. Certainly, diplomatic backing by Pakistan and China has been crucial in defeating efforts at the United Nations to put Azhar on the list of banned terrorists. Early details indicate that a sports utility vehicle laden with a huge quantity of explosives targeted the convoy of 78 buses carrying about 2,500 soldiers from Jammu to Kashmir. The video of the presumed suicide bomber too hints at an altered standard operating procedure meant to provoke and escalate tensions. Forensics teams have already begun work and answers to the disturbing questions the attack has raised on intelligence gathering, dissemination and coordination in the Valley must be pieced together. Beijing too must not, and cannot, evade questions about its previous blocking of action at the UN, specifically against Azhar. Post-Uri, after terrorist attacks the air is always thick with calls for retributive cross-border strikes. The past history of limited, if any, returns from such precipitate action must serve as a cautionary check. Instead, the effort must be to isolate Pakistan for its support to the Jaish and seek substantive action, to effectively upgrade intelligence and plug security gaps, and to win the confidence of the local population in the Valley."[16]

On 26 Feb 2019 India launched air strikes against militants in Pakistani territory, in a major escalation of tensions between the two countries. The government said strikes targeted a training camp of the Jaish-e-Mohammad (JeM) group in Balakot. India accuses Pakistan of allowing militant groups to operate on its territory and said Pakistani security agencies played a role in the 14 February attack claimed by JeM. Pakistan denies any role and says it does not provide safe haven to militants. Indian Foreign Secretary Vijay Gokhale told a news conference that the strikes had killed a "large number" of militants, including commanders, and had avoided civilian casualties.

Pakistan's Foreign Minister, Shah Mahmood Qureshi, told a media briefing that Pakistan was planning its response. "This is an aggression against Pakistan and Pakistan will respond," he said. Islamabad released pictures on social media showing uprooted trees and cratered soil, which it claimed was the extent of the damage from the Indian bombing. The Indian military action was foretold after the Pulwama suicide bomb attack on a paramilitary convoy that killed over 40 Indian personnel in Kashmir. In the context of a war between two nuclear-armed states, the consequences can be far more severe. The repercussions of nuclear war between India and Pakistan would have to borne by the entire region, if not the whole world. Finally Pakistan responded by down-in-the-mouth two India jet fighter on 27 February 2019. During the Soviet invasion of Afghanistan, several militant sectarian groups emerged in Pakistan to fight against Russian forces. These groups received military training and financial support from the army and Afghan mujahedeen leaders. After the Soviet withdrawal in 1980s, these sectarian groups retuned to Pakistan and embroiled in an endless war sectarian and ethnic war. Prominent Pakistani journalist and expert, Kamila Hyat (The News 28 February 2019) argued that Pakistan needs the culture of peace:

"Pakistan then has more motive than any other nation to act against extremism itself. It also has the experience to do so. It has seen since the 1980s how extremism and the sectarianism that comes with it can quickly expand its grasp over people and result in a cycle of death and killings. The emergence of new groups putting forward hatred only adds to the violence. The arrest of leaders of the Tehreek-e-Labbaik Pakistan indicates a move in the right direction. More such measures need to follow. More than arrests, it is wiping out the culture that underlies such extremist behaviour that will be the hardest task of all. If the environment in which extremism and hatred thrive can be altered, then we would have moved a very long way forward in controlling the problem and eventually eradicating it from everywhere in the country. We are already aware of the need to do so. The tedious task of pulling out the roots of hatred, one by one, like a weed that has worked its way into a garden, slowly taking over more and more space, must be begun. Removing it is a slow task, but it is one that will have to be performed if anything resembling true change is to come".[17]

On 27 February 2019, Deepika S reported China's abutment to India by asking Pakistan to stop its support of terror groups and use of them in geopolitical goals. During a joint statement by India, Russia and China, China cold shouldered Pakistan with respect to its support to terror groups. "They reiterated that states and their competent agencies play a central role in both national and international counter-terrorism efforts. They also stressed that terrorist groups cannot be supported and used in political and geopolitical goals," the communiqué said. However China also warned that those inciting or supporting terrorist acts must be held accountable and brought to justice in accordance with existing international commitments on countering terrorism.[18]

The 16th Foreign Ministers Meeting of Russia-India-China warned that Pakistan remains a terror haven. Indian Foreign Minister said that the airstrike in Pakistan, in light of the terror attack, was not a military action. "It wasn't a military operation, no military installation were targeted. The objective was to act against terrorist infrastructure of JeM to pre-empt another terror attack in India. India doesn't wish to see further escalation of situation. It'll continue to act with responsibility and restraint," she said.

In the past, terrorists attacked Pakistan's nuclear installations. In 2007, they attacked two air force facilities in Sargodha, associated with nuclear installations. On 21 August, 2008, terrorists attacked the Ordnance factories in Wah. In July 2009, a suicide bomber struck a bus that may have been carrying A Q Khan Research Laboratory scientists, injuring 30 people. Moreover, two attacks by Baloch militants on suspected Atomic Energy Commission facilities in Dera Ghazi Khan have also drawn international attention to the security of the country's nuclear installations. On 10 October, 2009, nine terrorists, dressed in army uniform, attacked the GHQ. In June 2014, two suicide bombers killed high ranking military officers linked to Pakistan's nuclear programme in Fateh Jang.[19]

The internal security problems being faced by Pakistan are a result of its own machinations of the past. The policy of the Pakistani 'deep state' to use terrorism as an instrument of state policy, combined with nuclear coercion, subterfuge, blackmail and denial, to wrest Kashmir from India and take control of Afghanistan, which it considers as its strategic backyard, has led it inexorably down the path of self-destruction. Today, when home-grown terror groups like the TTP challenge the might of the Pakistani state and its military, it would cause no surprise that many of its cadres have been originally trained in its own training camps run by the ISI, the Pakistani state's intelligence agency. Further, it has also been assessed that it is Pakistan, the fastest producer of nuclear weapons, and one of the worst proliferators of its technology, which is likely to witness such weapons falling into the hands of its 'non-state' actors.[20]

Both of Pakistan's neighbours, India and Afghanistan, have suffered the results of the former's devices, recent examples being Mumbai, Samba, Pathankot, Kabul, Kandahar, Mazar-e-Sharif and Herat. Consequently, they have made it very clear to Pakistan and the international community that they are not going to negotiate with or talk seriously to Pakistan unless the latter displays credible intent to dismantle its terror networks. Till then, both will do what they deem fit, to protect their people and their interests. The world, hopefully, has seen through all the subterfuge, blackmail and nuclear coercion that Pakistan has indulged in over the years, thanks also to its over-indulgent friends in the international community, who have provided it political, material and financial support and other resources, while pursuing their own interests. It is well known that, in 2010, it was one of them, at the behest of Pakistan, who prevented the ban by the UN of the JeM and its terrorist leader Masood Azhar. In fact, it is also time for these so called benefactors to take a call. Do they want to help stop the freefall or do they want to speed it along?[21]

In view of the foregoing, what are the options available for India now? There are only two options to fight against Pakistan's hybrid war. Either fights within enemy territory and attack his weak or vulnerable points or fight from own side and take it to the enemy territory. If India chooses to fight it from own territory and take it to the enemy side, in that case, first priority is to 'harden your targets' and minimize exposed flanks. Make attacks and counter-attacks by non-state actors difficult on high value targets. Ruthlessly eliminate nexus between politicians, proxies and anti-national elements operating within. Strangulate flow of funds and take the investigation of money trail from Pakistan and Jihadis to its logical end. Selective prosecution of a dozen members of Hurriyat is only cosmetic and tokenism. The threads leading to big fish at Srinagar, Delhi and Pakistan must be exposed and prosecuted. At the same time prepare ground conditions to penetrate, gain foothold and then strike at the vulnerable points within Pakistan to unhinge the anti-India forces.......Hybrid war can be defeated if it is taken to the point of origin and from where it gets impetus to sustain. Endeavour should be to fight from within Pakistan so that collateral damages do not impact your assets and capabilities. Cyber, economic, information, perceptional and psychological domain can have crippling impact.[22]

The Politics of Counter-Terrorism in India: Strategic Intelligence and National Security in South Asia is a book which examines the role of our intelligence agencies in managing the national security and in particular in the counterterrorism efforts of our country. Author Prem Mahadevan, argues that any evaluation of intelligence performance needs to take into account the limited resources of national level agencies. He concludes that given the defensive nature of the Indian security policy, the Intelligence Bureau (IB) and Research and Analysis Wing (R&AW) have performed fairly well. However, either by design or by default, he omits to mention Military Intelligence.

Terrorist organizations like al Qaeda, Al Shabab, Boko Haram, the Taliban, Arab extremists and Takfiri jihadists in Europe, Pakistan and Afghanistan, through face book, YouTube and twitter invite young people to join their networks, using various marketing techniques. These terror groups are marketers as well as consumers to a degree; their recruiters 'market' boys. They supply suicide bombers across Asia and the Middle East for just $ 20,000 for each bomber. Religious and political vendettas are being settled by using suicide bombers against rival groups or families in Pakistan.

This generation of fear and panic is controlled by extremist elements and non-state actors in Waziristan, Kabul and Quetta. Fear and terror marketing systems are updated every year and new techniques of destruction are being introduced every so often.

The greatest threat to the national security of Pakistan and India stems from nuclear smuggling and terror groups operating in Punjab, Baluchistan, Assam and Kashmir. Increasingly sophisticated chemical and biological weapons are accessible to organizations like IS, Mujahedeen-e-Hind (MH), and the Taliban and their allies, which is a matter of great concern. These groups can use more sophisticated conventional weapons as well as chemical and biological agents in India and Pakistan in the near future, as they have already experimented in Iraq and Syria. They can disperse chemical, biological and radiological material as well as industrial agents via water or land to target schools, colleges, civilian and military personnel. On June 6, 2015, Pajhwok News reported that dozens of schoolgirls were targeted by unknown terrorists using biological agents in Panj Aab district of Bamyan province. This could also happen in Punjab, Baluchistan, Sindh and Khyber Pakhtunkhwa or Delhi and Mumbai unless the export control regime is tightened.[23]

As international media focuses on the looming threat of chemical and biological terrorism in Asia and Europe, ISIS is seeking nuclear weapons but retrieving these weapons from the country is not an easy task. Pakistan has established a strong nuclear force to safeguard all nuclear sites 24 hours a day with modern military technology. The crisis is going to get worse as the exponential network of IS and its popularity in Afghanistan creates deep security challenges for Pakistan and its Taliban allies. This group could use chemical and biological weapons once it gains footing in Afghanistan. For this reason, Pakistan is trying to push the Afghan Taliban towards a political settlement in Afghanistan to prevent IS from gaining control of the country. IS and the Taliban are not the only security challenges for Pakistan; the country is also facing many social and economic problems, including electricity shortages.

In 2013, chemical attacks in the outskirts of Damascus posed a direct threat to the US and its allies, causing the UN Security Council to adopt a resolution on chemical weapons in Syria. The international operation of transporting the components of these weapons out of Syria was completed in the first half of 2014. In 2015, ISIS tried to gain access to these weapons in Syria and, in some cases, used chlorine bombs for terrorist activities in Iraq and Syria. On January 6, 2015, cases of ISIS using chemical weapons in Iraq and Syria emerged. These chemical attacks illustrate that IS and the Syrian opposition chose to use chemical weapons preferentially in Iraq and Syria. In Pakistan and Afghanistan as well, ISIS is seeking these weapons to use them against the armed forces. In the latest issue of its magazine (Dabiq), Islamic State claimed that it wants to buy nuclear weapons from Pakistan but experts view this claim as baseless, saying that a country likes Pakistan would never allow IS to purchase nuclear weapons from the country.

As Islamic State (IS) now controls parts of Iraq and Syria and has carried out successful attacks in Pakistan and Afghanistan, the group now wants to expand its terror networks from Afghanistan to Kashmir. According to some confirmed reports, hundreds of Pakistanis have joined the army of IS in Syria and Iraq. In October 2014, six leaders of the TTP announced their allegiance to IS. IS propaganda material has begun to crop up in various parts of Pakistan. Secret networks of IS are in contact with different sectarian and political groups in Khyber Pakhtunkhwa province and receive financial assistance from business communities. The TTP commanders of Orakzai Agency, Kurram Agency, Khyber Agency, Peshawar and Hangu district have announced their allegiance to the IS military command.

The problem of nuclear and biological terrorism deserves special attention from the governments of Pakistan and Afghanistan because the army of IS can develop a dirty bomb in which explosives can be combined with a radioactive source like those commonly used in hospitals or extractive industries. The use of this weapon might have severe health effects, causing more disruption than destruction. Political and military circles in Pakistan fear that, as IS has already seized chemical weapons in Al Muthanna, in northern Iraq, some disgruntled retired military officers or experts in nuclear explosive devices might help the Pakistan chapter of the group deploy biological and chemical weapons. A letter by the Iraqi government to the UN warned that the militant-captured chemical weapons site contains 2,500 chemical rockets filled with the nerve agent Sarin.

Pakistan has all the signs and symptoms of ailing state that may not be able to sustain itself at the current rate of deterioration. It feels wretched from the crisis of self-reliance at home. People, an important constituent of the elements that defines a State, are fast losing faith in their institutions. The democratically elected governments has been shamelessly accusing of inability and inefficiency in handling the tottering state since the last four decades. Professor Yunis Khushi in her paper highlighted some aspects of internal and external squeezing on Pakistan:

"Pakistan is at war with itself. This partial civil war is caused due to misadventures of many internal and external forces. All these forces are working on their agendas without worrying about the future of Pakistani people and implications of these deadly agendas on South Asia region and rest of the world. Among the internal forces, religious parties are promoting extremism, jihad, and intolerance and preparing Muslim youth from Ghalba-e-Islam (promulgation of Islam in the whole world). This job is being done in 2.1 million religious seminaries spread all over Pakistan. Initially the religious parties were providing jihad training to youth in collaboration with those who were heading jihad and providing training to Mujahedeen and these Mujahedeen were being exported to Afghanistan and Kashmir to fight freedom war. But, all this was being done with dollars from CIA via ISI. Net result is that Mujahedeen, which were created by CIA and ISI, are now fighting against Americans in Afghanistan, and against Pakistan army in Swat, Waziristan and other tribal areas of Pakistan.[24]

Poverty-stricken and economically failing state has become headache of its neighbour. Pakistani commentator, Jan Muhammad Achakzai in his recent article (25,Dec 2018) warned that Pakistan needs to specify its direction of either join the path of Singapore and Malaysia, or join the club of failed states: "Pakistan is facing worse challenges never seen before", is more relevant today than ever before; economically failing state, dysfunction political system, corrupt political elite, unemployed youth bugle, extremism both religious and now ethnic mix intend to denuclearize Pakistan, the only Muslim country to have nukes, and the list goes on. The most worrying aspect of all is the lack of capacity of the current system to cope with these challenges. Even worse is the agony of realizing that the current system is beyond repair. It is so rotten that any fix will take decades which we do not have to wait for. Whereas the country is going to be on the edge not after a decade from now, not five years from today but the likely year is going to be 2019, as it will determine our direction to join the path of the countries like Singapore and Malaysia, or enter the club of failed states; Syria, Iraq, and Libya[25]".

Chapter 7

Explaining Recent Intelligence Reforms in Bangladesh[1]

A.S.M. Ali Ashraf

Abstract

This paper surveys the major intelligence reform initiatives in Bangladesh and examines the determinants of such reforms. Drawing on the secondary literature and expert interviews, it argues that recent intelligence reforms in the country can be explained by four factors: capacity gaps, coordination needs, crisis-driven demands, and external influence. The effects of these four variables are examined with empirical evidence. The paper concludes with a brief discussion of policy imperatives and directions for further research.

Introduction

Intelligence reform is one of the most important but least understood phenomena in the political discourse of Bangladesh. What is intelligence reform and why should we care about such reform? In their seminal works on intelligence agencies, Ami Pedahzur and Amy B. Zegart identify two major styles of reform: innovation and adaptation.[1] The former involves introducing new intelligence agencies and doctrines, whereas the latter emphasizes

---

1   This article was first published in the *Journal of the Asiatic Society of Bangladesh* (Hum.), Vol. 59 (1), 2014, pp. 65-94. This paper has been reproduced here with the special permission of the author, Dr. ASM. Ali Ashraf, Ph.D. Associate Professor Department of International Relations, University of Dhaka.

reorganizing existing agencies and their coordination structures. Loch Johnson suggests that the differences between innovation and adaptation are often vaguely defined, and the two styles may interact very closely in shaping the intelligence reform practices in a state. For instance, when the Central Intelligence Agency (CIA) was established in 1947, the Truman administration thought it to be an innovation in intelligence coordination. However, in the 1980s, the CIA chiefs recognized that smooth integration of intelligence was a distant reality, which led them to create several inter-agency centers and task forces at the CIA to adapt to the problems of coordination by focusing on "Community-wide cooperation."[2]

The issue of intelligence reform is quite puzzling in Bangladesh. This is due to the fact that after years of slow responses to change, the intelligence community in Bangladesh has recently gone through a process of innovation and adaptation. For instance, the fight against organized crime and terrorism has led to the creation of new intelligence entities and the expansion of existing ones. In addition, ad hoc structures for central intelligence coordination have been replaced with formal coordination mechanisms. In some cases new laws have replaced old ones providing more clarity to the mandates of security and intelligence agencies. In this backdrop, two central questions emerge:

- How has the intelligence community in Bangladesh changed over time?

- Which factors shaped the intelligence reforms in Bangladesh?

In addressing these questions, this paper is organized into several parts. First, it discusses the research methodology and provides a literature review. Next, it profiles the intelligence community of Bangladesh, and offers a quick snapshot on the major intelligence reform initiatives in the country. The author then develops a few hypotheses on intelligence reform and tests their utility with empirical evidence. The concluding section proposes some policy recommendations, and stresses the need for further research.

Research Methodology

This paper employs the method of structured and focused comparison to analyze various intelligence agencies and their reform practices in Bangladesh.[3] It also examines the extent to which changes in the Bangladeshi intelligence community resembles or differs with other countries. For brevity and rigor, such cross-country comparisons are restricted to India, Pakistan, the United Kingdom and the United States. Data for this paper were generated from standard published materials, such as books, newspapers, peer-reviewed journals, and official reports of concerned government organizations. The author also conducted a few interviews with serving and retired officials having firsthand knowledge of the security and intelligence agencies in Bangladesh.

Two types of data are of particular interest here: (a) major intelligence reform initiatives taken by successive governments; and (b) immediate and long-term causes of those intelligence reform initiatives. The timeline covered in this paper includes the reform initiatives introduced in the years between October 2001 and December 2013. This timeline enables us to look at the initiatives taken by three distinct political regimes: (a) the BNP (Bangladesh Nationalist Party)-led four-party alliance government (Oct. 2001-Oct. 2006); (b) the military-backed interim government (Jan. 2007-Dec. 2008); and (c) the AL (Awami League)-led fourteen party alliance government (Jan. 2009-Dec. 2013).

It is widely held that political confrontation between the BNP and the AL has strongly encouraged the military to intervene in domestic politics by supporting an interim government from 2007 to 2008.[4] Despite sharp differences in their political ideologies, successive governments have tended to use intelligence agencies for the consolidation of their power and the suppression of political dissent. The timeline covered in this paper also coincides with the post-9/11 era. This offers an additional advantage of exploring the effect of the U.S.-led global war on terrorism on the intelligence reform practices in Bangladesh.

Literature Review

James J. Wirtz, a prominent intelligence studies scholar, once observed that unlike the United States, where "intelligence studies are considered to be a legitimate academic field," the study of intelligence is relatively "underdeveloped "and a "taboo outside the official circles" in other countries.[5] This is certainly a valid statement while referring to intelligence in Bangladesh context. Evidence can be found in the way most Bangladesh observers discuss intelligence issues on the margins of security sector reform (SSR) and counterterrorism studies, instead of treating intelligence as a distinct field of study. For instance, in their studies on SSR in Bangladesh, Imtiaz Ahmed and Jashim Uddin provide more emphasis on government efforts to reorganize the police, the judiciary, and the prison system, and less emphasis on intelligence agencies.[6]

While Amena Mushin and Siegfried Wolf include the issue of politicization of intelligence, their central focus is on civil military relations and the prospects of democracy in Bangladesh.[7] The conspicuous absence of intelligence issues as a central theme in the SSR literature is perhaps caused by a culture of silence, established by the colonial-era Official Secrets Act 1923 and sustained by the Right to Information Act 2009.[8] Successive governments have used these laws, and a host of others, to deny any disclosure of information on the intelligence agencies.

In contrast to the SSR literature, the study of counterterrorism has offered a useful starting point to analyze intelligence reform in Bangladesh. For instance, a study conducted by the Bangladesh Enterprise Institute, a local think tank, stresses the need for intelligence reform in the fight against terrorism.[9] The reports of the BDR Mutiny inquiry committees have also identified loopholes in the intelligence process and suggested greater coordination efforts to synchronize the intelligence production process.[10]

Recent reports on police reform, terrorist financing, and tax intelligence, produced by the UNDP, the Bangladesh Bank, and the National Board of Revenue have also emphasized the need for intelligence reform.[11] While the existing literature on intelligence issues in Bangladesh covers a broad spectrum of administrative reforms, they lack any thorough analysis of intelligence reforms in Bangladesh and their causal explanations. The central goal of this paper is to address this deficiency by developing hypotheses and testing their utility with empirical evidence. A general overview of the intelligence community is presented below before analyzing the reform initiatives.

The Intelligence Community in Bangladesh

The term 'intelligence community' is used to refer to disparate security and intelligence agencies working for the protection of internal stability and external security of a country. Since the independence of Bangladesh in 1971, successive governments have established four major categories of intelligence agencies, with often overlapping responsibilities in the domains of: (a) national security; (b) defense services; (c) law enforcement; and (d) financial crime.[12]

The first category of intelligence agencies mainly represent the Directorate General of Forces Intelligence (DGFI) and the National Security Intelligence (NSI) but may also include the Special Security Force (SSF), and the Border Security Bureau (BSB). Collectively, they are responsible for safeguarding vital national interests, physical protection of very important persons (VIPs), and territorial integrity of the country.

Among them, the DGFI, the NSI, and the SSF report to the Prime Ministers' Office (PMO), while the BSB reports to the reconstituted BGB, an entity under the Ministry of Home Affairs (Mohan). The DGFI and the NSI have some foreign intelligence collection capabilities, and they can access the intelligence resources of any other agencies in Bangladesh. The SSF focuses on VIP protection, which gives it the authority to demand information from any security service. Although the BSB operates under the Mohan, the Bangladesh Army maintains considerable influence through commanding and staffing the border force.

A brief profile of the intelligence outfits will provide insights into their origin and development. The DGFI and the NSI were formed in the immediate aftermath of the independence war.[13] Currently the DGFI is headed by a serving major general while the NSI is led by a retired major general of Bangladesh Army. The two agencies have some overlapping responsibilities, especially in the domains of intelligence, counterintelligence, and counterterrorism. Critics observe that the DGFI and the NSI have often deviated from their original goals of providing impartial assessments on vital issues of national interests, and instead turned into the coercive instruments of political control by successive governments.[14]

The twists and turns in the political history of Bangladesh are responsible for such politicization of intelligence agencies. In contrast to the DGFI and NSI, the SSF has a more recent origin. It was established in June 1986 as the President's Security Force (PSF), and was later renamed to Special Security Force in 1991 after the fall of the Kershaw regime and the reintroduction of parliamentary system of government.[15] A senior army official at the rank of major general heads the SSF. The force has four bureaus, including operation and protection, intelligence, logistics and training. Among the four agencies working on national security, the BSB has exclusive responsibility for producing and disseminating intelligence regarding border crimes. It was created in 2010 as part of a larger reform initiative in the defunct Bangladesh Rifles.

The second category of intelligence agencies represents three defense services. It includes the Directorate of Military (Army) Intelligence, the Directorate of Naval Intelligence, and the Directorate of Air Intelligence. They report to the Ministry of Defense (MoD), controlled by the Prime Minister. There are few publicly available data on such agencies, and hence they are excluded from further discussion. The third type of intelligence agencies works on law enforcement and crime prevention. It includes the Special Branch (SB), the Criminal Investigation Department (CID), and the intelligence wing of the Rapid Action Battalion (RAB). Although these spy agencies work under the authority of Bangladesh Police, and report to the home ministry, critics observe that the police headquarters and the home ministry have less control over the operations of the RAB than over the SB and the CID.

This is largely due to the fact that although RAB is headed by an additional inspector general of police, RAB's administrative and operational activities are heavily dominated by officials deputed from military services, who often interact more closely with the armed forces and the DGFI rather than the police headquarters and the home ministry.[16] The SB, the CID, and the RAB have both clearly defined and overlapping responsibilities. Among its various statutory obligations, the SB works for the collection and analysis of political intelligence and immigration intelligence. It also provides immigration services to Bangladeshi nationals and persons of foreign origin.[17]

In that capacity, it plays a crucial role in analyzing political intelligence, and cross-border movement of persons using land, air, and maritime borders. By contrast, the CID is the lead agency for the investigation and analysis of criminal offenses such as murder, human trafficking, and terrorist attacks. Interestingly, the RAB is tasked with some of the core responsibilities, which are also carried out by other police agencies. For instance, the Armed Police Battalions (Amendment) Act of 2003 authorizes the RAB to collect intelligence in respect of crime and criminal activities; and investigate any offence.[18]

These are precisely the domains of the SB, the CID, and their sister organization— the Detective Branch (DB). As a result of such overlapping responsibilities, various entities in the police intelligence network often engage in a turf battle over criminal investigation and crime analysis. Why is the RAB tasked with some shared responsibilities, and in what ways does it differ from other law enforcement intelligence entities? As explained later in this paper the inability of the law enforcement and intelligence agencies in the countries to contain the growing level of crime and terrorism, especially in the late 1990s and early 2000s, have compelled the government to create a new police unit with more power and legal mandates.

In doing so, RAB maintains an organizational structure which is sharply different from other police entities. For instance, as of June 2014, the operations of RAB are organized around fourteen battalions. This 'battalion-based' jurisdiction is sharply different from the traditional 'Thana' or police station-based anti-crime actions and law and order operations of the Bangladesh Police. The fourth group of intelligence entities focuses on financial crime analysis. It concerns the acquisition of intelligence role by the Bangladesh Bank (BB) and the National Board of Revenue

(NBR). The BB is the central bank and the monetary authority in Bangladesh, while the NBR is the central tax administration in the country.

Financial crimes such as money laundering and terrorist financing were long ignored and it was not until 2002, when a new anti-money laundering law was enacted paving the way for the creation of the Anti-Money Laundering Department (AMLD) at the central bank. The AMLD was later renamed Bangladesh Financial Intelligence Unit (BFIU) in 2012 with expanding remits in detecting and analyzing terrorist financing and money laundering.[19] On the other hand the Central Intelligence Cell (CIC) was established by the NBR to detect large tax fraud and related financial crimes.[20]

The BFIU and the CIC report to the central bank and the NBR, respectively, both of which operate under the Ministry of Finance (MoF). It is quite interesting that the Bangladesh Ministry of Foreign Affairs (MOFA) does not have any separate intelligence agency. Instead, various geographical and functional wings of the MOFA and diplomatic missions of Bangladesh conduct research and analysis on foreign policy matters.[21]

There is no precise data on why the research wing of the MOFA has little competence in the domains of intelligence analysis. This is perhaps due to the fact that in making key decisions on external affairs, the foreign minister is heavily dependent on the prime minister who is the executive head of the government. In addition, the prime minister's foreign policy advisor, a post created by Prime Minister Sheikh Hasina, offers his expertise on vital issues. It is widely held that the prime minister relies on the assessments provided by the DGFI and NSI on important questions of foreign affairs.

In summary, two discerning trends can be observed in the composition of the Bangladeshi intelligence community. First, agencies working on national security and defence services are controlled by the armed forces. By contrast, agencies working on criminal offences, including financial crimes, are controlled by the civilian police, the central bank, and the tax administration, respectively. The first two groups report to the prime minister, while the latter two groups report to the home and finance ministers. Although the independent Anti-Corruption Commission does not belong to any of the category discussed above, it has emerged as a key agency in investigating corruption charges.

Recent Intelligence Reforms in Bangladesh: A Snapshot

Since 2002, successive governments have taken more than a dozen initiatives to reorganize the intelligence agencies in Bangladesh. These reforms have focused on counterterrorism, coordination structure, financial crime, and border intelligence (See table 1).

Table 1: Major Intelligence Reforms in Bangladesh, 2002-2012 Year Reform Initiatives

2002	Enacting Anti-Money Laundering Act; Creation of Anti-Money Laundering Department (AMLD) at the Bangladesh Bank (BB)
2002	Opening of DGFI Counterterrorism Wing
2003	Enacting Armed Police Battalion (Amendment) Act
2004	Enacting Anti-Corruption Commission Act; Creation of an independent Anti-Corruption Commission (ACC)
2004	Creation of Central Intelligence Cell (CIC) at the National Board of Revenue (NBR)
2004	Creation of RAB under Bangladesh Police
2004	Creation of NSI Counterterrorism Cell (CTC)
2006	Creation of DGFI Counterterrorism Intelligence Bureau
2007	Reconstitution of Anti-Corruption Commission (ACC) by appointing a new ACC chief
2008 -present	Modernization of the Special Branch (SB) and the Criminal Investigation Department (CID) as part of the Police Reform Project (PRP)

2009	Creation of National Committee for Intelligence Coordination (NCIC) at the Prime Minister's Office (PMO)
2009	Creation of National Committee on Military Resistance and Prevention (NCMRP) at the Ministry of Home Affairs (MoHA)
2009	Creation of National Coordinating Committee (NCC) on financial sector reform at the Ministry of Finance (MoF)
2010 -2010	Disbanding the Bangladesh Rifles (BDR) and Creation of Border Guard Bangladesh (BGB) under the Ministry of Home Affairs (MoHA)
2010 -2012	Replacement of BDR's Rifles Security Unit (RSU) with Border Security Bureau (BSB) at the Border Guard Bangladesh
2012	Creation of NSI Combined Threat Assessment Center (CTAC) 2012 Enacting Money Laundering Prevention Act and Anti-Terrorism Act
2012	Replacing the AMLD with the Bangladesh Financial Intelligence Unit (BFIU) at the Bangladesh Bank.

Sources: Media reports and author's interviews.

While the existing list of intelligence reforms presented in table 1 does not provide an exhaustive catalogue, it certainly represents most of the recent reform initiatives discussed in the public domain. One is curious to know the determinants of such reforms. It is in this context, we now turn into the theoretical explanations of intelligence reform in Bangladesh.

Explaining Intelligence Reforms: Some Plausible Hypotheses

Which factors influenced the recent intelligence reforms in Bangladesh? How can one explain the timing of the reforms? In addressing these questions, I argue that it is possible to generate a set of testable propositions on intelligence reform and examine their utility in the context of Bangladesh. According to Richard A.

Best, Jr., most intelligence reforms in the United States have come to address three goals: to improve efficiency of the intelligence community, to respond to specific intelligence failure, and to refocus intelligence community requirements and structure.[22] Writing in the U.K. context, Ken Kotani also makes a similar observation.

Kotani's analysis of the Joint Intelligence Committee (JIC) reforms focuses on the British Government's desire to improve the coordination structure by removing intelligence analysis from the influence of policymakers and politicians.[23] For post-colonial states like Bangladesh, India and Pakistan, such coordination reform cannot be achieved without changing the redundant laws and reducing the political role of secrete services.[24]

Regarding the timing, most studies suggest that although intelligence reform is a continuing process, the incidence of a major security crisis or intelligence failure can act as a catalyst for drastic reforms. For instance, the Institute of Defence Studies and Analyses (IDSA) reveals how the Research and Analysis Wing (RAW) was created splitting the Intelligence Bureau (IB) in the aftermath of the Indo-China and Indo-Pakistan wars.[25] The failure of the IB to predict the war plans of China and Pakistan have played a significant role in shaping the formation of the RAW.[26] The reports of the 9/11 Commission and the Silberman-Robb Commission in the United States, and the Butler Committee in the U.K. also offer similar views toward the need for intelligence reforms after major failures.[27]

The role of external actors is also quite important in understanding the timing of intelligence reform. This is mostly evident in the case of the U.S.-led global war on terrorism. In response to al Qaeda's 9/11 terrorist attacks, the United States invaded Afghanistan and called for an international coalition to fight transnational terrorism. The United Nations and its numerous conventions, protocols, and resolutions on counterterrorism also put enormous pressures on countries to reform their legal and intelligence structures.

As a corollary to the UN-led global counterterrorism regime, the Paris-based Financial Action Task Force (FATF) emerged as an initiative of the G-7 industrialized countries in setting international standards on fighting money laundering, terrorist financing, and proliferation financing. Security studies literature is rich with the description of how countries across the world are forced to amend their legal frameworks and intelligence practices to comply with global standards.

On the basis of the above discussions, four hypotheses on intelligence reform can be derived. These hypotheses focus on four independent variables –capacity gaps, coordination needs, crisis-driven demand, and external pressures. The first three variables provide domestic level inputs whereas the remaining variable presents external inputs to shaping the intelligence reforms. The hypotheses and the logic behind them are presented below.

Hypothesis 1: *If serious capacity gaps exist in the security and intelligence agencies of a country, a government will respond by creating new agencies or expanding the remits of existing ones.*[28]

The logic of the first hypothesis is clear. If capacity gaps in the intelligence agencies are identified in a country, the cost of inaction is prohibitive, as this may increase the possibility of intelligence failure.[29] Therefore; national decision makers have an incentive to bring necessary changes to address capacity gaps. Several Bangladeshi scholars have also stressed the need for capacity building in law enforcement and intelligence agencies to bolster the counterterrorism efforts of the government.[30] Capacity gaps can be measured by looking into the shortfalls in human, financial, and technical resources, as well as the lacking in legal mandates.[31] As illustrated by the 9/11 terrorist attacks, the effect of capacity gaps should not be overestimated. This is due to the fact that coordination demands may also play a useful role behind intelligence reform. This leads us to develop a second hypothesis:

Hypothesis 2: *If the demand for intelligence sharing increases, a government will respond by changing the existing coordination mechanism.*

The logic of coordination reform hypothesis is straightforward. Intelligence agencies often work in compartmentalized environment and thus inhibit the demand for sharing.[32] Therefore, enhancing the capability of existing agencies will be necessary but not sufficient. Most governments will complement such capacity building approaches by reforming the intelligence coordination structure.[33] Coordination reform may require replacing ad hoc practices with formal structures or creating a new authority to lead the intelligence community. In the backdrop of the 9/11 terrorist attacks, United States took several initiatives to facilitate coordination reform: the creation of the Department of Homeland Security (DHS) and the introduction of the post of Director of National Intelligence (DNI) are noteworthy here.[34] The DHS was designed to bring together various internal security institutions while the DNI would replace the Director of Central Intelligence (DCI) as the new intelligence czar.[35]

While capacity gaps and coordination needs may be addressed as part of routine transformations in the intelligence community, this is hardly the case. For instance, Amy Zegart argues that, the due to their bureaucratic organizational ethos, which discourages drastic change, the U.S. intelligence community failed to adapt to the changing realities of the post-Cold War era.[36] She also suggests that unless intelligence failures exposed the limits of American security system, major reforms were not initiated. As stated before, Richard Best's analysis of the U.S. intelligence community and the IDSA report on India's intelligence agencies also stress that intelligence reform initiatives are often taken in response to a specific failure. This leads us to develop a third hypothesis:

Hypothesis 3: *If a crisis exposes the failure of intelligence agencies, government officials tend to respond to the crisis by drawing crucial lessons from past failures.*

As explained before, the logic of such crisis-induced reform hypothesis is simple: intelligence agencies are bureaucratic organizations, and therefore resistant to change.[37] In addition, governments may use such agencies as the political police, and ignore the demand for necessary reform.[38] The effects of such challenges–bureaucratic inertia and politicization will be weakened in the aftermath of a major intelligence failure. This is due to the fact that the governing elites will learn from past failures, and introduce necessary changes.[39] The three hypotheses presented above illustrate the effects of domestic level variables on intelligence reform. By contrast, the next hypothesis stresses the effect of external influence on intelligence reform.[40]

Hypothesis 4: *If national decision makers are unwilling or unable to respond to the needs for intelligence reorganization, external influence will facilitate such reform.*

External influence may come from diverse actors such as international allies, foreign adversaries, powerful states and international organizations. Foreign actors may use both positive incentives and coercive pressures to persuade intelligence reform in a state. In making crucial decisions on intelligence reform, states may wish to resist coercive external pressures but appreciate any positive incentives such as the offer of financial and technical assistance. However, when the cost of resisting an external pressure outweighs the benefits of doing so, a state is likely to respond positively by introducing intelligence reform. Since this essay examines intelligence reforms in Bangladesh, it is possible that some hypotheses are more valid than others in explaining a particular reform initiative. It is also possible that the explanatory variables–capacity gaps, coordination needs, crisis moments and external pressures–may interact with each other in causing certain types of reforms.

Research Findings

This section tests the utility of the four hypotheses.

Hypothesis 1: *Capacity Gaps*

Recent reforms in the domain of counterterrorism intelligence provide useful evidence to support the capacity gaps hypothesis. Let us begin with the DGFI and the NSI—the two most powerful intelligence agencies in the country, which have gradually adapted to the threat of terrorism by opening new cells, wings, and bureaus on counterterrorism. The evolution of the DGFI's Counter Terrorism Intelligence Bureau (CTIB) from the agency's counterterrorism wing and the introduction of the Combined Threat Assessment Center (CTAC) at the NSI reveal that the two agencies have not only been competing against each other but also addressing their capacity gaps in producing all source intelligence on the radical Islamist groups and their clandestine networks.

An interesting question emerges: although civilian law enforcement and intelligence agencies are primarily responsible for fighting terrorism, why did the DGFI as a military-controlled agency and the NSI as a mostly civilian agency come to acquire overlapping responsibilities over counterterrorism intelligence? The answer is straightforward: groups, motivated by left-wing revolutionary ideology and radical Islamism, have often attempted to "undermine the national and territorial integrity of Bangladesh, whether directly or indirectly."[41]

Therefore, terrorism is not considered to be a mere internal security problem, which can be controlled by civilian agencies. Instead, it is rightly seen by the government as a national security threat, the assessment of which requires the involvement of both military and civilian intelligence agencies, with an extensive collection efforts at the national level.

If the acquisition of new counterterrorism responsibilities represented an adaptation for the DGFI and the NSI, the creation of the Rapid Action Battalion (RAB) as a paramilitary force was seen by many as an innovation in law enforcement and intelligence. This is due to the fact that RAB was established in 2004 to augment the capability of Bangladesh Police in fighting serious crime and terrorism.[42] Former law Minister Moudud Ahmed's testimony reveals the utility of capacity gaps hypothesis. Ahmed, who played a vital role in creating RAB, said: "Our police are inadequate. They do not have sophisticated weapons nor do they have sufficient training. It is not possible to raise the police to a sufficient standard."[43]

The creation of RAB, in Ahmed's view, offered a useful tool to address these concerns with police. This is due to the fact that about half of RAB's 10,000 personnel are supposed to come from the armed forces whose rigorous physical training and better weapons and tactics were thought to overcome the deficiency in existing law enforcement agencies. Law Minister Moudud and other proponents of the capacity gap hypothesis suggest that government responses to address the deficiency in police came in several stages. Initially, Prime Minister Khaleda Zia's administration (2001-2006) tried with a few ad hoc police teams, such as the Rapid Enforcement Force, the Rapid Action Team, the Cheetah and the Cobra.

These short-term police teams gained initial successes but failed to restore the law and order situation. Khaleda Zia's government also deployed the army and border force to combat serious crime and terrorism.[44] Successes achieved during these anticrime drives by police, army, and border forces were limited and short-lived.[45] Drawing on the lessons of these anti-crime drives, in 2003 the government amended The Armed Police Battalions Ordinance 1979 to establish the RAB. The Armed Police Battalions (Amendment) Act 2003 authorizes the RAB to perform several internal security duties such as recovery of illegal arms, apprehension of armed gangs of criminals. As stated before, it also gives the RAB two exclusive duties: intelligence and investigation.[46]

Successive governments have not only equipped the RAB with sophisticated weapons, but also provided it with the indemnity for excessive use of force against criminal suspects. This is evident in numerous extrajudicial killings in RAB operations, some of which are attributed to RAB's intelligence wing.[47] RAB defends its position by asserting the right to use proportionate force during gunfight with criminal suspects. It also claims that all incidents of gunfight with suspect are investigated either by the police or by judicial magistrates.[48]

The effect of capacity gap is also evident in the SB and the CID. The longstanding employment of these two agencies in spying on private citizens and political parties have not only eroded their professional competence but also turned them into the political police of the incumbent governments. Recognizing their limits, the donor-funded police reform project has targeted, among other strategic priorities, improved efficiency of immigration service, criminal intelligence, and crime investigation. Some of these goals in better policing and intelligence were accomplished by providing new training modules, scientific equipments, and teaching professional ethics.[49]

Recent trends in the domain of financial intelligence seem to further confirm the effect of capacity gap hypothesis. Prior to the creation of the Anti-Money Laundering Department at the Bangladesh Bank in 2002, which was later renamed to Bangladesh Financial Intelligence Unit in 2012, the government possessed no dedicated agency to collect and analyze information on money laundering and terrorist financing. Similarly, prior to the formation of Central Intelligence Cell at the National Board of Revenue, the tax investigation unit of NBR had serious shortfalls in detecting tax evasion.[50]

The government responded to such limitations by creating the BFIU and the CIC. Support for the capacity gap hypothesis can also be found in the fact that the Anti-Corruption Commission was formed in 2004 and later reconstituted in 2007. Here the political will of the government proved to be a decisive factor in strengthening the anti-corruption investigations. For critics, corruption charges against the lawmakers of the ruling party are hardly investigated and prosecuted, whereas similar charges against the opposition parties are taken quite seriously by the ACC. Interestingly, the partisan role of the ACC was quite different when the military-backed caretaker government of Fakhruddin Ahmed appointed retired army chief General Hassan Moshhud Chowdhury as the ACC chairman.

During his tenure as the ACC chairman, Moshhud Chowdhury initiated corruption investigations against many political leaders including the BNP and Awami League party chiefs Khaleda Zia and Sheikh Hasina, respectively. It became quite apparent that while some of the corruption charges against Khaleda and Hasina might have been well substantiated, the ACC was used as an instrument of the military-backed caretaker government to implement a 'minus two' formula.[51] The goal of the 'minus two' formula was to cleanse Bangladeshi politics by removing the corrupt and the criminals so that a third force of civil society leaders with clean image could come to govern the country.[52] In summary, recent intelligence reform practices in the domains of counterterrorism, immigration service, criminal investigation, and financial crime provide useful evidence to support the capacity gap hypothesis.

Hypothesis 2: *Coordination Needs*

The second hypothesis focuses on coordination needs. Coordination can be centralized or decentralized. The former provides a strategic tool for intelligence sharing by bringing up various agency heads, whereas the second offers a useful mechanism to synthesize field-level intelligence efforts. Evidence suggests that the absence of an effective intelligence sharing mechanism led to the creation of at least three coordination bodies–the National Committee for Intelligence Coordination (NCIC), the National Committee for Militancy Resistance and Prevention (NCMRPP), and the National Coordination Committee (NCC-AML/TF) on anti-money laundering and terrorist financing. Prior to the formation of these coordinating committees, there was hardly any central coordinating body to facilitate intelligence sharing.

Instead, national core committees of senior officials worked on intelligence cooperation on an ad hoc basis, which was hampered by bureaucratic inertia, and competition between various agencies.[53] After the BDR Mutiny in February 2009 revealed the cracks in the ad hoc intelligence coordination structure, Prime Minister Sheikh Hasina established the NCIC in July 2009 to centralize the intelligence coordination process. Located at the Prime Minister's Office, the NCIC is composed of the cabinet secretary, principal secretary to the prime minister's office, director generals of NSI, DGFI, SSF, and inspector general of police.[54] The chiefs of RAB, SB, and CID assist the NCIC in performing its activities.[55]

A close look at the composition of the NCIC suggests that it addressed the thorny issue of bureaucratic competitions, by giving due importance to both civilian and military intelligence agencies. For instance, in the past the Prime Minister would give disproportionately more importance to the intelligence assessments of the DGFI and the NSI, and cared less about what analytical reports the other agencies could offer.[56] However, the government struck a balance between the civilian and military agencies by ensuring that the list of NCIC participants was expanded to include the national police chief, and heads of principal security and intelligence agencies which work under the Ministry of Home Affairs. For many analysts, compared to

169

the past practices of informal coordination, the NCIC represents a major transformation in which various agency heads meet the prime minister on a regular basis and share their assessments with the apex committee members.

According to home ministry officials, the formation of NCMRP in May 2009 was also an innovation in coordinating strategic communications against terrorism and religious militancy.[57] Although the NCMRP comprises seventeen delegates from various ministries such as the home, law, education, religious affairs, local government, and information ministries, officials from the principal law enforcement and intelligence agencies also attend its meetings. The anti-militancy committee mobilizes concerned agencies at the district, sub-district, and local government levels to denounce terrorism and all forms of extremism. According to former police chief Muhammad Nurul Huda, district level coordination bodies still exist but they lack any authority to synthesize operational intelligence.[58]

The NCMRP has the potential to address this gap, but critics observe that the NCMRP is overrepresented by the government ministries and security agencies and under-represented by the members of civil society and human rights bodies. This has created a danger of abuses of power by the government and its agencies.[59] Like the NCIC and the NCMRP; the National Coordination Committee (NCC) on financial crimes was formed in August 2009 under the leadership of finance minister Abul Maal Abdul Muhith. The finance minister chairs the NCC, and its membership comprises the central bank governor, and secretaries of finance and bank divisions, and ministries of home, foreign, and law.[60]

Over the last few years, the NCC was responsible for the formulation and implementation of policies regarding money laundering and terrorist financing.[61] According to one senior official in the Bangladesh Bank, the main task of the NCC was to reform the legal regime so that Bangladesh could gradually improve its compliance with global standards set by the United Nations and other multilateral bodies such as the Financial Action Task Force (FATF).

Although the NCIC, the NCMRP, and the NCC emerged as fully operational coordinating bodies, a few other proposals on intelligence coordination mechanism did not gain any currency. The concepts of the National Crisis Management Committee (NCMC) and the Quick Reaction Force (QRF) are two such cases. In the backdrop of the BDR Mutiny, there were repeated calls for creating a crisis management committee, which would not only include the prime minister and key cabinet members, but also the chair of parliamentary committee on national security, and leader of the opposition party in the parliament.[62] Given the highly polarized political culture in the country, in which personal hatred between the key leaders of mainstream political parties often impede the process of democracy; the idea of a crisis management committee was a utopia. Recognizing that NCMC has no future, the Bangladesh Army proposed the formation of a readily deployable quick reaction force, which could be used to deal with mutiny, terrorism, and hostage situations.[63]

If established, the QRF could also be deployed to the United Nations peace keeping missions. Till date, no concrete actions have been taken to raise the QRF. The preceding discussion shows the existence of three high level coordinating bodies. Although the NCIC is the most powerful coordination body, it does not include border and financial intelligence agencies. The newly created border intelligence agency BSB is absent from the NCIC structure due to its lack of competence and maturity. On the other hand, since the financial intelligence agencies participate in a finance ministry-led committee, they are perhaps excluded from the NCIC to avoid any duplication of efforts. For critics, the absence of border and financial intelligence entities is largely due to their infancy. Since both entities have been recently formed, their potential contribution to national intelligence coordination is under appreciated at the moment but may increase over time.

Hypothesis 3: Crisis-driven Demand

The third hypothesis posits that intelligence crises and failures can act as a catalyst for major reform. Consistent with the expectation of this hypothesis, intelligence failure leading up to the BDR mutiny had a decisive effect on reshaping the border intelligence.[64]

The reconfiguration of border force intelligence and the creation of two national coordination bodies provide useful evidence to test the crisis-driven reform hypothesis. The chain of events during the BDR Mutiny suggests that members of the Rifles Security Unit (RSU) failed to report to its higher authorities any sensitive information regarding disaffected border soldiers. Instead of delivering advanced information to their superior authorities, several dozen RSU members actively participated in the mutiny.[65]

Other agencies also failed to predict the outbreak of a mutiny, which destroyed the BDR's command structure. Lessons learned from the BDR mutiny influenced the way the border guard has been reconstituted since 2010. This is evident in disbanding the BDR and creating the Border Guard Bangladesh (BGB) with newly screened personnel. The RSU was also replaced with a new BGB intelligence network, which emphasizes fusion of information among analysts at the battalions, regional sectors, and central headquarters. In retrospect, intelligence failure prior to the BDR mutiny provides useful lessons, which have strongly shaped the Sheikh Hasina government's decision to form the two coordination committees such as the NCIC and the NCMRP.

The national probe committee on BDR mutiny, led by retired government official Anis Uz Zaman, found that the complicity of RSU members with the mutineers, and lack of inter-agency collaboration between the BDR headquarters and the home ministry officials contributed to intelligence failure prior to the mutiny. Therefore, the committee recommended that two intelligence coordinating bodies be established – a central intelligence coordination structure; and a national crisis management committee.[66]

The Anis Uz Zaman committee also emphasized better coordination between various intelligence and law enforcement agencies.[67] As explained before, the government responded positively to the idea of a central intelligence coordination structure and ignored the concept of crisis management committee. While the events of BDR Mutiny have had a quick effect on the government's decision to form the NCIC, the idea of creating the anti-militancy national committee (NCMRP) has had a long period of gestation.

Political observers suggest that the rise of militant Islamist groups such as the Harkat ul Jihad al Islami (HuJI), the Jamaat ul Mujahedeen Bangladesh (JMB), and the Jagrata Muslim Janata Bangladesh (JMJB), and their alleged involvement in several high profile terrorist attacks from 1999 to 2005 have encouraged the previous governments of Khaleda Zia and Fakhruddin Ahmed to form an inter-agency anti-militancy committee. In fact, both the BNP-led four party alliance governments (2001-2006) and the military-backed caretaker government (2007-2008) recognized that an anti-militancy committee would not only coordinate the works of various ministries but also allow the intelligence agencies to share their terrorist threat assessments.

Why was then May 2009 chosen as the timeline for establishing the NCMRP? There are two possible answers: First, although the idea of a similar anti-militancy committee were contemplated for quite some time, especially since the JMB's 2005 country-wide terrorist bombings, bureaucratic inertia and lack of inter-agency collaboration put enormous pressures impeding the birth of the committee. It appears that the home ministry exploited the crisis moment of the post-mutiny period in 2009 to establish the NCMRP. Second, widespread concerns over possible connections between radical Islamist groups and the BDR mutineers offer an additional explanation.[68]

Although no conclusive evidence was found to establish militants-mutineers connections, intelligence assessments warned of the possibility of looted weapons and explosives falling into the hands of criminals and terrorists, who might be intent on destabilizing the country.[69] Senior officials at the home ministry and the major intelligence agencies note that the NCMRP was created in response to such threat assessments. In summary, intelligence failures leading to JMB's country-wide terrorist bombings in 2005 and the BDR mutiny in 2009 have significantly shaped the structures of the border intelligence agency and the formation of the national coordination committees.

This paper has also mentioned similar crisis-driven reforms in India, the U.K. and the U.S. Are there any historical precedents aside from the 2005 JMB bombings and the 2009 BDR Mutiny, which may provide further credence to the crisis-driven reform hypothesis in Bangladesh? The answer is yes. The creation of the paramilitary Jatiya Rakkhi Bahini (National Defence Force) as an auxiliary police force in February 1972 and its absorption into the Bangladesh Army in October 1975 also illustrate the crisis-driven reform hypothesis. Although Bangladesh's independence leader Sheikh Mujibur Rahman established the Rakkhi Bahini as a loyal militia force to contain organized crime and terrorism and to consolidate his regime security, the Rakkhi Bahini was eventually turned into a state within state with huge mandates in intelligence gathering and law enforcement.[70]

The creation of the paramilitary Jatiya Rakkhi Bahini (National Defence Force) as an auxiliary police force in February 1972 and its absorption into the Bangladesh Army in October 1975 also illustrate the crisis-driven reform hypothesis. Although Bangladesh's independence leader Sheikh Mujibur Rahman established the Rakkhi Bahini as a loyal militia force to contain organized crime and terrorism and to consolidate his regime security, the Rakkhi Bahini was eventually turned into a state within state with huge mandates in intelligence gathering and law enforcement.[70]

Despite widespread criticisms of human rights abuses including torture, enforced disappearance, extrajudicial killings, Sheikh Mujib not only planned for the expansion of the Rakkhi Bahini but also enacted the Jatiya Rakkhi Bahini Amendment Act 1974 to give it "immunity from prosecution and other legal proceedings."[71] It was not until the assassination of Mujib in a military coup in August 1975 that the Rakkhi Bahini was abolished and merged with the armed forces through the Jatiya Rakkhi Bahini Absorption Ordinance 1975.[72]

Several questions flow from the above analysis: To what extent have the DGFI and the NSI see Mujib's killing in 1975 and Zia's murder in 1981 as cases of intelligence failure? How have successive governments reformed the DGFI and the NSI to enhance their professional competence? It is beyond the scope of this paper to examine the utility of the crisis-driven reform hypothesis with further historical evidence. Further studies should address this deficiency. The preceding discussions demonstrate the effect of domestic factors on intelligence reform. The next hypothesis examines the effect of external influence on intelligence reform.

Hypothesis 4: *External Influence*

The fourth hypothesis suggests that if national decision makers fail to respond to the needs for intelligence reform, external influence will facilitate such reform. External influence may come in two forms: carrots and sticks. The first refers to the offer of incentives, while the latter implies the use of coercive pressures. The incentive structure may include funding and technical supports whereas coercive pressures may focus on punitive actions against noncompliant practices. As stated before, external influence may come from two major sources: states and international organizations. For the purpose of brevity, this paper examines the effects of influence from several sources: the United States, the European Union, the United Nations, and the Financial Action Task Force.

Data on criminal and financial intelligence reform in Bangladesh support the validity of the external influence hypothesis. With an estimated US$45 million multi-year and multi-donor support, Bangladesh Police and the UNDP have embarked on the Police Reform Project, which has not only worked on gender mainstreaming and strategic leadership issues, but also targeted improvement in criminal investigation and criminal intelligence analysis.[73]

As part of the police reform initiative, funding support from the European Commission, the executive organ of the European Union, has offered an incentive to create the Trafficking in Human Being (THB) Unit at the CID. Although the newly created anti-trafficking unit is too small to cover the mammoth task of investigating hundreds of cases, it offers a useful example of how donor-driven reform agenda can assist an intelligence agency to adapt to the growing threat to human security.[74]

In addition to foreign aid, external pressures have also had positive effect on intelligence reform. This is sharply evident in the case of constant pressures of the U.S. State Department to improve the anti-trafficking regime in Bangladesh.[75] In a similar manner, pressures from the U.S. Treasury have also had significantly influenced the way the Bangladesh Bank has reformed its financial intelligence unit. According to one Bangladeshi analyst:

> The US [United States] has been keeping a close watch over the terror situation in Bangladesh. This is evident from the US pressure on the [Bangladesh] government in 2002 for the enactment of the AMLA [Anti Money Laundering Act], long before the surfacing of JMB [Jamaat ul Mujahedeen Bangladesh–a radical Islamist group]. Since then it has been hammering the government to complete probe into the alleged money laundering cases and to take some actions (emphasis added).[76]

In addition to the U.S Treasury, the Financial Action Task Force (FATF) has also put enormous pressures on Bangladesh to introduce a series of legal and administrative reforms in the domain of financial intelligence. The FATF is a global standard setter in the fight against money laundering, terrorist financing, and proliferation financing. During interviews, senior officials at the central bank and the ministries of home affairs, foreign affairs, and law and parliamentary affairs describe how Bangladesh risked being blacklisted for noncompliance with the global standards on anti-money laundering and countering of terrorist financing (AML/CFT). According to a senior official at the central bank, Bangladesh has been committed to bringing necessary reform in the financial sector "to avert any global negative impact" and to "meet the demand of global watchdog [such as FATF]."[77]

In order for Bangladesh to improve its compliance with the global AML/CFT regime, there was a need for changing the existing laws regarding antiterrorism, anti-money laundering, and countering of terrorist financing. These legal reforms would ensure that money laundering, terrorist financing, and proliferation financing are adequately criminalized and an independent financial intelligence unit is created to detect, analyze, and help prosecute such crimes. As stated before, in accordance with the requirements set by the FATF, the finance ministry-led national coordination committee steered the process of legislating the Money Laundering Prevention Act 2012 and the Anti-Terrorism Act 2012.[78]

The new laws have repealed their past versions in an effort to comply with the global AML/CFT standards. As a result, banks and nonbanking financial institutions are now required to report suspicious transactions to the Bangladesh Financial Intelligence Unit (BFIU). International pressures also came from the United Nations Security Council (UNSC) and various multilateral conventions. To understand how the UN pressures were channelled, one has to look at the UNSC Resolutions 1267 and 1373, both of which focus on targeted sanctions on terrorist financiers. The UN Counter Terrorism Committee also requires member states to assess their legislation regarding UNSCR 1373.

In addition, a host of UN conventions on transnational organized crime and terrorist offences, such as the 1998 Vienna Convention on drugs trafficking, the 1999 UN Convention on the suppression of terrorist financing, and the 2000 Palermo Convention on transnational crime had significantly influenced the way the security and intelligence agencies in Bangladesh have adapted to the evolving threats of transnational crime and terrorism. It is abundantly clear that the cumulative effects of pressures from the FATF and the UN have strongly shaped the way Bangladesh has introduced reforms in the financial intelligence sector.[79]

External influence can also explain the expansion of counterterrorism capabilities of the DGFI, the NSI, and the RAB, each of which competes to become the lead counterterrorism agency in the country. Participants in this research suggest that after the 9/11 terrorist attacks, U.S. pressures played a crucial role in encouraging the DGFI to acquire new counterterrorism responsibilities. These pressures would often come from senior officials at the U.S. State Department's Office of Coordinator of Counterterrorism as well as the Department of Treasury's Financial Crimes Enforcement Network.

Although external variables can provide useful insights into understanding reforms in the domains of counterterrorism and financial intelligence such variables appear to have less utility in analyzing reforms in the border intelligence apparatus, national intelligence coordination, and tax intelligence. As described before, the latter three changes were influenced by domestic pressures such as capacity gaps, coordination demands, and intelligence failure.

Policy Recommendations

Several policy recommendations flow from the central research findings.

1. First, capacity building should be an ongoing process. Intelligence practitioners and national decision makers should not wait until a major failure to initiate necessary changes. Although this paper focuses on the capacity of individual agencies, it also recognizes the importance of improving the capability of intelligence coordination structures.

2. Second, national level intelligence coordination is necessary but not sufficient. There is an urgent need to promote operational collaboration among field level intelligence agencies. In addition, border intelligence and financial intelligence entities need to be strengthened and brought under the purview of the National Committee for Intelligence Coordination.

3. Third, an autonomous research centre outside the intelligence community should be formed to examine the cases of intelligence failures. The proposed centre should study missed opportunities and lessons learned.

4. Fourth, external assistance from the EU and the UNDP

has brought useful changes to the criminal investigation capability. In addition, pressures from the FATF, the United States, and the United Nations have helped developing the financial intelligence unit and a national coordination body on anti-money laundering. Building on the pre-existing reforms, Bangladesh should continue to enhance the capability of intelligence agencies and their coordination structures.

Conclusion

This paper has accomplished several tasks. First, it profiled the intelligence community in Bangladesh and mapped out the major intelligence reforms in the country. Next, it developed a set of testable propositions on intelligence reforms, and examined their utility with empirical evidence. The central research findings show that recent intelligence reforms in Bangladesh can be explained by four factors–capacity gaps, coordination needs, crisis-driven demands, and external influence. Despite its accomplishments, this paper has a few limitations. It does not address the issue of democratic control of intelligence agencies. Although Bangladesh claims to be a parliamentary democracy, there is no legislative oversight body to control the budgets, personnel or acquisition policy of the intelligence agencies. The judiciary also lacks any control mechanism over the intelligence agencies. In the absence of any legislative or judicial oversight mechanisms, the executive branch in general and the prime minister in particular have effectively monopolized the control over intelligence agencies.

The executive monopoly over the intelligence community has created several problems. It has certainly reduced the possibility for bringing greater degree of transparency and accountability in the way security and intelligence agencies operate. Other problems relate to the absence of any overarching intelligence law and an intelligence strategy which could provide well defined tasking for intelligence community suggests that in the absence of any well defined tasks and clear legal mandates, the security and intelligence agencies remain vulnerable to manipulation by the incumbent political regimes.[80]

In conclusion, the four hypotheses tested in this paper offer only plausible explanations. It is important to conduct further research to learn about the changes and continuities in the security and intelligence agencies of Bangladesh. Future studies should expand the timeline of analysis, and include more variables and country cases. They should also give adequate emphasis on the issue of democratic control over the intelligence agencies.

Courtesy: Journal of the Asiatic Society of Bangladesh (Hum.), Vol. 59 (1), 2014, pp. 65-94. This paper has been taken with the special permission of Dr. ASM. Ali Ashraf, Ph.D. Associate Professor Department of International Relations, University of Dhaka, Dhaka 1000, Bangladesh.

Chapter 8

Intelligence without Ambition: National Directorate of Intelligence (NDS) of Afghanistan

The US so called war on terror in Afghanistan that impacted liberal societies in the West unfathomably in many ways have now entered a crucial phase. Russia and China have joined the theatre of war as the strongest stakeholders, and dancing in the combat zones. After a dishonourable and discreditable defeat in Afghanistan, the US President Donald Trump prepared a strategy to pull thousands of US troops out of the country, but faced irritability in White House and Pentagon. The allies also got out of joint and felt sore due to their whitewashing and embarrassment. They have now dog-tired to stand or act professionally.

The US and NATO forces used all means of viciousness, including unwarrantable dog-rape, and dropped the most powerful Nonnuclear-Mother-of-Bombs which caused incurable disease, death and suffering. They bombed houses, killed children and women with impunity, destroyed the Kunduz hospital and MSF's fully functioning trauma centre, but never succeeded in winning the loyalty of the Afghan nation.[1] Resentful by their kill and burn tactics, Afghan army turned its guns on their officers and soldierskilled hundreds inside forts and battlefield.[1] Throughout its three decades of war in Afghanistan, Washington's military operations have never been helpful to stabilize the country. Its strongest intelligence infrastructure failed (Fixing Intel, General Flynn 2010) to understand the mental outlook of the people of Afghanistan.

After the fall of the Taliban regime in 2001, the CIA and Pentagon reinvented Afghan intelligence and trained it on controversial streaks. The CIA, and Pentagon armed, trained, and used NDS for their own operational purposes. Afghan intelligence units needed more advanced technology, intercept capabilities and cross-communication between the National Directorate of Security (NDS) and security forces in the field, but the US and NATO forces failed to meet their requirements. The National Directorate of Security (NDS) continued to suffer key intelligence capabilities, especially in gathering intelligence information from remote areas in order to prevent neighbouring states from interfering in the internal affairs of Afghanistan.

In spite of their sweat and continuous combat since the invasion of October 2001, the CIA, MI6, and Eye-5 Intelligence Alliance failed to put the Taliban insurgency in nutshell. With the US forces demoralised faces, and the Taliban aggressive fighters-equipped with night-vision and sophisticated weapons, airstrikes became the last tenuous line of defence.[2] The failure of America's intervention in Afghanistan offered broader insight into the limits to its global power. President Trump, instead of the promised fundamentally different approach, repeated President Obama's go off in smoke and miss and boat strategy-to cut a deal with the Afghan Taliban, for which the U.S. needed the full backing of Pakistan's military establishment.[3]

Failure of Afghan intelligence agencies to defeat the Taliban in Afghanistan has deeply gloomed international community that consequences of wrongly designed counterinsurgency and counterterrorism strategies are consistently substandard. Disorder and complications the United States and its allies created in Afghanistan are more evident than ever before. Through its appalling and unsuccessfully engineered strategies and military adventures, the CIA, MI6, the NATO spy agencies, and Pentagon facilitated the rise of a new terrorist group (ISIS) that never existed prior to the war on terrorism in Afghanistan. The US civilian and military intelligence fashioned a strategic mistake-reasoning that military action can put the state back in order, but unfortunately failed. The British MI6 came to nothing to collect high-quality intelligence information from Helmand, while the EU intelligence agencies were also running wrong horses to meet security challenges in Afghanistan.[4]

With the geographical expansion of the Islamic state (ISIS), and the emergence of Khurasan group (KIS) in Jalalabad, Russia and China comprehended that these developments were a direct threat to their national security and territorial integrity. Russia established its own Taliban, and adorned the group with sophisticated weapons to counter the Islamic State and exponentially growing US influence in Afghanistan and Central Asia.[5] China supported the Russian plan. Russia also reinvented its old intelligence and political contacts in Afghanistan, while China deployed its army alongside Afghan-China border. Russian military intelligence (GRU) and MGB organized its old cadre in Afghanistan and created an environment, in which neither the US and NATO military commanders, nor Afghanistan's army commanders have been capable to cruise between small and big cities in open air.[6]

In the contemporary international system, states are the fundamental customer of classified and processed intelligence information for security, law enforcement and policymaking. However, Islamic State (ISIS) and the Taliban also perceive a need to collect and process advance information to protect their networks against the theft of their strategic, defense and political secrets. As intelligence is more than an organized collection of targeted information, processing can include technical issues such as transcribing and translating intercepted telephone conversations and verifying the reliability of information. In modern philosophy, intelligence involves a real struggle with human opponents, carried on to gain some advantage over them. Michael Warner understands that argument over the definition of intelligence resembles perhaps nothing so much as a trademark dispute. In essence, the debate among intelligence experts has caused deep confusion over the basic job of an intelligence agency during war and peace times.[7]

During the last 14 years, we have heard or seen no success story from the National Directorate of Security (NDS) in the country because it adopted a political culture and its leadership acted like politicians. The fall of Kunduz, consecutive terror attacks in Kabul and the abrupt appearance of (ISIS) in Afghanistan, raised important questions about the credibility and competency of the Afghan intelligence agencies. Before the Taliban attack on Kunduz, NDS operatives safely left the city without informing the government in Kabul.[8] Large-scale desertion of the Afghan army soldiers, intelligence units and the police enabled the Taliban to enter the city unopposed. After their capture of the city, they looted weapons, including tanks. The president's appointed investigative team in its 30-page summary report also noted that there was coordination among the police, intelligence and Afghan army commanders.

The CIA and Pentagon killed innocent patients and doctors shamelessly and apologized that their five billion dollar intelligence computer system went offline the day of the bombing on Kunduz hospital. Human rights groups termed it a serious violation of human rights and an unprecedented war crime. In fact, writing on the intelligence mechanism and operation of the NDS is an industrious task as there is limited information available to analysts and researchers in libraries and market. The NDS is a remnant of the Khidmat-e-Etlaat-e-Dulat (KHAD), established in the 1980s, and trained by KGB experts. However, from 1980 to the collapse of the Afghan state in 1992, no intelligence reforms have been undertaken by successive governments in the country.

In 1992, the mujahedeen undermined the basic structure of intelligence and used it against each other. In 2002, when the CIA reorganized the scattered pieces of Afghan intelligence under the name of NDS and trained its officers, two ideological camps emerged. The Soviet trained agents and CIA trained agents opposed each other, and established secret contacts with various mafia groups across the country. The presence of Russian and Chinese intelligence in Afghanistan further complicated the process of intelligence sharing and cooperation between Afghan and western intelligence agencies in the country. The state and system of government has ultimately been hijacked by these agencies. The secret war between Russian, Chinese and US Defence clandestine intelligence agency in northern Afghanistan raised serious question about the intensifying great game in the country, which might possibly prompt a destructive nuclear war in Central Asia.

The exponentially spreading web of foreign espionage in the region and the recruitment of Afghans agents for it cause fear and anxiety. Dr Abdullah in his recent statement raised concern about the existence of foreign spies within the state institutions. "Double agents are more dangerous than insurgents," he said.[9] The fall of Kunduz, Pakistan's re-engagement in the peace process and policy differences between the president and Intelligence Chief Rahmatullah Nabil forced him to resign. He was, in fact, unprofessional, and an incompetent chief who knew nothing about the way intelligence operates. He was acting like a politician.[10]

His precursors were also street children who made the agency ethnicised, sectarianised and regionalized. Now, with the appointment of Major General Masoud Andarabi as the chief of the NDS, it was hoped that he could introduce some structural reforms and changes within the controversial intelligence infrastructure of his half Sovietised and half Americanized agency. Yesteryears' news stories showed that former Afghan intelligence chiefs also acted like politicians and interfered in the decision making process in the country.[11]

Distrust between the government and intelligence chiefs affected friendly relations between Afghanistan and its neighbours. They openly issued statements on television channels and criticized Presidents and their diplomatic approach. They opposed Pakistan's role in the peace process and branded the country an enemy of the Afghans. The way the NDS operates needs to be changed now, introducing wide-ranging intelligence reforms to make effective the NDS and its countrywide networks, which may lead the fight against ISIS and the Taliban in the right direction. The Afghan leadership needs to depoliticize the agency and expel illiterate elements appointed on ethnic and sectarian lines. The mujahedeen and Taliban supporters within the intelligence agency are making things worse. The roots of the NDS must be re-established in the south and east, and the influence of drug smugglers and war criminals needs to be undermined.

The stories of the failure of Afghan intelligence agencies and their political and religious affiliations and loyalties have badly affected military strategies and counter insurgency measures of NATO and US intelligence circles; secret political and military reports are feared to have gone into the hands of war criminals, regional states and the Taliban insurgents. As per the nature of their controversial work, Afghan agents belong to various ethnic and political groups; therefore, they are bound to report to their masters. Like the Afghan police and army, intelligence network has also been divided between states, warlords, NGOs and foreign intelligence agencies. On July 13, 2012, Khaama Press reported that intelligence organizations of neighbouring states had acquired Afghan intelligence cards and operated independently.[12]

There are many sections within the intelligence agencies; some report about the NATO, US, UK and ISAF military activities to the Taliban; some report to 'war criminals'; some report to Karim Khalili; some report to the vice president and leader of the Northern Alliance and some report to Iran and Pakistan. An addition to the political and ethnic influence of the Taliban and the former Mujahedeen war criminals in KHAD, the influence of foreign intelligence networks is further making the task of the agency controversial. Recently, a source within the agency told me that the leakage of many important political and military reports has put in danger the lives of many Afghan and NATO soldiers. From a membership card to important intelligence reports, everything is for sale cheaply.[13]

All players in the battlefield used Afghan intelligence for their own purposes while the recruitment of its members on ethnic basis is more worrisome. Experts say that this is the main cause of the failure of the Afghan, US and NATO forces in undermining insurgency and terrorism in Afghanistan. Mujahedeen, Taliban, Iran, Pakistan, Saudi Arabia, India, China and Russia play their own roles. Afghan intelligence is playing a double game, providing false information to international community about the military plans of insurgents. The former Pakistani president Musharraf once alleged that Afghan intelligence was being used by the RAW against Pakistan. "Afghan intelligence, the Afghan president and the Afghan government don't talk of them. I know what they do.

They, by design, mislead the world...The Afghan intelligence is entirely under the influence of Indian intelligence. We know that." Mr. Musharraf said.[14]

The way intelligence works is a joke. Appointments on political and ethnic bases are an irksome story. No professional measures of intelligence are adopted; every sectarian and ethnic member of the agency is bound to report his leader, not to help the state in fighting Taliban insurgency. In his well-written book, Michael Herman understands, "We have already seen how national intelligence can be used for mediation and conflict resolution, including such means as its provision to potential antagonists as a stabilizing measure; its use in international cooperation on counter terrorism and limiting international arms transfer; and the verification of arms control and other international agreements. Afghan intelligence with its non-professional strategies and security measures, never served the interests of the Afghan state, it served the interest of other states".[15]

In October 2012, a radicalized member of the Afghan intelligence blew himself up using a suicide vest, killing two US soldiers and four Afghan intelligence men. This is a new and secret tactic of war against the US and NATO forces. The prominent Afghan intellectual and historian, Muhammad Hassan Kakar, in his research book (1982-2004) complains, "The Afghan society may now be regarded a murderous society. The sad thing about it is that there is no investigation for murder cases. Human life has become the life of sparrow, and the principle that might is right dominates. In the past, murder cases were investigated not only among the people where the murder had taken place but also among neighbours, who were summoned to the security centres for questioning. In this way social conscience against murder was awakened."[16]

On December 13, 2014, the NATO and International Security Assistance Force (ISAF) mission in Afghanistan came to an end with the transfer of security responsibilities to the Afghan National Security Forces (ANSF) but they could not succeed in establishing the writ of the government in all parts of the country. The challenges of building a strong army for the country remains a dream because the power of the central government depends on negotiations with the Taliban, Islamic State (IS) and regional criminal militias. In the US-led war on terrorism in Afghanistan and the ongoing civil wars in the Middle East and Pakistan, professional intelligence was the only way to assess the strength and lethality of terrorists and insurgent groups. However, the Afghan government never focused on reforming the National Directorate of Security (NDS), Khadamat-e-Aetela'at-e-Dawlati (KHAD) or strengthening the intelligence structure.[17]

The withdrawal of US and NATO intelligence staff from Afghanistan (2014) and the desertion of NDS professional officers to join the Taliban and private militias has left a vacuum that has facilitated IS and the Taliban in their fight against the unity government. Regrettably, one of the major problems of Afghan intelligence is that the relationship between the local population and policy makers has broken down. Two weeks ago, during ISIS's attacks on Kunduz province, the NDS's local officials could not accurately estimate the Afghan army's strength and resources. The NDS misled the army commander to take pre-emptive action and disrupt the terrorists' supply line. Since the role of intelligence agencies in the Afghan conflict has expanded and they now are a core element in conflict management, coordination and cooperation between the NDS and policing agencies is important.[18]

The NDS does not share all information with the police department and has failed to provide intelligence information to policy makers, Afghan army commanders or other agencies about IS and Taliban activities. The other major challenge is the lack of experience and education within the NDS's ranks. They have no knowledge of modern intelligence systems or their role in conflict management across the world. Another challenge is adapting intelligence to local needs. The NDS supports and provides intelligence information to leaders, commanders and warlords of a specific community because the Sovietised agency still needs to be adapted to Afghanistan.

The Afghan Military Intelligence (AMI) is also facing numerous difficulties in collecting information about the war strategies of IS and Taliban commanders from remote districts. The agency lacks trained officers to reach remote districts or even those outside the provincial headquarters to interact with the local population. If the AMI and NDS agents in war zones try to collect analyze and process intelligence information, their efforts can allow policy makers and the army commanders to discern friend from foe, and thus apply professional measures with precision and minimal collective damage, human or material.

A major portion of intelligence information collection and analysis for countering insurgency in Afghanistan is labour intensive and relies on the local commanders being able to interact with farmers, Maliks, educated people and religious clerics regularly. The agencies do not rely on modern methods and cannot differentiate between Pakistani and Afghan Pashtuns or between Afghan Tajiks, Turks and their Central Asian friends. The NDS has often been repudiated by parliamentarians, press analysts and ordinary Afghans for its unprofessional modes of operation, torture and death in custody. The agency has been targeting specific communities and operating on ethnic lines since 2001. Because the agency's roots are in the north, most of its agents do not know the security parameters of the southern, eastern and western provinces of Afghanistan.

Afghan intelligence agencies ultimately rely on human intelligence because they still lack the availability of modern intelligence collection technologies. The NDS and RAMA (a research and intelligence agency) have a weak human intelligence network in the cities and most of their sources are unreliable. The information they receive is useless because the agencies are unable to analyze or process it. There are numerous factors that hinder the performance of the Afghan intelligence agencies. For instance, many NDS agents cannot use Facebook, e-mail and the internet for intelligence purposes. After the US invasion in 2001, the Afghan National Military Intelligence Centre (ANMIC) was established to support senior military commanders in the battlefield but the president and army chief have not been satisfied with its performance in the past.[19] The Directorate of Policing Intelligence (DPI), which provides intelligence information about the arrest and prosecution of criminals, National Information Management System (NIMS), Wolfhound Information System (WLS), National Target Exploitation Centre (NTEC) and dozens of other military and police intelligence organizations have so far failed to lead countrywide military operations in the right direction.[20]

Two months ago, ISIS kidnapped 31 people from Zabul province but Afghan intelligence was unable to determine their whereabouts. After two months, the government swapped 26 prisoners for 19 hostages and millions of dollars. On May 14, 2015, Tolo News reported the closure of 69 schools in Uruzgan province due to the security situation. Some 14 civilians, including nine foreigners, were killed after Taliban gunmen stormed a guesthouse on the outskirts of Kabul.[21] On May 16, the Pajhwok News Agency reported that IS had kidnapped 27 passengers in Sayed Karam district of the south-eastern Paktia province. The residents said gunmen took passengers with them in Badam Kanda. The Taliban forced passengers out of 30 vehicles and took them to an undisclosed location. All these fatalities occurred due to the inability of NDS and AIM to inform the authorities in time.[22]

In November 2018, President Ashraf Ghani said that more than 28,529 Afghan soldiers and officers killed since 2015, which made an average of 25 per day. He also said 58 American soldiers were also killed during the same period. In July 2018, the UNAMA in its report noted the killing of more than 1,692 civilians in June 30, 2018. UNAMA also noted that anti-government forces were responsible for 67 percent (1,127 deaths and 2,286 injuries) of the casualties.[23] However, on 25 February 2019; Daily Outlook Afghanistan reported the UNAMA calculation of civilian deaths in the country:

"In total, UNAMA documented 10,993 civilian casualties (3,804 deaths and 7,189 injured), representing a five per cent increase in overall civilian casualties and an 11 per cent increase in civilian deaths compared to 2017. UNAMA attributed the majority of civilian casualties –63 per cent– to Anti-Government Elements (AGEs), 37 per cent to Taliban, 20 per cent to Daesh/Islamic State Khorasan Province (ISKP), and 6 per cent to undetermined AGEs. Pro-Government Forces caused 24 per cent of civilian casualties --14 per cent by Afghan national security forces, six per cent by international military forces, as well as four per cent by other pro-Government armed groups and forces. Anti-Government

Elements were responsible for 6,980 civilian casualties (2,243 deaths and 4,737 injured), a three per cent increase on 2017, which mainly resulted from the indiscriminate use of suicide improvised explosive devices (IEDs) and the deliberate targeting of civilians with these devices. Taliban caused 4,072 civilian casualties (1,348 deaths and 2,724 injured), seven per cent down on 2017, while Daesh/ISKP caused 2,181 civilian casualties (681 deaths and 1,500 injured), an increase of 118 per cent. UNAMA attributed a further 678 civilian casualties (196 deaths and 482 injured) to undetermined AGEs. Anti-Government Elements' use of IEDs in both suicide and non-suicide attacks reached extreme levels and remained the leading cause of civilian casualties in 2018, accounting for 42 per cent of the total. Suicide IED attacks caused 2,809 civilian casualties (886 deaths and 1,923 injured), almost 26 per cent of all civilian casualties, while non-suicide IEDs caused more than 16 per cent, resulting in a combined total of 4,627 civilian casualties (1,361 deaths and 3,266 injured)[24].

The UNAMA report noted 63 percent of civilian causalities caused by anti-government groups, thus 37 percent reflects to Taliban, 20 percent to Daesh, and 6 percent other anti- government elements. The report noted 24 percent of the civilian causalities posed by pro-government forces; 14 percent Afghan National Forces and six percent Resolute supports and four percent other pro-government armed groups. On 25 February 2019, Afghanistan Times reported former President Hamid Karzai's resentment over targeting of civilian population in military's retaliatory actions against what the government called militants. However, continuation of targeting the civilian population in air strikes and ground attacks of armed forces has been a matter of great concern, which also made disgruntled those who had attached hopes and expectations with the US brokered peace efforts.

According to Hamid Karzai office statement, once again like of recent past, the civilian population was targeted in Jalga district of Maidan Wardag province of Afghanistan, inflicting losses to human lives and properties in that already affected area. Targeting of civilian population in a village of Maidan-Wardak is not first ever incident. Earlier similar innocent and helpless civilians throughout the country suffered a lot. In fact these civilians are unable to shift and live like internally displaced people near to urban cities and towns. Even they couldn't afford transportation charges and were compelled to stay in the areas which were converted into battle ground between the parties involved in encounter or conflict against each other's since a long. However, tens of people from Wardak province have staged demonstration in Kabul city on 26 February 2019 to protest military operations by the security forces that caused civilian causalities there. The protestors called on the government to avoid operations targeting civilian causalities. They claimed that a recent operation in the Julga district killed a number of civilians including children.[25]

On 21 February, 2019 Daily Outlook Afghanistan noted weaknesses of the Afghan government in maintaining good governance: In fact, judiciary and law enforcement agencies must be capable to hold the law as the top priority matter. In Afghan political system the separation of powers is not clear and the judiciary is composed of what the Presidential Office decides. Moreover, the powerful and the rich are mostly considered above the law and the poor and weak have to go through the 'quagmire of law and order system'. The capacity of good governance is judged by its potential to offer the basic requirements of life to the people easily and readily. Moreover, it must strive to raise the standard of living of the masses. There are certain important characteristics that must be achieved so as to establish it. Good governance has to be participatory, consensus oriented, accountable, transparent, responsive, effective and efficient, equitable and inclusive and follows the rule of law".[26]

Good governance requires that institutions and processes try to serve all stakeholders within a reasonable timeframe. It means that it should be responsive. In the same way it should also ensure equity and inclusiveness. This requires all groups, but particularly the most vulnerable, have opportunities to improve or maintain their well being but what Afghan government has to offer us is the negligence of the most vulnerable. The minority groups in fact suffer from lack of proper participation in decision making and they find their existence threatened within the society.

Chapter 9

Instability in Afghanistan: Implications for Pakistan[1]

Mohammad

Abstract

In terms of foreign policy, Afghanistan is the most important determinant for the policy makers in Pakistan. Since its formation in 1947, Pakistan's relations with Afghanistan have not been cordial. In the aftermath of 9/11, this country has become a flash point of clashing interests among different powers. Due to the Indian involvement in the country, the western borders between Pakistan and Afghanistan have become very insecure. Pakistan has always been a victim of the instability in Afghanistan. In this study an effort is made to evaluate the impacts of instability in Afghanistan on Pakistan. Also it aims at sorting out factors and policy goals of actors involved in the war on terror in Afghanistan. A historical and analytical research effort has been made to bring about the real facts and the prospects of the issue.

Introduction

For the last three decades or so Afghanistan faces serious challenges of instability due to internal stripe and wars. Firstly, the internal race for power between different groups since Sardar Daoud took over the government of his cousin in 1971; secondly,

---

1   This article was first published in the Journal of Political Sciences & Public Affairs 4: 213. This has been reproduced here with the permission of the author.

the USSR supporting groups made different Coup from time to time[1]. In 1979 USSR entered their troops into Afghanistan and a war started between the Mujahedeen and the Red Army. This battle created destruction, ruined the infrastructure and made the country instable. Due to war the country became underdeveloped. Their people had to take refuge in different countries to save their families and children. They were striving to find food and shelter for their children. To make their own hands strong they used army to kill the innocent people, create terror and fear in their hearts. Due to eleven years long war in Afghanistan its people suffered and also the neighbouring countries especially Pakistan.

Reasons behind long lasting wars in Afghanistan

The war brought instability, hater, disparities and destruction in Afghanistan. This war was imposed by the Afghan elite and the credit goes to their wrong decisions. Afghanistan was a prosperous country before the war. A large number of tourists were coming to Afghanistan which in return provided huge amounts of revenue to the national exchequer. The main cause of instability was the ideological war of two super powers USSR and USA during the cold war era. Both had their own interests in Afghanistan. USSR wanted to reach warm waters and have access to the Middle East's oil resources. While USA wanted to contain USSR with the help of her allies Saudi Arabia, Pakistan and the Afghan Mujahedeen.

The main elements which smoothen the way for hatching the eggs in Afghanistan were; (a) political and military elite; (b) rural people; (c) insurgent groups; (d) war lords; (e) geographical location; (f) roughly terrain and hilly areas, having no road connection with central government; (g) poverty; (h) and extremism. When the government fails to provide employment to its masses, remove poverty and change their life standards, then the huge bulk of youth could take guns and join terrorist group[2]. Extremist thoughts also played very decisive role in destabilizing the country. Due to illiteracy of her people the mullahs could easily misguide the innocent people in the name of religion. After the withdrawal of USSR from Afghanistan the USA and her allies left alone those Mujahedeen who fought against the USSR. They were once called by the allies as holly warriors. But after, no attention was given to

194

establishing a unity government in Afghanistan. The arms which were taken by the fighters against the foreign invader were turned against each other.

This battle for power continued for six year. The war lords introduced their self imposed punishments which were enough to speak for its cruelty and barbarism. The Afghan society became wild, brutish and nasty. There was no sign of rule of law because there was no law at all. There was no concept of centre governmental. The conditions resembled the Hobbs state of nature. Powers who could bring war destiny to the Afghanis did not look back for peace. All the people were fed up from these wild animals.

Rise of the Taliban

A new group came into the front which was called the Taliban. The word means those students who received religious education from madrasas[3]. Many of them fought against Russia and were familiar with the war tactics. Ninety percent (90%) area of Afghanistan was captured by them very quickly. They imposed Islamic law or the Sharia law as the state law. Pakistan was the first to recognize the Taliban government. As compared to the past there was peace and stability during the Taliban regime.

After 9/11 terrorist attacks on the USA, Taliban were demanded to hand over Osama Bin Laden to them. Denying which brought another devastating war to Afghanistan. The USA and her allies attacked the country with sophisticated technology and modern arsenal. The soil of Afghanistan became a weapon test-ground where everyone had the opportunity to test his own weapon. They had no concern with the consequences. They had no answer to the question –what is the target! And who is killed? Many children were killed, many wounded and many affected psychologically. Many of them flew to neighbouring countries to find shelter. A huge number of came to Pakistan as refugees. Some of them had to find shelter in Iran and other neighbouring countries.

Strategic importance of Afghanistan

The main cause behind the instability in Afghanistan is the involvement of neighbouring states and world powers. They want to grind their own axis by establishing puppet governments to take advantages of the geo-strategic and geo-political importance of Afghanistan and have an access to the energy rich CARs. The USA wants to make strong position in Afghanistan to contain Russia, China and Iran. But on the other hand want a permanent air base to explore the central Asian resources[4]. Afghanistan is a gateway which every state wants to use on his own style. During the last century it had been a focal point between USSR and British India at last an agreement was reached between the two which gave it the status of a buffer state.

In 1947, after the partition of India cold war started between the two super powers[5]. When USSR attacked Afghanistan, the USA had a policy to stop them on the Pak-Afghan border. She succeeded in her antagonistic designs to stop the USSR with the help of Saudi Arabia and Pakistan. The two neighbouring states Pakistan and India were against each other in Afghanistan. Each of them wanted to have their supported government which would guarantee their interests in Afghanistan.

The New Great Game

Since long, India has been using the Afghan soil for her own interests. She wants to reach the energy rich CAR's. Pakistan has an advantage over India because it borders Afghanistan. Being landlocked Afghanistan depends on Pakistan's Sea ports for mobility and trade. Gwadar port and Pak China Economic Corridor (PCEC) will be equally beneficial to Central Asian countries and Afghanistan. Pakistan is also working on a motorway project from Gawader to Peshawar then Torkhum and Kandahar to provide transit trade facilities to Afghanistan and Central Asian Republics. On the other side India made Iranian port Charbahar functioning. Iran through an agreement has given Charbahar port to India for ten year lease. Also a 300 km road from Charbahar to Afghanistan is constructed.

With the advent of USA and NATO a new great game has been started in Afghanistan. Saleem Safi an anchor person and journalist in Pakistan called the situation as the game of Buzkhashi[6]. He compares Afghanistan's situation to this game of Buzkashi and calls it a great game[7]. In which all the countries involved are trying to fulfill their interests by exploiting Afghanistan. That is why Afghanistan becomes so important for the world powers. Afghanistan is located amidst of Central Asia, South Asia and Far East which increases its significance several times inside and outside the region. Afghanistan is also positioned at the crossroads of three most important powers of Asia Iran, Pakistan and China while the other two major powers Russia and India are located at a short distance from Afghanistan which makes it exposed to the outside interference[8].

No state in its neighbourhood near or far is ready to permit other states to achieve dominance in Afghanistan. Such behaviour has destroyed greater part of Afghanistan. Blame for much of the political instability and flight of its people goes to the external powers – struggling hard to attain their strategic, ideological and economic interests in the country. Afghanistan is a pearl in pursuit of which different powers are involved. India, Iran and US factors are very crucial because their involvement is destabilizing Afghanistan, and have direct bearing on Pak-Afghan relations.

Afghan instability, implications for Pakistan

Due to civil wars no group is in a position to form multi ethnic government in which due share is given to everyone on the population basis. Due to the rivalries of different world and regional powers, peace is far away dream in Afghanistan[9]. The last three decades of war has darkened the destiny of Afghanistan people it has also brought destruction and affected the whole region in general and Pakistan in particular. The instability in Afghanistan is impacting the order of life in Pakistan. Due to wars, instability and involvement of world and regional powers, Pakistan has been affected very severely. The details are as followed:

Socio-political impacts: Afghanistan has been facing instability, wars and destruction for the last three decades or so. Afghanistan is not affected alone but the neighbouring countries also do. Pakistan being a front line state affected very severely. Pakistan is a poor country which was not in a position to face such huge bulk of refuges which came to Pakistan due to war. About 3 million people came to Pakistan which is a great challenge for the poor country having fragile economy. The daily cost of the Afghan refugees is $1 million in which half is donated by UN and the remaining half comes from Pakistan. It is raises the debt burden on Pakistan economy[10]. It also affects Pakistan's education, health and infrastructure. When the Russia returned and new government formed, very small number of refugees went back to Afghanistan.

After 9/11, America attacked Afghanistan which generated afresh inflow of refugees to Pakistan. Due to this unchecked inflow of refugees militancy has grown in Pakistan. Pakistan is not in a position to handle such a huge number of refugees and the international community is not seriously supporting Pakistan[11]. Another great impact is that camps of Afghan refugees are becoming nurseries of terrorists and militants which is a great threat to the security of Pakistan.

Since her independence Pakistan has been facings a big enemy in the shape of India. The eastern border has remained insecure due to India war like attitude. She spares no efforts to harm Pakistan and till to date three wars have been fought between the two. Now India is involved infiltrating terrorists into Baluchistan, KPK and other parts of the country to destabilize the law and order situation and posture Pakistan as a failing and terrorist state in the world. The Indian intelligence agency RAW is involved in distributing weapon and financial support to the rebels of BLA (Baluchistan Liberation Army) and BLF (Baluchistan Liberation Front). She has opened consulates in Jalalabad and Kandahar near Pakistani border. Where insurgents are trained and equipped with arms and weaponry to carry out terrorist activities in Baluchistan and KPK[12].

To stop the infiltration of terrorists, militants and extremists Pakistan has deployed more than 80,000 army personals on her western border. Due to long stay of Afghan refugees, Pakistani society has been infected with sectarianism, Kalashnikov culture, drugs, puppy and religious extremism[13]. Sophisticated and conventional weapons were supplied to Afghanistan for war purpose but instead they were supplied to, and used in Pakistan. Camps where Afghan refugees stayed inside Pakistan became places of criminals and gangsters. Due to instability in Afghanistan drug trade is high because on large area of Afghanistan puppy is cultivated.

The income coming from heroine trade is used by terrorist because its cultivation is mostly done in terrorist dwelling areas. According to a report all the region is affected by the drugs and about 800,000 people in Pakistan alone are abused. About 400,000 in five Central Asian countries and almost 2 million in Iran are drug addicts[14].

Insurgency, the rise of TNSM and Taliban

After 9/11 a new wave of terrorism began in Pakistan's tribal areas and KPK. The USA and NATO strikes in Afghanistan made the terrorists and foreigners take shelter in the FATA and tribal area of Pakistan. From these attacks Afghanistan once again became a battle field. Pakistan being a front line state decided to become ally of USA in the war against terrorism. Because of long border consisting mountains and terrain area between the two states, it was easy for the militant to safely escape from Afghanistan to FATA. After this many local group started kidnapping, robbing, looting and even killing innocent people. These developments affected the socio economic and political arena of day today life.

They became so proud that they challenged the writ of government in FATA, tribal areas and Malakand division. In reaction Mulla Fazal Ullah with his group started their activity in Malakand division in the name of Sharia and Islamization. Fazal Ullah called it TNSM (Tehreeke-Nifaz Sharia-e-Muhammadi). Due to this the group was once imagined to have been creating a state within the state. They enforced their laws and installed self-structured courts system which had nothing to do with Islam and Sharia. One who disobeyed and went against their orientation was given severe punishment. These practices greatly disturbed the socio economic and political life of the common people in Malakand division.

TNSM movement of the Taliban destroyed schools, hospitals, colleges, cinemas, robbed banks and centres where people were engaged in their daily businesses. Even they threatened government servants who were working in different departments. The government decided to take military action against the group. In the wake of it a large number of people were internally displaced

(IDP's). They were temporarily settled in the districts of Mardan and Swabi. It was a difficult task but Pakistan done it well [15]. Rail, roads and infrastructure was damaged by it in the entire country. In swat also called "the Switzerland of Pakistan" tourism the main source of economy was greatly affected. Tourists were discouraged by the group activities, so the country tourism industry was damaged.

Prevailing State of Insecurity

These wild acts of terrorism have challenged Pakistan's security, integrity and defense. There is a feeling of insecurity in the mind of every citizen because men of law enforcement agencies and VIP personalities have been targeted by them. For example ex-president Musharraf was attacked, attack was made on ex-PM Shaukat Aziz, and Suicide attack was made on the leader of ANP a political party. An attack was made on Sri Lankan cricket team in Lahore which closed the doors of international cricket on Pakistan.

The ICC cricket world Cup matches were scheduled in India, Pakistan Bangladesh and Sri Lanka but due to security reasons all the cricket matches which were to be played in Pakistan had been cancelled and rescheduled. Pakistan's important places such as GHQ Rawalpindi, PNS Mehran Karachi, Police stations in different parts of the country were targeted by the terrorists. FC training centre, Army public school Peshawar, International Islamic University Islamabad, Manawa police training school and Bacha Khan University Chersada were attacked by terrorists. Terrorism had greatly affected the education and health sectors.

The terrorist had targeted the polio vaccination teams and leady health workers. Many have lost their lives and most of them became disabled. Terrorists attacked the schools in different parts of the country. The education department of KPK has reported that nearly 65% of schools had been affected due to terrorist attacks. Majority of them were girls' schools and colleges and 42% were boys' schools and colleges. Due to which 150,000 students left their education incomplete. Due threats from these groups almost 8000 lady teachers have become jobless[16].

Operation Zarb-e-Azab

To eradicate terrorism from its roots, Pakistan army started operation Zarb-e-Azab in Waziristan Agencies. Due to which millions of its residents were affected and took shelter in plan areas. According to reports 929,859 people migrated from the area and took refuge in camps in Kohat and Banu area. The government provided them with food, medicine and other goods of daily use from its own resources not demanding international community support[17].

The Violations of State's Sovereignty by US Drones

Another serious impact is the violation of sovereignty and integrity of Pakistan by drone attacks, which are carried out by USA in FATA and Waziristan. These drones not only killed the terrorists but also innocent people and children's. Pakistan raised her voice against it at different forums on different occasion. Since 2005 till 2016, 320 drone attacks were made in which 2,806 people killed and 353 injured. The following table shows the number of drone attacks and its impacts: Table 1.

Rise in Sectarian Violence

Another impact is sectarian violence which destabilizes Pakistani society very badly. The terrorists are taking great advantage of Shia and Sunni divide and using it for their own evil gains. This strife is considered to be the fossil of Afghan Jihad. During Soviet invasion Pakistan became safe haven for those elements that had to participate in Afghan Jihad. It was also the beginning of sectarian tussle between Shia and Sunni and other groups.

They started targeting one another places of worships and religious rituals, which affected Pakistani society and outlook very deeply. From sectarian stripes, since 1999 till 2009, some 22,000 Shia became victims of terrorist attacks. Most of these sectarian attacks took place in Kurram agency; Para Chinar, Hungo and Orakzai agency, majority of affected were Shia population[18]. These sectarian attacks not only paralyzed Pakistani society but also created internal security problems. In response to it, the government banned some jihadists groups like Sipah-e-Sahaba,

Sipah-e-Muhammad, Jaish-e-Muhammad, etc. These groups were mainly responsible for sectarian violence. The number one enemy of Pakistan, India took advantage of the situation and used these groups for her own evil designs. India supplied arms and provided financial support to these jihadists to destabilize Pakistan. About 80,000 people have died and thousands injured in the war on terror. Some $70 billion were lost in this war.

Year	Incidents	Killed	Injured
2005	1	1	0
2006	0	0	0
2007	1	20	15
2008	19	156	17
2009	46	536	75
2010	90	831	85+
2011	59	548	52
2012	46	344	37
2013	24	158	29
2014	19	122	26
2015	14	85	17
2016	1	5	0
Total	320	2806	353+

Source: http://www.satp.org/satporgtp/countries/pakistan/ database/ Droneattack.htm

Table 1: Drone attack in Pakistan: 2005-2016.

Another very affected city from terrorism is Karachi, which is economic and social hub of Pakistan. About 60% of our revenue comes from Karachi. But for the last two decades or so, Karachi has become a battle ground for different ethnic groups like, MQM (Muhajir Qaumi Movement), Pashtuns and Sindhi. All these groups are against each other and target killing each other workers. MQM had strong hold in Metropolitan Karachi. Like all other cities, Karachi is also affected from war on terror. Many gangster groups have strengthened their positions.

TTP and other terrorist organizations are found involved there. They kidnap people, doing bank robberies, street extortion and ransom. Some foreigner elements are also involved in terrorist activities in Karachi. NATO used the Karachi port for transportation of weapons and other equipment's of their forces in Afghanistan. Some NATO containers were stolen by terrorists containing weapons, which they used for their terrorist activities in Karachi. Due large population, its residents have been limited to their residences due to terrorist activities. Anything can happen at any time there, one would see roads are blocked, and someone is killed by someone unknown. The ransom and money raised from illegal means is used in these kinds of activities which aim at terrifying the government to stop operations against these groups in different areas.

Due to long lasted war, insurgency, bomb blasts and suicide attacks, Pakistani people have become psychological patients. Majority of the people are suffering from stress and strain. Some have become mentally disturbed because their relatives were killed in bomb blasts and suicide attacks. Most of them become disable after survival due to which street begging is rising. Many of them are children who have lost their parents and now having no resources cannot get education and striving hard for their livelihood. The estimates and analysis drawn from the available data suggests that Pakistan has suffered more than Afghanistan from the war against Al-Qaeda and terrorism.

Economic impacts: Peace and stability is the primary concern of every country. If there is peace and stability then the economy will be ok, more people, companies, will come and invest there. This will raise the life standard of the native people and employment opportunities would increase. Literacy rate will rise and people life standard go up. On the other hand a country which is facing long term war and instability then there will be no development and the infrastructure will be destroyed. A huge bulk of people would migrate to other countries to save their lives. Same was the case with Afghanistan, when Russia attacked on it; about 3 million migrated towards Pakistan. It had a great economic burden for economically weak state, almost unprepared to face this challenge. The daily cost of the Afghan refugees was $1 million, in which, half was donated by UN and half by the government of Pakistan. It raised the debt burden on Pakistan economy. It also affected education, health and infrastructure. The Afghan government refused to receive them back due to lack of resources. When the Russia withdrew, new government was formed in Afghanistan but only a small number got back.

Refugees Influx

After 9/11 a new dilemma in the shape of refugees' influx started. In the shape of refugees some militants also entered Pakistan which disturbed law and order situation in the country. Pakistan was not in a position to handle this new inflow of refugees without international community support. This also affected the development and growth rate in all sectors of economy. For the last three decades, Pakistan has been paying a huge price in men and material. The instability in the neighbouring country has created security challenges for Pakistan. A huge amount of economy is spent on war on terror. This situation is impacting the export order around the world. Due to which Pakistan failed to meet the requirements of world business community. Pakistan has not been in a position to meet her competitors in the world market.

The export targets fixed in the annual budgets is not met which slows down the economic growth rate of the country. In this critical situation, the world business community had shifted their capital and businesses to the economically stable countries of the region. This affected the entire economic fabric, and inflation rate went high. This instability cause unemployment, and jobless youth is produced, which is a great burden on the fragile economy. Our population consists of about 80,000 million youth but the government had scarce resources to handle them. In developed countries of the world such a huge number of youth (if skilled) is a sign of development but in Pakistan it is a sign of underdevelopment. Due to governments' inability to provide jobs to them, they can easily be deceived the by terrorists for their evil designs.

The ministry of industries and some autonomous bodies of provincial governments presented a report which shows the yearly losses in Pakistan due Afghan instability (Table 2). From this report we can conclude that from 14 years war on terror Pakistan has lost $106.98 billion which is a big amount for an economy facing instability. Pakistan needed to extend its resource base, to enhance economic growth rate. Terrorism has been destroying Pakistan physical and human capital since 2001. Terrorism destroyed our health, education, water sanitation, medical care centers and infrastructure which are basic elements for economic development. Due to it trade activities becomes limited and economic growth slowing down. It also restricted the Foreign Direct Investment (FDI).

Years	$ Billion	Rs Billion	% Changes
2001-02	2.67	163.9	-
2002-03	2.75	160.8	3
2003-04	2.93	168.8	6.7
2004-05	3.41	202.4	16.3
2005-06	3.99	238.6	16.9
2006-07	4.67	283.2	17.2
2007-08	6.94	434.1	48.6
2008-09	9.18	720.6	32.3
2009-10	13.56	1136.4	47.7
2010-11	23.77	2037.3	75.3
2011-12	11.98	1052.8	-49.6
2012-13	9.97	964.24	-16.8
2013-14	6.63	681.68	-33.5
2014-15	4.53	457.93	-31.7
Total	107	8702.8	

Source: Report presented by the (MoF), Ministry of Interior, Ministry of Foreign Affairs and Joint Ministerial Group. Table 2: Estimated Losses in Pakistan (2001-2015).

Public development funds are used in purchasing sophisticated and modern weaponry to meet the challenge of terrorism. The terrorist activities have far reaching impacts on the economic system. It not only creates social problems but also economic problems. Due to terrorism and less economic output our GDP dropped from 7.5 to 1.6 in 2010. To fulfill the annual budget deficits the government has to take foreign loans from international monetary organizations, like, IMF and World Bank with high interest rates which is also weakening our economy. The war on terror Coalition Support Fund (CSF) given by USA cannot be spent on developmental activities.

Due to terrorism FATA is very severely affected where almost 60% people are living below the poverty line. Education ratio there is very low as compared to other areas, and female education ratio is 0%. Another impact is drug trafficking and smuggling of daily life commodities from Afghanistan to Pakistan. They are cheaply available in Bara market in Peshawar. Which is duty free and cheaper compared to Pakistani products, this also impacts the state of economy. Karachi is the major contributor of Pakistan's economy, which produces 60% of the total budget. Due to sea ports, it plays a vital role in Pakistan's economy. But for the last two decades Karachi has become a terrorist zone which not only affects the social and economic life of its masses but also the economy of the country. Karachi is economic power hub; people come to work here from different parts of the country.

In the after math of 9/11, it is also under the sway of terrorists. Many terrorists came to Karachi and started to receive Bata, bank robbery; kidnapping and ransom were taken from the business community. Due to risk and terror they shifted their businesses to other countries of the region. The money collected through these means is used in terrorist activities. The activities are also supported by some leading political parties for their own interests. In result of all that goes on either in the sub rubs or in the metropolitans, beside all, severely impact the state of Pakistan's economy.

Conclusion

Pakistan is the neighbouring country having very close and brotherly relations with Afghanistan. She hosts almost 3 million Afghanistan refugees. A stable prosperous and developed Afghanistan is in the greater interests of Pakistan. To use Afghanistan as a gateway to Central Asian Republics Pakistan wants cordial relations with Afghanistan. She wants a friendly government in Afghanistan which could guarantee her interests inside and outside the country. Pakistan wants peace in Afghanistan which would make possible the withdrawal of US and NATO forces from Afghanistan. The stability in Afghanistan will pave the ways for the return refugees which are a big burden on her economy. The instability creates a lot of problem for Pakistan socio, economic and political sectors. A number of criminals and extremists come to Pakistan in the shape of refugees, which is disturbing the internal peace and stability of Pakistan. Pakistan faces joblessness, inflation, no foreign investment. Therefore, for the stability, peace and development in Pakistan, a stable and peaceful Afghanistan is a prerequisite.

Courtesy: Mohammad (Department of Political Science, Hazara University Mansehra, Pakistan-2016). Instability in Afghanistan: Implications for Pakistan. J Pol Sci Pub Aff 4: 213. doi:10.4172/2332-0761.1000213. Journal of Political Sciences & Public Affairs, The Journal provides the Quarterly publication of articles in all areas related to Political Science, Public Affairs, Law and order, Political Regime, Public Awareness, Public Health, Public Interest, Public Policy, Political Economy, Trade Policy etc.

Notes to Chapters

Chapter 1: The Changing Fight of Indian Intelligence Agencies: Jihadism in Kashmir, Reforms, and Bureaucratic Stakeholdrism

1   50 years of R&AW. Is India's Foreign Spy Agency Dreaded or Dreadful: Satyen K. Bordoloi, 21 September 2018. http://www.sify.com/news/50-years-of-r-aw-is-india-s-foreign-spy-agency-dreaded-or-dreadful-news-columns-sjvjvebjcaaij.html

2   RAW: India's External Intelligence Agency, Jayshree Bajoria, 07 November 2008, Council on Foreign Relations.

3   Intelligence failure and reforms, Stinath Raghavan, Paper presented in Indian Seminar in 2009 http://www.india-seminar.com/2009/599/599_srinath_raghavan.htm

4   After Uri, a look at why intelligence failure happens? 18 Soldiers dead in Uri, marking one of the worst Indian intelligence failures of recent times. Pradip R. Sagar, The New Indian Express 24 September 2016. http://www.newindianexpress.com/magazine/2016/sep/24/Quicksand-of-espionage-why-intelligence-failures-happen-1524631.html

5   The peril of Prediction: Indian Intelligence and the Kargil Crisis, Prem Mahadevan Paper No-29, 2011, Centre for Land Warfare Studies India

6   India's Intelligence War in Afghanistan, Musa Khan Jalalzai, Daily Times, 21 September 2016

7   Investigating Crisis: South Asia's Lessons, Evolving Dynamics and Trajectories. Intelligence Strategic Assessment, and Decision Process Deficits. Saikat Datta, the Stimson Centre, 2018

8   Ibid

9   Ibid

208

10 Policy Report No-3: Why Intelligence Fails? Janani Krishnaswami, The Hindu centre for Politics and Public Policy, 2013

11 Ibid

12 The Making of the Kargil Disaster, Nasim Zehra, Daily Dawn 02 Jul, 2018

13 A Case for Intelligence Reforms in India. IDSA Taskforce Report, Institute of Defense Studies and Analysis, New Delhi. 2012

14 India's spy Agencies more Toothless than ever. India has been forced to rely for information on Legal Requests to Service Providers-Responses to which often arrive too late to be of Use. Praveen Swami, Indian Express, 01 December 2014, https://indianexpress.com/article/india/india-others/indias-spy-agencies-more-toothless-than-ever/

15 Pervez Musharraf Crossed LoC before Kargil War. V K. Singh praises ex Pak army Chief's Courage. The Times of India, 01 February 2013, https://timesofindia.indiatimes.com/world/pakistan/Pervez-Musharraf-crossed-LoC-before-Kargil-war-V-K-Singh-praises-ex-Pak-army-chiefs-courage/articleshow/182

16 The Kargil Adventure was four men Show. General Khaleeq Kiani. Dawn 28 January 2013

17 ibid

18 The Terror challenge in South Asia and Prospect of Regional cooperation. Anand Kumar. Institute for Defense Studies and Analysis. 2012, India

19 Pakistani terrorists made a big mistake. Prime Minister Modi, 15 February, 2019 Asia Times

20 Has The Pulwama Attack Shown An Intelligence Failure? Anurag Paul, 15 February 2019

21 India's Intelligence Agencies: In Need of Reform and Oversight. Manoj Joshi and Pushan Das, Observer Issue Brief-98, July 2015

22 Asma Khalid 12 February 2018, South Asian Journal

Chapter 2: The Jaish-e-Mohammed, Lashkar-e-Toiba, and Pakistan's Intelligence War

1   Lal Khan, Daily Times 18 February, 2019

2   An Idea or a Threat? Islamic State Jammu & Kashmir, AMIRA Jadoon Combating Terrorism Centre, February, 09, 2018

3   Ibid

4   22 February 2019, Dawn reported Pakistan's Director General (DG) Inter-Services Public Relations (ISPR), Maj Gen Asif Ghafoor resentment against India on the Pulwama incident.

5   26 Feb 2019 India launched air strikes against militants in Pakistani territory, in a major escalation of tensions between the two countries. The government said strikes targeted a training camp of the Jaish-e-Mohammad (JeM) group in Balakot.

6   The News International on 02 March 2019

7   Pakistani deep state miscalculates on India, Prakash Katoch, Asia Times, 01 March 2019

8   27 February, 2019, the Hindu Newspaper in its editorial comment reported the resolve of the Indian government: The government said all other options had been exhausted in making Islamabad keep its commitments since 2004 on curbing the activities of groups like the JeM.

9   The Hindu, 27 February 2019

10 In the Line of Fire, Pervez Musharraf, Simon and Schuster, 04 Sep 2008

11 Praveen Swami, "Pakistan and the Lashkar's Jihad in India," The Hindu, 09 December, 2008.

12 Stephen Tankel, "Lashkar-e-Taiba, Mumbai, and the ISI," Foreign Policy, 20 May, 2011.

13 The Future of Intelligence Vikram Sood, from The New Arthashastra: A Security Strategy for India, edited by Gurmeet Kanwal, HarperCollins India.

14 Times of India, September 15, 2013

15   Times of India, September 15, 2013

Chapter 3: India's Intelligence Agencies: In Need of Reform and Oversight. Manoj Joshi and Pushan Das

1   The National Intelligence Strategy of the United States of America, 2014, p. 2

2   Satish Chandra, "National Security System and Reform, "India's National Security Annual Review 2005, p 211

3   The IB's manpower is of the order of 25,000 plus personnel, but it actually needs double that number, primarily among intelligence collectors and technical staff. R&AW has some 9,000 personnel, but only about 3 per cent of these are posted abroad. Its officer cadre is even smaller than that. The issue of manpower actually runs across the intelligence services, whether it is the JIC, DIA or the economic intelligence agencies.

4   "Boundless Informant: the NSA's se. Sandeep Joshi, "India gets ready to roll out cyber snooping agency," The Hindu, June 10, 2013; Reuters, "India sets up nationwide snooping programme to tap your emails, phones", June 20, 2013. A smaller system called Network Traffic Analysis or NETRA system has been around since 2009 accessing Indian cyber traffic for the IB. Praveen Swami, "Hands tied on tech, India's digital eye is half shut," Indian Express, August 11, cret tool to track global surveillance data," http://www.guardian. co.uk/   world/interactive/2013/jun/08/boundless-informant-nsa-full-text.

5   2014http://indianexpress.com/article/india/india-others/hands-tied-on-tech-indias-digital-eye-is-halfshut/ 99/. The big problem Swami, however, points out, is that lack of decryption skills results in a great deal of the intercepted material remaining unused.

6   Rashmi Rajput, "Maharashtra ATS contests Delhi police claim on IM operative," The Hindu September 9, 2014 http://www.thehindu. com/news/national/maharashtra-ats-contests-delhi-police-claim-on-indianmujahideen-operative/article6391728.ece; Praveen Swami, "Pressure for results skewing terror investigations?" The Hindu September 15, 2011http://www.thehindu.com/news/national/pressure-for-results-skewingterror-investigations/article2456267.ece

7   Soumen Dutta, "Burdwan Blasts: Is Bengal Police Shielding Ac-

cused," Hindustan Times October 8, 2014 http://www.hindustan-times.com/india-news/west-bengal-police-shielding-burdwan-bombers/article1-1272828.aspx

Chapter 4: Why Intelligence Fails. Janani Krishnaswamy

1   Interview with the Minister, New Delhi, August 6, 2013.

2   Sources privy to such kind of information say the Indian government will spend approximately Rs.6000 crores on intelligence reforms over a five-year-period between 2010 and 2015.

3   Prem Mahadevan, 'Politics of Counterterrorism in India: Strategic intelligence and national security in South Asia. (I.B.Tauris: London), p22

4   Name withheld for protecting identity

5   See Anthony Glees, 'The Future of Intelligence Studies,' Journal of Strategic Security, 6 (5): 124-127, last accessed on September 5, 2013, at: http://scholarcommons.usf.edu/jss/vol6/iss5/15

6   The allegations listed above were pointed out by the Ram Pradhan Inquiry Committee.

7   It is because of the secretive nature in revealing sufficient information about the nature of intelligence that I was in no position to develop a database of past failures or identify a pattern in such failures of the intelligence community.

8   Indian Express, The intelligence failure: the buck stops nowhere, May 14, 2012, last accessed on September 15, 2013 on http://newindianexpress.com/nation/article9991.ece

9   Reuters, 'Post-9/11 US intelligence reforms take root, problems remain,' September 8, 2011, last accessed on September 15, 2013 at http://www.reuters.com/article/2011/09/08/us-sept11-intelligencei-dUSTRE78714D20110908.

10   Interview with former additional secretary, Cabinet Secretariat and R&AW, Jayadeva Ranade, New Delhi, August 8, 2013

11   CNN, 'Why FBI and CIA didn't connect the dots,' May 2, 2013, last accessed on September 18, 2013 at: http://edition.cnn.com/2013/05/02/opinion/schneier-boston-bombing/index.html

12 Interview with terrorism studies expert, Ajai Sahni, New Delhi, August 7, 2013

13 Prem Mahadevan skilfully dealt with the tricky subject of policy failures and political perspectives in intelligence in his book Politics of Counterterrorism in India.

14 As a former director of Intelligence Bureau points out in an interview, 'Success stories often go unreported because intelligence agencies often cannot reveal other spies.' In fact, 'only rogue agencies disclose'. (Name withheld for protecting identity)

15 On the basis of revelations made by alleged Indian Mujahedeen terrorist Sayed Maqbool, the Delhi Police Special Cell had issued a warning in October 2013 that the banned outfit planned to target the Buddhist shrines in Bodh Gaya. The police claimed to have shared intelligence about a fidayeen (suicide) attack with the state agencies concerned nearly nine months earlier. There were at least two alerts issued to Bihar within the preceding three months warning of terror attacks in the light of the ethnic conflict in Myanmar. However, the local intelligence agencies and the government in Bihar were accused of failing to act on available inputs.

16 Henry Kissinger's article on Washington Post, 'Lessons from four failures,' August 16, 2004, last accessed on September 18, 2013 at http://www.henryakissinger.com/articles/wp081604.html

17 See Wilson John, 'Intelligence agencies in India: Need for a public interface,' ORF Issue Brief: 28, June 2011, last accessed on September 15. 2013, at http://www.observerindia.com/cms/sites/orfonline/modules/issuebrief/attachments/ORFIss28_1309513248636.pdf

18 See Danish Sheik, 'Locating India's intelligence agencies – in a democratic framework,' ORF Issue Brief, last accessed on September 15, 2013

19 See Anand, Vinod, 'An integrated and joint approach towards defence intelligence,' Strategic Analysis, Vol XXIV/8,(2000), p408-409

20 Locating India's intelligence agencies – in a democratic framework, p6

21 Ibid

22 See Kanti Bajpai, 'Internal Security: The Indian Way,' Strategic Analysis, 34:5, 697-701

23 See C. Christine Fair, 'Prospects for effective internal security reforms in India,' commonwealth & Comparative Politics, 50:2, 145-170

24 See Praveen Swami, 'Stalled reforms,' The Hindu, May 9,2003, last accessed on September 15, 2013, at:http://www.hindu.com/thehindu/thscrip/print.pl?file=20030509002108700.htm&date=fl2009/&prd=fline&

25 Interview with Sahni, New Delhi, 7 August 2013

26 The paper examines the important strides in intelligence reform that India has undertaken in the aftermath of Kargil 1999 and 26/11. The two cases have been considered not just because of the intensity of the attacks, but because of the controversial reforms that were made following it.

27 The terminology is adopted from the usage of terrorism studies expert Sahni who referred to sweeping organizational reforms as 'meta-institutional'.

28 Making an observation about the state of reform making in India, former director of R&AW Sood said in an interview that 'reforms in the country have often focused on controlling the system, rather than addressing the deep-seated problems within the intelligence agencies'. Reforms, he insists, should be addressed 'from the very bottom focusing on recruitment, training and curriculum for intelligence analysts'.

29 For instance, V. Balachandran, a co-author of the Ram Pradhan Committee report, noted in an article entitled 'The signal through the noise- NCTC's role in sifting through the intelligence glut,' published in Indian Express, that the NCTC is a 'needless irritant on Centre-State relations'. Further, he called the former home minister P. Chidambaram's proposal on NCTC — with investigation and operations responsibility—as 'overzealous'. During an interaction on September 5, 2013, he said that he had written several times earlier that the original version of US NCTC created in 2004 which P. Chidambaram and his team studied in 2009 did not have this role.

30 Interview with Sahni, New Delhi, 7 August 2013

31 Former additional secretary (R&AW) Kalyan K. Mitra highlights the impromptu nature of intelligence reforming in India at a workshop on 'Intelligence Failures in the USA, UK and Russia: Lessons for India,'

Observer Research Foundation at New Delhi on October 20, 2004, last accessed on Aug 28, 2013, at: http://orfonline.org/cms/export/orfonline/modules/report/attachments/intlrep_1162888665766.pdf

32 Interview with a former Intelligence Bureau director, New Delhi, August 8, 2013 (Name withheld for protecting identity).

33 See Srinath Raghavan, Intelligence failures and reforms, Seminar, July 2008, last accessed on August 23, 2013, at:http://www.india-seminar.com/2009/599/599_srinath_raghavan.htm

34 The Hindu, 'A big blow to Indian Mujahideen's bomb-making, recruitment skills,' August 30, 2013, last accessed on September 28, 2013 at http://www.thehindu.com/news/national/a-big-blow-to-indian-mujahideens-bombmakingrecruitment-skills/article5072449.ece

35 Interview with former, IB Director, Delhi, August 8, 2013 (Name withheld for protecting identity)

36 Ibid

37 Interview with Sood, Delhi, August 8, 2013

38 See Anthony Glees, 'The Future of Intelligence Studies,' Journal of Strategic Security, 6 (5): 124-127, last accessed on September 5, 2013, at: http://scholarcommons.usf.edu/jss/vol6/iss5/15

39 See Kargil Review Committee Report (henceforth KRC report)

40 See Prem Mahadevan, 'The perils of prediction: Indian intelligence and the Kargil crisis,' Centre for Land Warfare Studies, No. 29, (2011)

41 Intelligence Failures in the USA, UK and Russia: - Lessons for India, ORF Workshop, New Delhi.

42 See Srinath Raghavan's essay on 'Intelligence failures and reforms' that throws light on some of the pressing issues of the intelligence community by drawing on the history of intelligence failures in India. In particular, it examines why New Delhi failed to anticipate the 'surprise attacks' by China in 1962 and Pakistan in 1999.

43 Kapil Kak, 'India-China war of 1962: Higher defence management: Then and now,' CLAWS, (2012), accessed on August 28, 2013 at http://strategicstudyindia.blogspot.in/2013/01/india-china-war-of-1962.html

44 See Srinath Raghavan, 'Intelligence failures and reforms,' Seminar

45 See B.N. Mullik, 'My Years With Nehru: The Chinese Betrayal,' Allied Publishers, Bombay, 970, pp. 329-30.

46 KRC report

47 The review is based on a series of news reports by The Hindu

48 Interview with Manish Tewari

49 India Today, "Mumbai blasts: Chidambaram denies intelligence failure," July 15, 2011, last accessed on September 28, 2013 at http://indiatoday.intoday.in/story/mumbai-blasts-chidambaram-denies-intelligencefailure/1/144890.html

50 CNBC TV18, "Mumbai blasts: Failure of intelligence?" July 15, 2011, last access on September 28, 2013 :http://www.moneycontrol.com/news/current-affairs/mumbai-blastsfailureintelligence_565777.html?utm_source=ref_article

51 In his concluding remarks at Wednesday's Chief Ministers' conference on internal security, home minister, Sushilkumar Shinde had said that a decision on setting up of the controversial National Counter Terrorism Centre will be taken only after full consensus.

52 Interviews with V. Balachandran, Mumbai, August 9, 2013

53 Interview with former additional secretary, Cabinet Secretariat and R&AW, Mr.Jayadeva Ranade, and former director, R&AW, Vikram Sood, New Delhi, August 8, 2013

54 Interview with Sood

55 Interview with Ranade

56 Interview with a former director, IB, New Delhi, August 7, 2013

57 Interviews with Sood and former (unnamed) IB director

58 Interview with Sahni

59 Interview with Sood

60 Interview with Sood and D.R.Karthikeyan

61 Name withheld for protecting identity

62 Times of India, 'Indian intelligence system needs urgent reforms,'

September 15, 2013, last accessed on September 25, 2013 at http://
blogs.timesofindia.indiatimes.com/ChanakyaCode/entry/indian-
intelligence-system-needsurgent-Reforms

63 Ranade pointed out how the inefficient working of MAC was apparent during the 26/11

64 This statement was also verified by K.V.Thomas during an interview, where he said, 'Out of the total of 15,000 intelligence personnel
in the country, hardly 300 personnel have been deployed towards
counterterrorism intelligence.'

65 Interviews with K.V.Thomas.

66 Sahni, in an interview, noted that the chowkidar system set-up in
colonial India is no more active.

67 David Kahn, "A Historical Theory of Intelligence," Intelligence and
National Security, Vol. 16, No. 3, (September 2001): 79–92.

68 John A. Gentry, Assessing intelligence performance, The Oxford
handbook of national security intelligence,

69 Roberta Wohlstetter's doctrinal conclusions in her classic book Roberta Wohlstetter, 'Pearl Harbor: Warning and Decision. Stanford
University Press, 1962.

70 Richard K. Betts, 'Analysis, War, and Decision: Why Intelligence
Failures Are Inevitable', World Politics 31/1 (Oct. 1978) p.88.

71 See Prem Mahadevan, 'Politics of Counterterrorism in India: Strategic intelligence and national security in South Asia. I.B.Tauris: London

72 See Charles Cogan, 'Hunters not gatherers: intelligence in the twenty-first century', Intelligence and National Security, Vol. XVIII/4
(2003), p42

73 See Michael Herman, 'Ethics and Intelligence after September 2001,'
Intelligence and National Security, Vol. 19, Iss. 2, (2004)

74 Glenn Hastedt, 'The Politics of Intelligence and the Politicization of
Intelligence: The American Experience,' Intelligence and National
Security, Vol. 28, Issue 1, (2013), last accessed on August 28, 2013

75 For instance, Amy Zegart points to bureaucratic resistance to reform
and structural flaws within the US intelligence community as the

main causal factor that prevent them from averting 9/11.

76 See Peter Gill, 'Reasserting control: Recent changes in the oversight of the UK intelligence community,' Intelligence and National Security, Vol. 11, 2, (1996)

77 See Stephen Marrin, 'Revisiting Intelligence and Policy: Problems with Politicization and Receptivity,' Intelligence and National Security, Vol. 28, Issue1, (2013)

78 See Anthony Glees, 'The Future of Intelligence Studies,' Journal of Strategic Security, 6 (5): 124-127. Available at: http://scholarcommons.usf.edu/jss/vol6/iss5/15

79 See Anthony Glees, 'The Future of Intelligence Studies,' Journal of Strategic Security Available at: http://scholarcommons.usf.edu/jss/vol6/iss5/15

80 Loch K. Johnson and Allison M.Shelton, 'Thoughts on the State of Intelligence Studies: A Survey Report,' Intelligence and National Security, (2013), Vol. 28, No. 1, 109–120

82 After Mumbai – India's response, RUSI

83 See Vinod Anand, 'An integrated and joint approach towards defence intelligence,' Strategic Analysis, Vol XXIV/8, (2000), p408-409

84 Interview with V. Balachandran, Mumbai

85 Interview with V. Balachandran, Mumbai

86 As pointed out by the Ram Pradhan Committee Report, 'Intelligence arbitration - a vital stage in intelligence processing that includes analysis and appreciation to operational units - is neglected.'

87 Interview with Sood

88 Srinath Raghavan, 'Intelligence failures and reforms,' available at http://www.indiaseminar.   com/2009/599/599_srinath_raghavan. htm, accessed on July 01, 2013

89 This typology draws on Richard K. Betts, Enemies of Intelligence: Knowledge and Power in American National Security, Columbia University Press, New York, 2007.

90 Michael Warner, 'Introduction: Wanted: A definition of intelligence' in 'Secret Intelligence – A Reader' (eds.) Christopher Andrew Rich-

ard J. Aldrich, Wesley K. Wark (Routledge, 2009), p1 91 Troy, Thomas, The "correct" definition of intelligence, International Journal of Intelligence and Counterintelligence, Vol V/4, (1992), p.433, 443, 449

92   Michael Warner, 'Introduction: Wanted: A definition of intelligence' in 'Secret Intelligence – A Reader' (eds.) Christopher Andrew Richard J. Aldrich, Wesley K. Wark (Routledge, 2009), p3

93   Sood says this is also why scholars have been reluctant to be associated with intelligence activity in the country.

94   Stephen Marrin, 'Preventing Intelligence failures by learning from the past', International Journal of Intelligence and Counterintelligence, 17:655-672

95   The questions were drafted based on several interactions with former intelligence personnel.

96   Interviews with several past and serving intelligence personnel

97   This kind of approach is recommended because as strategic affairs expert, Mr.Manoj Joshi, says, 'Any attack indicates a failure. Is it a failure to act on actionable information or a failure of no intelligence at all? The nature of intelligence alert becomes crucial in determining the kind of failure to avert a terrorist attack.'

98   See Amy Zegart, 'September 11 and the Adaptation Failure of U.S. Intelligence Agencies,' International Security 29, no. 4 (Spring 2005): 78-111.

99   The method is derived from Amy Zegart (Spring 2005)

100 In this policy paper, I insist on taking a very balanced approach in categorising failures and holding particular stakeholders accountable. While some (unnamed) intelligence officials are against the terminology of 'intelligence failure,' greater circumspection should be employed to the term 'policy failure' too.

101 Interview with V. Balachandran, Mumbai

102 Ranade is known to have been involved in making an in-depth analysis of the 26/11 attack in its immediate aftermath. The report remains classified, and was therefore not shared with the author.

103 Such a deduction was made based on V. Balachandran's comments

who observed thenewness in terrorist tactics – the kind that was not witnessed in India before 26/11 happened.

104 Interview with Ranade

105 E-mail interactions with a source privy to such kind of information.

106 Mohan Singh, 'Failure of intelligence coordination - Did we learn anything from 26/11,' Centre for Land Warfare Studies, January 25, 2011, accessed on September 25, 2013 at http://www.claws.in/Failure-of-intelligencecoordination---Did-we-learn-anything-from-26/11-Centre-for-Land-Warfare-Studies.html

107 Interview with a former IB director (name withheld for protecting identity) 108Mohan Singh, 'Failure of intelligence coordination - Did we learn anything from 26/11,' Centre for Land Warfare Studies, January 25, 2011, accessed on September 25, 2013 at http://www.claws.in/Failure-of-intelligencecoordination---Did-we-learn-anything-from-26/11-Centre-for-Land-Warfare-Studies.html

109 I make the following assumptions: (1) Strengthening the intelligence apparatus can help avert failures in future. (2) Intelligence scholars can have a major influence over intelligence policy making. (3) Political perceptions about policy issues are created based on sound academic analysis.

111 By 'reliable scholars', I refer to the ones who are capable of dispassionately studying policy issues and making arguments based on 'facts rather than opinion'. In other words, intelligence agencies should consider sharing such limited information as listed above, with a set of objective and ethical researchers who also preserve the rights of those being researched.

112 I could not develop such a trend chart for this paper, because of the unavailability of such kind of information.

113 Locating India's intelligence agencies – in a democratic framework

114 ORF workshops on intelligence failures

Bibliography (Chapter 4)

Intelligence Review Committee Reports

1. From Surprise to reckoning: Kargil Review Committee report, Executive summary, July 29, 1999, available at http://www.fas.org/news/

india/2000/25indi1.htm

2. Report of High Level Enquiry Committee (HLEC) on 26/11, April 18, 2009, available at http://timesofindia.indiatimes.com/photo/5289981.cms

3. Standing Committee on Defence report (2006-07), Ministry of Defence, July, 2007, Lok Sabha secretariat, available at http://idsa.in/system/files/Standing%20Committee%20on%20Defence%20 22nd%20R eport%202006%202007.pdf

Policy Papers Relating to Indian Intelligence

1. Danish Sheik, 'Locating India's intelligence agencies – in a democratic framework,' ORF Issue Brief.

2. Kanti Bajpai, 'Internal Security: The Indian Way,' Strategic Analysis, 34:5, 697-701

3. Kapil Kak, 'India-China war of 1962: Higher defence management: Then and now,' CLAWS, (2012), accessed on August 28, 2013 at http://strategicstudyindia.blogspot.in/2013/01/india-china-war-of-1962.html

4. Mohan Singh, 'Failure of intelligence coordination – did we learn anything from 26/11,' Centre for Land Warfare Studies, January 25, 2011, available at http://www.claws.in/Failure-of-intelligence-coordination---Did-we-learn-anything-from-26/11-Centre-for-Land-Warfare-Studies.html

5. B.N. Mullik, 'My Years With Nehru: The Chinese Betrayal,' Allied Publishers, Bombay, 1970, pp. 329-30.

6. Prem Mahadevan, 'The perils of prediction: Indian intelligence and the Kargil crisis,' Centre for Land Warfare Studies, No. 29, (2011)

7. Srinath Raghavan, 'Intelligence failures and reforms,' available at http://www.indiaseminar.   com/2009/599/599_srinath_raghavan.htm, accessed on July 01, 2013

8. Vinod Anand, 'An integrated and joint approach towards defence intelligence,' Strategic Analysis, Vol XXIV/8, (2000), p408-409

9. Wilson John, 'Intelligence agencies in India: Need for a public interface,' ORF Issue Brief: June 28, 2011, available at http://www.observerindia.com/cms/sites/orfonline/modules/issuebrief/attach-

ments/ ORFIss28_1309513248636.pdf

Books

1. Prem Mahadevan, 'Politics of Counter-terrorism in India: Strategic intelligence and national security in South Asia. (London:I.B.Tauris,2009)

2. Peter Gill, Stephen Marrin, and Mark Phythian, eds., 'Intelligence Theory: Key Questions and Debates.' (New York: Routledge Press, 2009)

3. R.N.Kulkarni, 'Sin of National Conscience. (Mysore: Kritagnya Publication, 2004) 49

4. B.Raman, 'Intelligence: Past, present and future.' (New Delhi: Lancer Publishers, 2002) Media reports

Media Reports

1. Indian Express, 'the intelligence failure: the buck stops nowhere,' May 14, 2012, last accessed on September 15, 2013 on http://newindianexpress.com/nation/article9991.ece

2. Reuters, 'Post-9/11 US intelligence reforms take root, problems remain,' September 8, 2011, last accessed on September 15, 2013 at http://www.reuters.com/article/2011/09/08/us-sept11-intelligencei-dUSTRE78714D20110908.

3. CNN, 'Why FBI and CIA didn't connect the dots,' May 2, 2013, last accessed on September 18, 2013 at http://edition.cnn.com/2013/05/02/opinion/schneier-bostonbombing/ index.html

4. Washington Post, 'Lessons from four failures,' August 16, 2004, last accessed on September 18, 2013 at http://www.henryakissinger.com/articles/wp081604.html

5. The Hindu, 'Stalled reforms,' May 9, 2003, available at http://www.hindu.com/thehindu/thscrip/print.pl?file=20030509002108700.htm&date=fl2009/&prd=fline

6. India Today, 'Mumbai blasts: Chidambaram denies intelligence failure,' http://indiatoday.intoday.in/story/mumbai-blasts-chidambaram-denies-intelligencefailure/1/144890.html

7. Times of India, 'Indian intelligence system needs urgent reforms,'

September 15, 2013,available at http://blogs.timesofindia.india-times.com/ChanakyaCode/entry/indianintelligence-system-needs-urgent-reforms

Western Academic Papers in Intelligence Studies

1. Anthony Glees, 'The Future of Intelligence Studies,' Journal of Strategic Security, 6 (5): 124-127, available at: http://scholarcommons.usf.edu/jss/vol6/iss5/15

2. Amy Zegart, 'September 11 and the Adaptation Failure of U.S. Intelligence Agencies,' International Security 29, no. 4 (Spring 2005): 78-111.

3. C. Christine Fair, 'Prospects for effective internal security reforms in India,' Commonwealth & Comparative Politics, 50:2, 145-170

4. Charles Cogan, 'Hunters not gatherers: intelligence in the twenty-first century', Intelligence and National Security, Vol. XVIII/4 (2003), p42

5. David Kahn, 'An Historical Theory of Intelligence,' Intelligence and National Security, Vol. 16, No. 3, (September 2001): 79–92.

6. Glenn Hastedt, 'The Politics of Intelligence and the Politicization of Intelligence: The American Experience,' Intelligence and National Security, Vol. 28, Issue 1, (2013), last accessed on August 28, 2013

7. John A. Gentry, Assessing intelligence performance, The Oxford handbook of national security intelligence,

8. Loch K. Johnson and Allison M.Shelton, 'Thoughts on the State of Intelligence Studies: A Survey Report,' Intelligence and National Security, (2013), Vol. 28, No. 1, 109–120 50

9. Michael Warner, 'Introduction: Wanted: A definition of intelligence' in 'Secret Intelligence–A Reader' (eds.) Christopher Andrew Richard J. Aldrich, Wesley K. Wark (Routledge, 2009), p1

10. Michael Herman, 'Ethics and Intelligence after September 2001,' Intelligence and National Security, Vol. 19, Iss. 2, (2004)

11. Michael Warner, 'Introduction: Wanted: A definition of intelligence' in 'Secret Intelligence–A Reader' (eds.) Christopher Andrew Richard J. Aldrich, Wesley K. Wark (Routledge, 2009), p3

12. Peter Gill, 'Reasserting control: Recent changes in the oversight of the UK intelligence community', Intelligence and National Security, Vol. 11, 2, (1996)

13. Richard K. Betts, 'Analysis, War, and Decision: Why Intelligence Failures Are Inevitable', World Politics 31/1 (Oct. 1978) p.88.

14. Richard K. Betts, 'Enemies of Intelligence: Knowledge and Power in American National Security', Columbia University Press, New York, 2007.

15. Stephen Marrin, 'Revisiting Intelligence and Policy: Problems with Politicization and Receptivity', Intelligence and National Security, Vol. 28, Issue1, (2013)

16. Stephen Marrin, 'Preventing Intelligence failures by learning from the past', International Journal of Intelligence and Counterintelligence, 17:655-672

17. Troy, Thomas, The "correct" definition of intelligence, International Journal of Intelligence and Counterintelligence, Vol V/4, (1992), p.433, 443, 44.

Chapter 5: Pakistan's Secret Agencies, Miltablishment, Talibanization and the Tug-of-War

1 Pakistan's Anti-India Spy Network Eyes Vital Defense Infrastructure from Sri Lanka. Animesh Roul, Terrorism Monitor Volume: 12 Issue: 19, October 10, 2014

2 Reform of Pakistan's Intelligence Services, Hasan Abbas, Belfer Centre for Science and International Affairs, 15 March 2008. https://www.belfercenter.org/publication/reform-pakistans-intelligence-services.

3 Pakistan: Reorganization of Intelligence infrastructure. Jalalzai Musa Khan, Daily Times, 24 March 2014, https://dailytimes.com.pk/writer/musa-khan-jalalzai/page/9/

4 Jalalzai Musa Khan, Pakistan: Living with a Nuclear Monkey, chapter-12, PP, 172-173

5 Ibid, Chapter-11, PP-161

6 Ibid, PP-162

7   Pakistan: Reorganization of Intelligence infrastructure. Jalalzai
     Musa Khan, Daily Times, 24 March 2014, https://dailytimes.com.
     pk/writer/musa-khan-jalalzai/page/9/

8   Ibid

9   Jalalzai Musa Khan, Pakistan: Living with a Nuclear Monkey, PP-174

10   The growing 'tug of war' between Pakistan's Spy Agencies: The grow-
     ing 'tug-of-war' between Pakistan's spy agencies: F.M. Shakil, Asia
     Times, 04 October 2017. http://www.atimes.com/article/growing-
     tug-war-pakistans-spy-agencies/

11   Reform of Pakistan's Intelligence Services, Hasan Abbas, Belfer Cen-
     ter for Science and International Affairs, 15 March 2008. https://
     www.belfercenter.org/publication/reform-pakistans-intelligence-
     services.

12   Jalalzai Musa Khan, Pakistan: Living with a Nuclear Monkey, PP-
     165-167

13   Imad Zafar, Dawn Leaks: A Tweet that Underscored the State within
     State, 01 May 2017, https://nation.com.pk/01-May-2017/dawn-
     leaks-a-tweet-that-underscored-the-state-within-a-state

14   The Afghan Intel crisis, PP: 133

15   Jalalzai Musa Khan, Pakistan: Living with a Nuclear Monkey, Chap-
     ter, 10, PP-130-131

16   Ibid

17   Why Pakistan supports terrorist Groups. Vanda Felbab-Brown,
     Brookings, 05 January 2018. https://www.brookings.edu/blog/order-
     from-chaos/2018/01/05/why-pakistan-supports-terrorist-groups-
     and-why-the-us-finds-it-so-hard-to-induce-change/

18   Robert D. Kaplan, the Revenge of Geography: What the Map Tell us
     about Coming Conflicts and the Battle against Fate. Random House
     International, 01 November 2012.

19   Marketing Terrorism and Fear, Daily Times, 24 April 2016

20   Dawn, 28 February 2018

21   Jalalzai Musa Khan, Pakistan: Living with a Nuclear Monkey, Chap-
     ter-1, PP-4

22 A Landmark Verdict, Muhammad Zain, Weekly Cutting edge, 16 February, 2019

23 Pakistan's dismantling of its terror infrastructure. 04 February, 2016. By Lt Gen Philip Compose

24 18 March 2018, Dawn reported Major General Asif Ghafoor, the Director General of the Inter-Services Public Relations (ISPR), interview with Gulf News

25 South Asian intelligence review in its Pakistan: Assessment (2018

26 South Asian intelligence review in its Pakistan: Assessment (2018

27 Mainstreaming Jihad: Why Now? Pervez Hoodbhoy, Dawn, 16 December 2017. https://www.dawn.com/news/1376805.

28 Pakistan to become Singapore or Syria-the Choice is Starker, Jan Muhammad Achakzai, Global Village Space, 25 December 2018

29 BBC, 23 November 2016

30 Ibid

31 The Insurgent Sanctuary in Pakistan, Seth G. Jones, CSIS Briefs, September 11, 2018

32 Counter Terrorism Policy Measures: A Critical Analysis of Pakistan's National Action Plan, Farhan Zahid, 19 July 2016

Chapter 6: Intelligence Agencies, Sectarian Mafia Groups, Army, and the Culture of Jihadism

1 Is Pakistan's National Action Plan Actually Working? Two years after Pakistan unveiled its strategy for fighting terrorism, the results are mixed. By Zeeshan Salahuddin, Diplomat--December 24, 2016

2 Pakistan 'Unprepared' for refugees fleeing operation against Taliban, Jon Boone. The Guardian, 26 Jun 2014

3 Nuclear Jihad in South Asia, Algora, 2015, New York

4 Chief General Musharaf, 13 February 2015

5 India Today, 11 February 2016

6 Lt General Aslam resigns after being superseded, Pakistan Today, 28 November 2013, and Lt General Aslam resigns after he fails to be-

come Pakistan Army Chief, The Economic Times,28 Nov, 2013,

7   Military-Intelligence-Militant Nexus in Pakistan: Fighting a War of Asymmetry against India. Sanjeeb Kumar Mohanty and Jinendra Nath Mahanty.

8   Pakistan's Armed Forces: Impact on the Stability of the State. Dhruv C Katoch, Journal of Defence Studies, Vol. 5 No. 4 October 2011

9   On 14 February 2019, India warned that it would ensure the "complete isolation" of Pakistan after a suicide bomber killed 46 paramilitary police in Indian-administered Kashmir.

10 Terror at Pulwama–'Game Over' for Pakistan. Rajeev Agarwal, CLAWS Newsletter, 15 February 2019

11 India Today, 16 February 2019

12 US Today, 16 February 2019

13 Daily Times, 16 February 2019

14 Ibid

15 Afghanistan Times, 15 February 2019

16 The Hindu newspaper on 16 February 2019 noted some aspects of the incident in its editorial comment

17 Kamila Hyat, The News, 28 February 2019

18 On 27 February 2019, Deepika S reported China's abutment to India by asking Pakistan to stop its support of terror groups and use of them in geopolitical goals

19 Pakistan: Living with a Nuclear Monkey. Musa Khan Jalalzai, Vij Publishing India, 2018

20 Pakistan's Dismantling of its Terror Infrastructure, Lt Gen Philip Campose, CLAWS-04 February, 2016

21 Pakistan's Dismantling of its Terror Infrastructure, Lt Gen Philip Campose, CLAWS-04 February, 2016

22 India's Response to Pakistan Hybrid War in J&K is Skin Deep. By Brig. Narender Kumar, SM, VSM, CLAWS, 30 April, 2018

23 On June 6, 2015, Pajhwok News reported that dozens of schoolgirls

were targeted by unknown terrorists using biological agents in Panj Aab district of Bamyan province.

24   Fault Lines in Pakistan's Armed Forces: Impact on the Stability of the State. Dhruv C Katoch. Journal of Defence Studies. Vol. 5 No. 4 October 2011

25   The Menace That Is Lashkar-e-Taiba, Ashley J. Tellis. March 2012

26   Radicalisation of Pakistani Armed Forces. Alok Bansal, CLAWS, June 28, 2011

27   Pakistan's Internal and External Enemies. Yunis Khushi, International Relations Department, Lahore Garrison University, Pakistan, Submission: March 26, 2018; Published: September 05, 2018

Chapter 7: Explaining Recent Intelligence Reforms in Bangladesh. A.S.M. Ali Ashraf

1   Ami Pedahzur, The Israeli Secret Services & The Struggle Against Terrorism (New York: Columbia University Press, 2009); Amy B. Zegart, Spying Blind: The CIA, the FBI, and the Origins of 9/11 (Princeton and Oxford: Princeton University Press, 2007).

2   Loch K. Johnson, "Preface to a Theory of Strategic Intelligence," International Journal of Intelligence and Counterintelligence, Vol. 16, No. 4 (2003), p. 643.

3   For details on the comparative case study method, see, Alexander George and Andrew Bennett, Case Studies and Theory Development in the Social Sciences (Cambridge, MA: MIT Press, 2005), Chapter 3, pp. 67-72.

4   The two parties follow sharply different ideologies. The BNP is a center-right political party, founded by General Ziaur Rahman, whereas the Awami League is a center-left political party, which led the Bangladesh independence movement at the direction of Sheikh Mujibur Rahman. The two parties maintain a dynastic style of leadership evident in the fact that Zia's wife Khaleda Zia and Mujib's daughter Sheikh Hasina have effectively centralized all decision making powers regarding their respective parties. In addition to the BNP and AL, there are two other major parties: the center-right Jaitya Party established by former military dictator Hussein Muhammad Ershad, and the Jamaat-e-Islami, which adheres to a fundamentalist Islamist

ideology. For details, see Inge Amundsen, "Dynasty or Democracy? Party Politics in Bangladesh," CMI Brief, Vol. 12, No. 6 (2013), pp. 1-4.

5   James J. Wirtz, "The American Approach to Intelligence Studies," in Handbook of Intelligence Studies, edited by Loch K. Johnson (New York: Routledge, 2007), p. 36.

6   Imtiaz Ahmed, "Bangladesh," in Security Sector Reform and Democratization: A Comparative Perspective, edited by Heiner Hanggi and Carolina G. Hernandez (Geneva and Zurich: DCAF and Lit Verlag, 2013); M. Jashim Uddin, "Security Sector Reform in Bangladesh," South Asian Survey 16/2 (2009), pp. 209-230.

7   Amena Mohsin, "Bangladesh: An Uneasy Accommodation," in Muthiah Alagappa, Coercion and Governance: The Declining Political Role of the Military in Asia (Stanford, CA: Stanford University Press, 2001), pp. 209-225; Siegfried Wolf, Civil-Military Relations and Democracy in Bangladesh (Heidelberg, APSA, 2013).

8   Although the 2009 Right to Information Act created many provisions for public disclosure of information, Section 32 provides a legal blanket against disclosure of information by eight intelligence agencies in Bangladesh.

9   Bangladesh Enterprise Institute, Public Information: The Role of Intelligence Agencies in Bangladesh, A Strategy Paper (Dhaka: BEI, 2011).

10 Anis Uz Zaman Khan, Chairman of the Investigation Committee, Revolt at the BDR Headquarters situated at Peelkhana: Report of the Investigating Committee Created for Investigation of the Heinous Massacre, Submitted on 21 May 2009; Jahangir Alam Chowdhury, Chairman of the Investigation Committee, Opinion: Investigation by the 20 Members of Army, May 2009; Shah Mohammad Saifuddin, 'BDR Revolt: A Deadly Strategic Game Plan, South Asia, May 20, 2009.

11 Government of Bangladesh, Ministry of Home Affairs, Towards Police Reform in Bangladesh: Needs Assessment Report 2003 (Dhaka: UNDP, 2004); Police Reform Program, Baseline Survey on Personal Security and Police Performance in Bangladesh (Dhaka: UNDP, 2011); Bangladesh Bank, Recent Reform Initiatives (Dhaka: Bangladesh Bank 2012); Government of Bangladesh, National Strategy for

Preventing Money Laundering and Combating Financing of Terrorism 2011-2013 (Dhaka: Bangladesh Bank, 2012); National Board of Revenue, Outline of Modernization Plan (2011-2016) (Dhaka: NBR, 2011).

12 This typology is modeled on but expands Rob Johnston's analysis of U.S. intelligence community. Johnston identifies three broad categories: (a) National technical; (b) defense; and (c) Law Enforcement and Homeland Security agencies. See, Rob Johnston, Analytic Culture in the U.S. Intelligence Community (Washington, D.C.: Central Intelligence Agency, 2005), p.126.

13 After achieving independence from Pakistan in 1971, the new government in Bangladesh established the Directorate of Forces Intelligence (DFI) along the line of Pakistan's Directorate for Inter-Services Intelligence (ISI). The DFI was later renamed to DGFI in 1976.

14 Prime Minister Sheikh Hasina also made a similar observation during her visit to the DGFI headquarters in May 2014. See "Govt Does Not Want to Use DGFI Politically: PM," New Age (Dhaka), May 14, 2014; See also Mohsin, "Bangladesh: An Uneasy Accommodation," pp. 209-225.

15 Special Security Force (SSF), "History", http://www.ssf.gov.bd/content/2.html, accessed June 18, 2014. 16 Author's interview with retired and serving officials at various government agencies.

16. Author's interview with retired and serving officials at various government agencies.

17 The other key responsibilities of the SB include security planning, registration and control of foreigners and verification of personal identification for passport issuing purposes. SB also gives protection to very important persons (VIPs), and works on immigration and passport control. Information regarding the political intelligence reform is classified. See Government of Bangladesh, "The Immigration Service," Bangladesh Police' <www.immi.gov.bd/faq.php> (accessed February 19, 2013).

18 Government of Bangladesh, The Armed Police Battalions (Amendment) Act, 2003 (Act no. XXVIII of 2003) <bdlaws.minlaw.gov.bd/print_sections_all.php?id=593> (accessed April 26, 2013).

19 Bangladesh Bank, Recent Reform Initiatives, p. 25; "BB Forms New Intelligence Unit to Curb Money Laundering," New Age (Dhaka),

January 29, 2012.

20 Syed Md. Aminul Karim and Md. Alauddin, "Emerging Tax Issues in Asian Countries," IMF Japan High Level Tax Conference for Asian and Pacific Countries, January 31-Feburary 3, 2102, Tokyo, Japan, p. 27.

21 See Ashfaqur Rahman, "Whither Bangladesh Foreign Office?" The Daily Star (Dhaka), January 20, 2013; Staff Correspondent, "The Daily Star-CFAS Roundtable: Proactive Foreign Policy Sought," The Daily Star (Dhaka), May 8, 2008.

22 Richard A. Best, Jr., Proposals for Intelligence Reorganization, 1949-1996 (Washington, D.C.: CRS, 2004); Mark M. Lowenthal, Intelligence: From Secrets to Policy (Washington, D.C.: CQ Press, 2006), p. 275.

23 Ken Kotani, "Recent Intelligence Reform in the United Kingdom," The National Institute for Defense Studies News, 142 (2010), pp. 1-6.

24 Muhammad Nurul Huda, "Reforming Minds and Attitudes," The Daily Star (Dhaka), August 13, 2011; Hassan Abbas, "Reforming Pakistan's Police and Law Enforcement Infrastructure: Is It Too Flawed to Fix?" USIP Special Report, No. 266 (February 2011), pp. 9-12;

25 Institute of Defence Studies and Analyses (IDSA), A Case for Intelligence Reform in India: IDSA Task Force Report (New Delhi: IDSA, 2012)

26 IDSA, A Case for Intelligence Reform in India, pp. 15-16; See also, Shirin Mazari, "India's Unconventional War Strategy," Defence Journal, January 1999. http://www. defencejournal.com/jan99/rawfacts. htm, accessed June 18, 2014.

27 National Commission on Terrorist Attacks Upon the United States, The 9/11 commission Report (New York and London: W.W. Norton & Company, 2004); The Commission on the Intelligence Capabilities of the United States Regarding Weapons of Mass Destruction, Report to the President of the United States (Washington, D.C., March 31, 2005); Chairman Lord Butler of Brockwell KG, Review of Intelligence on Weapons of Mass Destruction: Report of a Committee of Privy Counsellors (London: TSO, 2004).

28 Stan A. Taylor and David Goldman, "Intelligence Reform: Will More Agencies, Money, and Personnel Help?" Intelligence and National Security, Vol. 19, No. 3 (2004), pp. 416-435.

29 According to Amy B. Zegart, "The vast majority, 268 recommendations, or 79 percent of the total [recommendations offered by various commissions to reform U.S. intelligence community], resulted in no action at all." Zegart suggest this inaction caused intelligence failure prior to the 9/11 terrorist attacks. See Zegart, Spying Blind, pp. 34-36.

30 M. Sakhawat Hossain, "Capacity Building of Law Enforcement and Intelligence Agencies," in Farooq Sobhan (ed.), Countering Terrorism in Bangladesh (Dhaka: UPL, 2008), pp. 37-82; People's Republic of Bangladesh, National Strategy for Preventing Money Laundering and Combating Financing of Terrorism 2011-2013 (Dhaka: BFIU, 2012), p. 16.

31 After the 9/11 terrorist attacks, the United States emphasized hiring more analysts with foreign language skills, and expanding the size of covert operators to fight against transnational terrorists. See National Commission on Terrorist Attacks Upon the United States, The 9/11 commission Report; Aris A Pappas and James M. Simon, "The Intelligence Community: 2001-2015: Daunting Challenges, Hard Decisions," Studies in Intelligence, Vol. 46, No. 1 (2002), pp. 39-47.

32 Sometimes the compartmentalized culture is created to protect data from adversaries. However, over-emphasis on secrecy may impede the prospect of timely action.

33 Muhammad Nurul Huda, "Capacity Building and Coordination at Field Level of the Government Agencies in Preventing Terrorism," in Farooq Sobhan (ed.), Trends in Militancy in Bangladesh: Possible Responses (Dhaka: UPL, 2010), pp. 101-107.

34 The position of Director of National Intelligence was created in the United States to ensure better coordination of disparate intelligence agencies. See Richard A. Best, Jr., Intelligence Reform After Five Years: The Role of the Director of National Intelligence (DNI) (Washington, D.C.: CRS, 2010).

35 In the past homeland security responsibilities were split among various agencies whereas the DCI would hold two hats – one for the Central Intelligence Agency and the other for the U.S. intelligence

community. In both cases, inter-agency collaboration was a major problem.

36 Amy B. Zegart, "September 11 and the Adaptation Failure of US Intelligence Agencies," International Security, Vol. 29, No. 4 (2005), pp. 78-111; Kotani, "Recent Intelligence Reform in the United Kingdom," pp. 3-6.

37 Stafford T. Thomas, "The CIA's Bureaucratic Dimensions," International Journal of Intelligence and Counterintelligence, Vol. 12, No. 4 (1999-2000), pp. 399-413.

38 For an excellent analysis of how intelligence agencies may turn into political police, see William W. Keller, The Liberals and J. Edgar Hoover: Rise and Fall of a Domestic Intelligence State (Princeton: Princeton University Press, 1989). See also,Loch K. Johnston, "Preface to a Theory of Strategic Intelligence," International Journal of Intelligence and Counterintelligence, Vol. 16, No. 4 (2003), pp. 654-655.

39 John Hollister Hedley, "Learning From Intelligence Failures," International Journal of Intelligence and Counterintelligence, Vol. 18, No. 3 (2005), pp. 435-450.

40 For a cogent analysis of the domestic versus external determinant of intelligence reform, see Jeanne K. Giraldo and Harold A. Trinkunas, "Terrorist Financing: Explaining Government Responses," in Giraldo and Trinkunas (eds.), Terrorism Financing and State Responses (Stanford: Stanford University Press, 2007), pp. 282-296.

41 ATM Amin, "Developing a Counter Terrorism Strategy for Bangladesh," in Farooq Sobhan (ed.), Countering Terrorism in Bangladesh (Dhaka: UPL, 2008), p. 30.

42 International Crisis Group, "Bangladesh: Getting Police Reform on Track," Asia Report, No. 182 (Brussels: ICG, 2009).

43 Quoted in Roland Buerk, "Bangladesh's Feared Elite Police," BBC News, December 15, 2005.

44 The Army-led Operation Clean Heart and the BDR-led Operation Spider Web were aimed at hunting down armed militants and terrorists in the country. See Rounaq Jahan, "Bangladesh in 2003: Vibrant Democracy or Destructive Politics?" Asian Survey, Vol. 44, No. 1 (2004), p. 59.

45 ABM Ziaur Rahman, "Countering Terrorism: Responses of Stake-holders," in Imtiaz Ahmed (ed.), Terrorism in the 21st Century: Perspectives from Bangladesh (Dhaka: UPL, 2009), p.169.

46 See Articles 6aa and 6bb of The Armed Police Battalions (Amendment) Act, 2003 (Act No. XXVIII of 2003) <bdlaws.minlaw.gov.bd/print_sections_all.php?id=593>(accessed 26 April 2013).

47 Human Rights Watch, Judge, Jury, and Executioner: Torture and Extrajudicial Killings by Bangladesh's Elite Security Force (New York: HRW, 2006); More recent allegations focus on a criminal case, in which senior RAB officials in Narayanganj city killed seven people in exchange for monetary benefits. See "Ex-RAB Officer Tareque Admits Link," The Daily Star (Dhaka), June 18, 2014.

48 Interview with a senior RAB official; Also see, M. Moyeenul Haque, "RAB Operations – An Insider's View," in RAB Journal 2008 (Dhaka: RAB Legal and Media Wing, 2008), pp. 84-85.

49 Author's interview with UNDP experts on police reform project in Bangladesh. 50 Karim and Alauddin, "Emerging Tax Issues in Asian Countries."

50. Karim and Alauddin, "Emerging Tax Issues in Asian Countries."

51 Iftekharuzzaman, "Can We Expect an Effective ACC? The Daily Star (Dhaka), February 23, 2010.

52 Inam Ahmed, "Walking the Edge," India Today, May 28, 2007.

53 Kawser Ahmed, "Defining National Security Matters and Need for Founding a National Crisis Management Body and Its Functionaries," in The Battle Without Borders (Dhaka: Osder Publications, 2010), p. 167.

54 M Abul Kalam Azad, "Work on Counterintelligence Unit Under Way," The Daily Star (Dhaka), January 23, 2010; "PM to Sit with Intel Agencies Today," News Today (Dhaka), December 26, 2010.

55 "Security Forces Capacity Building," Security Risks-Com, January 1, 2011.

56 Author's interview; "B'Desh Forms National Committee to Coordinate Intelligence Activities," Zee News (India), August 3, 2009.

57 Interview with senior officials at the Ministry of Home Affairs.

58 Huda, "Capacity Building and Coordination at Field Level," p. 104.

59 Ahmed, "Bangladesh," in Security Sector Reform and Democratization, p. 16.

60 See "National Committee Formed to Finalize Anti-Money Laundering Action Plan," The Financial Express (Dhaka), August 2, 2009.

61 GoB, National Strategy, Annexure, p. iv.

62 The three defense service chiefs, key intelligence chiefs, and police chief would also represent NCMC. See Azad, "Work on Counterintelligence Unit Under Way."

63 Shakhawat Liton, "Army Seeks to Form Crisis Unit," The Daily Star (Dhaka), June 8, 2009.

64 see Anand Kumar, "Reconstitution of the Bangladesh Rifles." Journal of Defense Studies, Vol. 4, No. 2 (2010), pp. 116-124.

65 After criminal investigations, the Bangladesh Government accused 113 RSU soldiers, of whom four were acquitted and 109 were given prison terms, ranging from four months to seven years. Each convict was fined Taka 100 (less than $1.5). Four of the accused RSU men were acquitted as allegations against them were not proved. See Staff Correspondent, "RSU Was Aware, but Kept Mum," The Daily Star (Dhaka), December 20, 2010; Staff Correspondent, "Intelligence Unit Let It Happen," The Daily Star (Dhaka), May 9, 2010.

66 "A Summary of the National Probe Report on the BDR Mutiny," The Daily Star (Dhaka), May 29, 2009.

67 Khan, Revolt at the BDR Headquarters, p. 26.

68 Md. Asadullah Khan, "Mutiny or Conspiracy?" The Daily Star (Dhaka), March 7, 2009. Also see Kumar, "The BDR Mutiny," pp. 109-111.

69 Shafqat Munir, "The BDR Mutiny in Bangladesh: Understanding the National and Regional Implications," RUSI Commentary, March 26, 2009; Anand Kumar, "The BDR Mutiny," pp. 109-110.

70 Talukder Maniruzzaman, "Bangladesh in 1975: The Fall of the Mujib Regime and Its Aftermath," Asian Survey, Vol. 16, No. 2 (1976), p. 121.

71 Human Rights Watch, Ignoring Executions and Torture: Impunity for Bangladesh's Security Forces (New York: HRW, 2009), p. 5.

72 See, Jatiya Rakkhi Bahini (Absorption into the Army) Ordinance, 1975 (Ordinance No. LII of 1975). http://bdlaws.minlaw.gov.bd/pdf_part.php?id=505, accessed June 20, 2014.

73 Bangladesh Police is the implementing agency and the UNDP is a donor coordinating agency for the police reform project. For a detailed critique of the police reform process in Bangladesh, see ICG, "Bangladesh: Getting Police Reform on Track."

74 The THB was created with nine officials only.

75 The State Department's pressure came in the form of its downgrading Bangladesh from 'Tier 2' to 'Tier 2 Watch List' in the 2009 Trafficking in Persons Report. This downgrading underscored the necessity of legal and intelligence reform to comply with the global anti-trafficking regime.

76 Rahman, "Countering Terrorism: Responses of Stakeholders," p. 175.

77 Nazmul Ahsan, "FATF Lists 5 Deficiencies in BD's Financial Sec" The Financial Express (Dhaka), July 9, 2012.

78 "National Committee Formed," The Financial Express (Dhaka), August 2, 2009.

79 Bangladesh Financial Intelligence Unit, Managing Core Risks of Financial Institutions: Guidance Notes on Prevention of Money Laundering and Terrorist Financing (Dhaka: Bangladesh Bank, 2012).

80 See, Frédéric Grare, Reforming the Intelligence Agencies in Pakistan's Transitional Democracy (Washington, D.C.: Carnegie Endowment for International Peace, 2009).

Chapter 8: Intelligence without Ambition: National Directorate of Intelligence (NDS) of Afghanistan

1 The Afghan Intel Crisis, Musa Khan Jalalzai, New York 2017

2 Ibid

3 No easy escape from Afghan war for Trump: Russia, China and Iran now backing Taliban and stymieing US peace efforts, Brahma Chellaney, 02 October, 20128

4 GCHQ: inside the top secret world of Britain's biggest spy agency:

Files leaked by Edward Snowden reveal how the NSA pays for and influences some of the UK's intelligence gathering programmes. The documents also give unique insights into the challenges faced by the agency and the concerns it has about how to tackle them. Nick Hopkins, Julian Borger and Luke Harding, The Guardian, 02 August 2013. https://www.theguardian.com/world/2013/aug/02/gchq-spy-agency-nsa-snowden

5   The Islamic State in 'Khorasan': How it began and where it stands now in Nangarhar, Author: Borhan Osman, Afghanistan Analysis network, 27 July 2016, https://www.afghanistan-analysts.org/the-islamic-state-in-khorasan-how-it-began-and-where-it-stands-now-in-nangarhar/

6   Ibid

7   The Afghan Intel Crisis: Satellite State: War of Interests and the Blame-Game, By Musa Khan Jalalzai, New York, 2017

8   Taliban launch large-scale assault on western Afghan city: Security forces reportedly rushing reinforcements to Farah as insurgents armed with captured weapons flood into city. Akhtar Mohammad Makoii in Herat and Emma Graham-Harrison in London, the Guardian, 15 May 2018

9   The Times, 21 March 2018

10 The Afghan Intel Crisis: Satellite State: War of Interests and the Blame-Game, By Musa Khan Jalalzai, New York, 2017

11 Ibid

12 Khaama Press, 13 July, 2012

13 Ibid

14 Whose Army? Afghanistan's Future and the Blueprint for Civil War. By Musa Khan Jalalzai, New York, 2014

15 Intelligence Power in Peace and War. By Michael Herman, Cambridge University Press, 1996

16 Afghanistan: The Soviet Invasion and the Afghan Response, (1979-1982), Mohammed Kakar. 1997

17 ToloNews, December 13, 2014

18 Ibid

19 The Afghan Intel Crisis: Satellite State: War of Interests and the Blame-Game, By Musa Khan Jalalzai, New York, 2017

20 Ibid

21 ToloNew, 14 May 2015

22 Pajhwok News, 16 may 2015

23 In July 2018, the UNAMA in its report noted the killing of more than 1,692 civilians in June 30, 2018. UNAMA also noted that anti-government forces were responsible for 67 percent (1,127 deaths and 2,286 injuries) of the casualties.

24 25 February 2019; Daily Outlook Afghanistan reported the UNAMA calculation of civilian deaths in the country

25 Collateral losses, damages, Afghanistan times, February 25, 2019

26 On 21 February, 2019 Daily Outlook Afghanistan noted weaknesses of the Afghan government in maintaining good governance

Chapter 9: Instability in Afghanistan: Implications for Pakistan by Mohammad

1   Kenneth K (2006) Afghanistan: Post-Taliban Governance, Security, and US Policy. CRS Report for Congress Prepared for Members and Committees of Congress 6.

2   Madrasa or Madrasah is a school where people go to learn about the religion of Islam.

3   Naseer SA (2011) Prospects for peace and stability in Afghanistan. Afghanistan Regional Dialogue Background 1

4   At that time the world was considered to be bipolar because there was two super powers i-e USA and USSR now Russia.

5   Buzkashi is a game very famous in Afghanistan, Central Asia and Pakistan's Tribal Belt, in which the horsemen try to snatch, died goat from each other and make a point.

6   Saleem S (2013) Pakistan and Afghanistan then what need to do?. Pakistan institute of legislative Development and transparency.

7   Kamal M (2001) The Taliban Phenomena: Afghanistan 1994–1997. International Journal of Middle East Studies 32: 586-588.

8   Haroun M. Through Their Eyes: Possibilities for a Regional Approach to Afghanistan.

9   Laura s (2007) Crises in Afghanistan & the need for a comprehensive strategy. Regional Studies 3: 20.

10 Safder H (2012) Issues and Challenges in Pakistan Afghanistan Relation after 9/11. A Research Journal of South Asian Studies 27: 6-7.

11 Khurshid H (1962) Pakistan and Afghanistan Relations. Asian Survey 2: 14-24.

12 Barnet RR, Andrea A (2003) Regional Issues and the Reconstruction of Afghanistan. World Policy Journal 20: 31-40.

13 Muhammad I (2011) Terrorism in Pakistan Causes and Remedy. Academic Journal 6: 224.

14 (2013) Mullah Fazlullah chosen as Tehreek-e-Taliban Pakistan Chief. November 7. The Express: Tribune.

15 Usman D (2012) Sociological Analysis of terrorism in Pakistan. Academic Research International. 3: 203-212.

16 Anthony HC, Varun V (2011) Pakistan Violence Vs Stability. Center for Strategic & International Studies.

17 (2015) 80,000 Pakistanis killed in US 'War on Terror': report. The Express: Tribune.

18 Shabir H, Naeem A, UI Haq PI (2015) Impacts of Terrorism on the Economic Development of Pakistan. Pakistan Business Review 8: 704-722.

Bibliography

Abbas Hassan. 2004. Pakistan's Drift into Extremism: Allah, the Army and America's War on Terror. M.E Sharp Inc.

Abid, Abdur Rehman, 22 April, 2009, "Buner Falls into the Hands of Swat Taliban," Dawn Karachi

Abrams Herbert L. 1991, "Human Reliability and Safety in the Handling of Nuclear Weapons," Science and Global security

Adams, Mark and Mark Bradbury, 1995, Conflict and Development: Organisational Adaptation in Conflict Situations; An Oxfam working Paper, Oxford.

Afghan people dialogue on peace: building and foundations for an Inclusive Peace Process. Local Roadmap for Peace.10 June 2014 UNAMA Office Kabul, Afghanistan

Ahmad Javid. 2018. The Major Flaws in Afghanistan's Intelligence War: The United States needs an honest reassessment of Afghanistan's defence capabilities as it ramps up its combat-training role. National Interests

Afghan people dialogue on peace: building and foundations for an Inclusive Peace Process. Local Roadmap for Peace.10 June 2014 UNAMA Office Kabul, Afghanistan

Ahmad Khalid. 2011. Sectarian War: Pakistan's Sunni Shia Violence and its Links to the Middle East, Oxford University Press.

Agha H. Amen. David J. Ossineke Paul Andre Deterges. 2010. The Development of Taliban Factions in Afghanistan and Pakistan: A Geographical Account. Edwin Millen

Agfa H. Amen. David J. Ossineke Paul Andre Deterges. 2010. The Development of Taliban Factions in Afghanistan and Pakistan: A Geographical Account. Edwin Millen

Ball, Nicole and Tammy Halevy 1996, Making Peace Work: The Role of International Development Community; Overseas Development Council USA.

Barakat, Sultan and Arne Strand 1995, Rehabilitation and Reconstruction of Afghanistan: A Challenge Afghans, NGOs and the UN Disaster Prevention and Management; Volume 4 No.1 MCB University Press UK.

Barakat, Sultan, Mohammed Ehsan and Arne Strand 1995, NGOs and Peace Building in Afghanistan; Workshop Report University of York UK.

Brian Glyn William. 2011. Afghanistan Declassified: A Guide to America's Longest War, University of Pennsylvania Press.

Brown Wahid and Don Rasher. 2012. Fountain of Jihad: The Haqqani Nexus. 1973-2010. Hurst & Co. London

Basrur, Rajesh, October 2002, "Kargil, Terrorism, and India's Strategic Shift," India Review

Bashkar Roy. 2008, "China Unmasked—What Next"? South Asian Analysis group Paper No. 2840.

Badash Lawrence, 1994. Scientists and the Development of Nuclear Weapons, Atlantics Highlands, Humanitarian Press

Coll Steve. 2018. Directorate S: The C.I.A. and America's Secret Wars in Afghanistan and Pakistan New York: Penguin Press

Crews, Robert D. and Tarzi, Amin. 2008. The Taliban and the Crisis of Afghanistan. Harvard University Press

Carlotta Gall, 2014. The Wrong Enemy: America in Afghanistan 2001–2014. Houghton Mifflin Harcourt, New York.

242

Chalmers Malcolm. 2012. Less is better: Nuclear Restraint at Low Numbers. Royal United Services Institute for Strategic Studies London.

Clarke, J.W.2007. Defining danger: American assassins and the new domestic terrorists, New Brunswick, N.J.: Transaction Publishers.

Collins Joseph J. 2016. Understanding war in Afghanistan, Create Space Independent Publishing Platform

Dimitrakis Panagiotis. 2013. The Secret War in Afghanistan: The Soviet Union, China and Anglo-American Intelligence in the Afghan War, I.B Tauris

Davis Anthony 1998, "How the Taliban Became A Military Force-Fundamentalism Reborn" in Afghanistan and the Taliban, edited by Maley William New York University Press USA.

Davies Philip H. J and Kristian C. Gustafson. 2013, Intelligence Elsewhere: Spies and Espionage Outside the Anglo-sphere, Georgetown University Press, Washington.

Dahl Robert, 1985, Controlling Nuclear Weapons: Democracy versus Guardianship. Syracuse University Press, New York.

Dando Malcolm. 2001. The New Biological Weapons: Threat, Proliferation and Control. Lynne Rienner Publishers, London

Dark Sun. 1995, the Making of the Hydrogen Bomb, by Richard Rhodes, Simon & Schuster, New York

Davies Philip H. J and Gustafson Kristian C, 2013; Intelligence Elsewhere: Spies and Espionage outside the Anglo sphere. Georgetown University Press, Washington DC USA

Emadi, Hafizullah. 2010. Dynamics of Political Development in Afghanistan: The British, Russian, and American Invasions. Palgrave Macmillan.

Ehrhart Hans Georg. 2012. Afghanistan in the Balance:

Counterinsurgency, Comprehensive approach and Political Order. McGill-Queen's University Press

Eager Paige Whaley, 2008, From Freedom Fighters to Terrorists: Women and Political Violence, Ashgate, Hampshire

Faruqui Ahmad, 2001. The Complex Dynamics of Pakistan Relationship with China, Policy Research, Islamabad

Farmelo Graham. 2013. Churchill's Bomb: How the United States Overtook Britain in the First Nuclear Arms Race. Basic Books, New York, USA

Fraser David Major General, Brian Hanington, Mcclelland & Stewart 2018. Operation Medusa: The Furious Battle that Saved Afghanistan from the Taliban

Forsberg, Carl. 2009. 'The Taliban's Campaign for Kandahar. Afghanistan Report, Institute for the Study of War

Ferguson Charles D, William C. Potter. 2004. The Four Faces of Nuclear Terrorism, Monterey Institute of International Studies.

Gera Y K Maj General. 2010. Peace and stability in Afghanistan: The Way Ahead, Vij books India

Giustozzi Antonio 2018. The Islamic State in Khorasan: Afghanistan, Pakistan and the New Central Asia

Gill Peter Stephen Marrin and Mark Phythian. 2009. Intelligence Theory: Key Questions and Debates, Studies in Intelligence series, Routledge, 2009

Gill Peter and Mark Phythian. 2006. Intelligence in an Insecure World, , Polity Press UK

Guhar Altaf, 1996, Ayub Khan: Pakistan's First Military Ruler, Oxford University Press.

Ganguli Sumit and S. Paul Kapur, 2009. Nuclear Proliferation in South Asia: Crisis Behavior and the Bomb. Routledge, New

York.

Hanifi Shah Mahmood. 2012. Power Hierarchies and Hegemony in Afghanistan: State Building, Ethnic Minorities and Identity in Central Asia. IB Tauris

Harpviken, Kristian Berg, 1997, Transcending Traditionalism: The Emergence of Non-State Military formations in Afghanistan, Journal of Peace Research Vol.34 No.3 Peace Research Institute Oslo and SAGE Publication UK.

Harpviken, Kristian Berg, 1999, Feature Review of Two titles on Afghanistan Third World Quarterly; Volume 20, No.4, CARFAX Publishing UK.

Hoffman Bruce. 1998. inside terrorism, Columbia University Press. New York.

Ismail, Ahmed I. and Reginald Green Herbold 1999, Rehabilitation, Sustainable Peace and Development Towards Reconceptualisation, Third World Quarterly, Volume 20 No.1 CARFAX Publishing UK.

Ibrahimi, Niamatullah. 2009. 'Divide and Rule: State Penetration in Hazarajat from Monarchy to the Taliban. Working Paper No: 42, series 2.

Jahan Rounaq. 1972. Pakistan: Failure and National Integration, Columbia University Press. New York.

Jalal Ayesha, 2011. The Past and Present in Pakistan: Beyond the Crisis State, Columbia University Press, New York.

Jadoon Amira Nakissa Jahanbani, and Charmaine Willis. 2018. Challenging the ISK Brand in Afghanistan-Pakistan: Rivalries and Divided Loyalties, Combating Terrorism Centre, Vol 11 Issue 4

Jackson Paul. 2003. 'Warlords as Alternative Forms of Governance. Small Wars & Insurgencies, Vol 14, No. 2

Jalalzai Musa Khan. 2014. Whose Army? Afghanistan's Future and the Blueprint for Civil War, Musa Khan Jalalzai, Algora Publishing New York, USA

Khan, Riaz M. 2011. Afghanistan and Pakistan: Conflict, Extremism, and Resistance to Modernity. John Hopkins University Press

Kumar Radha and Dnyanada Palkar.2014. Afghanistan and its neighbours, Regional View. Delhi Policy Group Publication

Lieven Anatol. 2018. Peace in Afghanistan: The Duty of Afghanistan's Region. Russia in Global Affairs, Moscow Russia

Khan Saira. 2009. Nuclear Weapons and Conflict Transformation (The Case of India– Pakistan). Routledge (Taylor and Francis Group), London.

Mir Amir. 2009. Talibanization in Pakistan, Pentagon Security International, Publisher, India.

Mujaddidi.Ghulam Farooq 23 June, 2017. Decoding Afghan Security Forces' Failures: Afghanistan's woefully unprepared intelligence and security agencies are as much of a problem as cross-border terrorism, The Diplomat.

Nawaz Shuja. 2009. FATA: The Most Dangerous Place, Centre for Strategic and International Studies. USA.

Nojumi, Neamatollah, Dyan Mazurana, Elizabeth Stites. 2008. After the Taliban: Life and Security in Rural Afghanistan. Rowman & Littlefield Publishers

Nojumi, Neamatollah. 2016. American State Building in Afghanistan and its Regional Consequences: Achieving Democratic stability and Balancing China's Influence, Lanham, MD: Rowman & Littlefield,

Nardin Terry 1998, The Comparative Ethics of War and Peace in The Ethics of War and Peace; Religious and Secular Perspectives edited by Terry Nardin; Princeton University Press USA.

Omarkhail Ihsanullah, 21 May 2018. Afghan security sector in dire need of reform, Asia Times,

Osama W.M. 2002, the Case of US Leadership in Rebuilding of Afghanistan, Analysis from East West Centre.

Philip H. J. Davies and Kristian C. Gustafson, 2013, Intelligence Elsewhere: Spies and Espionage outside the Anglo sphere. Georgetown University Press, USA

Raza Rumi. 2010–2011.The rise of Violent Extremism. Extremism Watch, Mapping Conflict trends in Pakistan, Jinnah Institute Islamabad. Raza Rumi is the editor of Daily Times Pakistan

Shulsky Abram N. and Schmitt. Gary J. 2002. Silent Warfare: Understanding the World of Intelligence. Potomac Books Washington, USA

Siddiqa Ayesha, Military Inc.: Inside Pakistan's Military Economy, Pluto Press 20 Apr 2007.

Shahrani. M. Nazif. 2018. Modern Afghanistan: The Impact of 40 years of War. Indiana University Press

Saikal Amin. 2016. Afghanistan and its Neighbours after the NATO Withdrawal (Contemporary Central Asia: Societies, Politic and Cultures), Lanham, MD: Lexington Books

Shahrani.M. Nazif. 2018 Modern Afghanistan: Impact of 40 Years War. Indiana University Press

Safi Khalilullah and Rutting Thomas. 27 June 2018. Understanding Hurdles to Afghan Peace Talks: Are the Taliban a Political Party? Afghanistan Analysts Network

Sultan Barakat and Zyck S.2010. 'Afghanistan's insurgency and the Viability of political Solution, Studies in Conflict and Terrorism, Vol. 33, No. 3.

T.Robert Fowler Dundurn. 2016. Combat Mission Kandahar: The Canadian Experience in Afghanistan. Dundurn

Theo Farrell. 2017. Unwinnable Britain's War in Afghanistan, 2001-2014, Bodley Head, Penguin Books Limited.

Theo Farrell. 2017. Unwinnable Brittan's War in Afghanistan. 2001-2014. Bodley Head Penguin Books Limited

Taj Farhat. 2012. Taliban and Anti Taliban, Cambridge Scholars Publishing.

Weller George. 2006. First into Nagasaki: The Censored Eyewitness Dispatches on Post-Atomic Japan and its Prisoners of War, Crown, New York

Wellock Thomas R. 1998. Opposition to Nuclear Power in California, 1958–1978. Madison, University of Wisconsin Press.

Yoshihara Toshi and James R. Holmes. 2012. Strategy in the Second Nuclear Age: Power Ambitions and the Ultimate Weapon. Georgetown University Washington DC

Yusafzai Hamid Iqbal. 2011. The US Factor in Pak–Afghan Relations Post 9/11. Lambert Academic Publishing, Germany

Zaeef, Abdul Salam, 2009. My Life with the Taliban, London: Hurst and Company.

Index

www.ingramcontent.com/pod-product-compliance
Lightning Source LLC
Chambersburg PA
CBHW031543260326
41914CB00002B/253